EYLAU—FRIEDLAND

The Polish Campaign

by F.-G. HOURTOULLE

Colour plates by André Jouineau
Maps by Denis Gandilhon and Jean-Marie Mongin
Translated from the French by Alan McKay

HISTOIRE & COLLECTIONS—PARIS

Once the Prussian army was routed, a number of groups of partisans roamed around the countryside, harassing the French troops. (RR)

Histoire & Collections © 2007

EYLAU—FRIEDLAND
The Polish Campaign

CONTENTS

FROM ONE WAR TO THE NEXT	4
THE PRUSSIAN ARMY	14
THE RUSSIAN ARMY	28
THE BATTLE OF EYLAU	45
FROM EYLAU TO FRIEDLAND	68
THE BATTLE OF FRIEDLAND	80
THE FRENCH ARMY	91
THE EMPIRE AT ITS ZENITH	143
Abbreviations	144

Cover picture © RMN

FROM ONE WAR TO THE NEXT

"Soldiers, the Russians are bragging about advancing towards us, so we'll march towards them, we'll save them half the trip. They'll get another Austerlitz, right in the middle of Prussia!"

On 27 October 1806, Napoleon entered Berlin two days after *Maréchal* Davout's heroic troops. In the space of eight weeks he had humiliated and brought arrogant Prussia to her knees, together with its beautiful Queen Louise and its insipid King Friedrich-Wilhelm, the Great Frederick's grandson. The Prussian army had ceased to exist - with the exception of General Kalkreuth's corps which slipped away in the direction of Konigsberg, and some small strongholds doomed to surrender shortly – even before it had been able to link up with Benningsen's Russian Army which only entered East Prussia on 29 October.

Napoleon remained in Berlin in November 1806 during which he was intensively active, as was his wont.

In order to weaken the Russian Eagle, he made use of diplomacy. He wrote to Selim II, the Sultan of Turkey, encouraging him to start campaigning again: *"... Have your soldiers march on Shoczim; you having nothing to fear from Russia..."* No sooner said than done and the Tsar, who had sent General Michelson into this sector, had to make do without 60 000 men dealing with the Sublime Porte.

Napoleon also covered his southern flank against any vague attempts by Austria. In order to guarantee this he proposed, in exchange for Galicia, to give the wealthy province of Silesia which had been taken over by Frederick the Great sixty years earlier back to Austria. Nevertheless, Jérôme and his 9th Corps were keeping an eye on things there.

Finally there was the problem of the eternal enemy, England, to deal with. In order to pre-empt any landings on the Baltic coast, the Emperor detached Brune's and Mortier's Corps, giving the latter the task of watching over Swedish Pomerania. But beyond this military decision, he also drew up a decree, one which was to have quite different repercussions, setting France on the downhill path which eventually proved fateful to her: on 21 October he decreed the beginning of the Continental Blockade: *"Any stores, any merchandise and any property belonging to an English subject are declared spoils of war; trading with English merchandise is forbidden, and all merchandise belonging to England or coming from its factories are also declared spoils of war; no English ships or ships coming from English colonies will be received into a French port or those of its allies."* Since France could not invade England directly, she wanted to stifle it by blocking the reason that made it powerful: its trade.

In the meantime, the strongholds at Magdeburg and Lübeck capitulated. So on 16 November, from the Charlottenburg in Berlin, Napoleon decided to impose his peace conditions on Prussia. He demanded that Prussia give up several strongholds (Danzig, Kolberg, Thorn, etc.); that French troops occupy all the southern part of

Top. **The Poles helping Ney's 6th Corps to cross the Vistula.**
(RR)

Above. **The only true ally that Frederick-William III (left), a sovereign left now without a state, had was Alexander I, the Tsar of all the Russias (right).**
(RR)

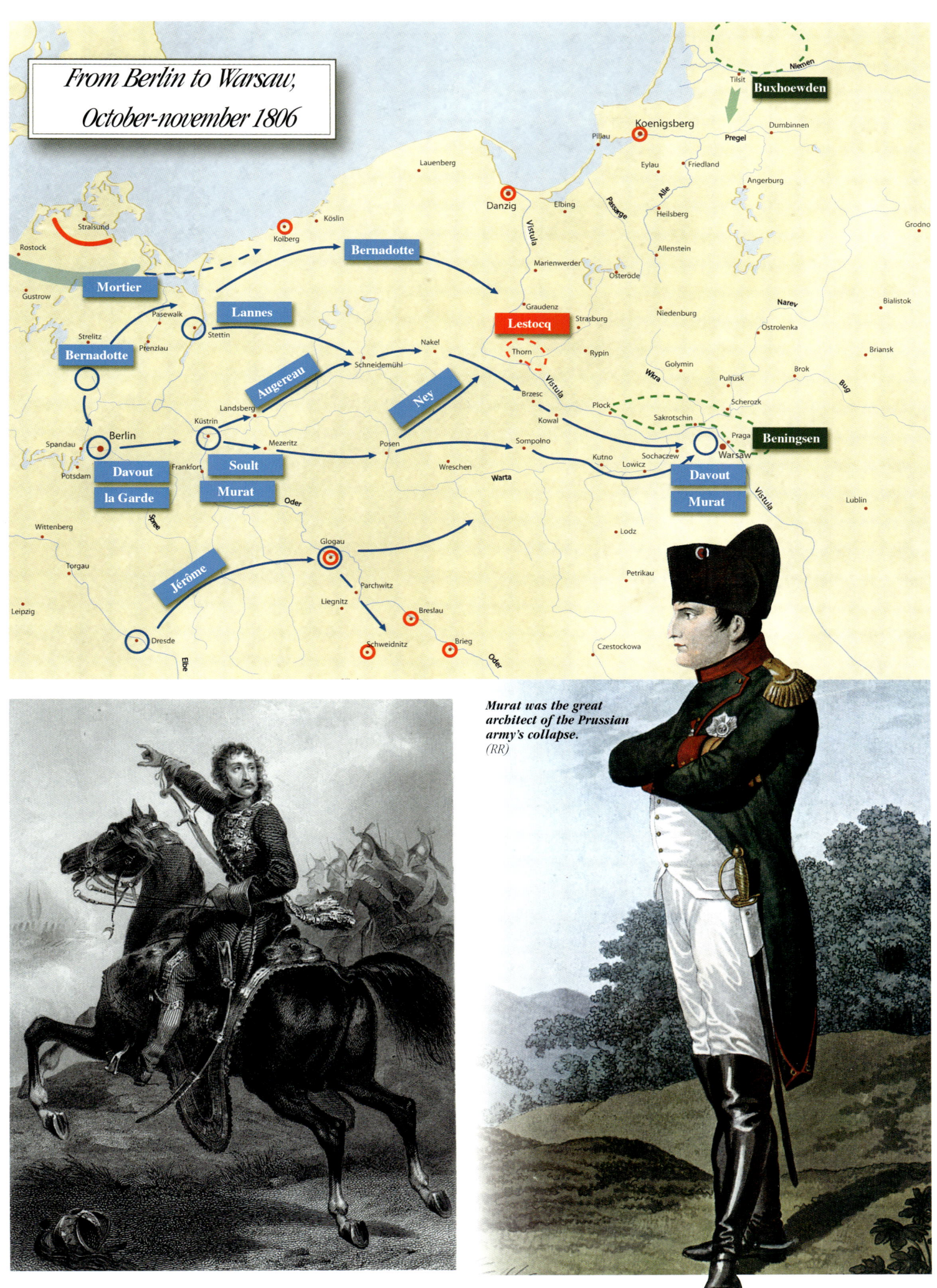

From Berlin to Warsaw, October-november 1806

Murat was the great architect of the Prussian army's collapse. (RR)

the kingdom which now gave up several areas to the benefit of their Rhine Confederation allies. On the 22nd, Friedrich-Wilhelm III rejected these conditions and decided to send his last troops to his Russian ally and to continue the war.

From Berlin to Warsaw

Alexander decided to come to the help of the defeated Prussians. The remains of their army were shut up inside Danzig where, under the orders of Kalkreuth, a corps was organised for Lestocq. The Tsar first got an army together under Benningsen, followed by a second under the command of Buxhoevden. Coming up from the Turkish border, Essen was advancing slowly with two divisions. All these troops were under the theoretical command of Field-Marshall Kamenski. He was 76 years old, tired and ill. He himself said to the Tsar *"that he could no longer see and could hardly ride a horse any more; he could hardly read a map and he did not know the country."*

At the end of October 1806, Napoleon ordered

The French army lived off the countryside across which men roamed foraging and looting.
(RR)

his army corps to move off in pursuit of the last Prussian troops or to besiege the last strongholds in the defeated kingdom. He was already pushing off towards the East: Lannes was at Stettin and moved towards Thorn. Augereau was due to meet him on the way. Davout was marching towards Frankfurt and Posen. To the south, Jérôme was moving up from Dresden towards Globau/Glogau with the Bavarians and the Wurtemburgers. The other corps followed in the second echelon as and when they could. The Emperor knew that the Russians were heading towards him, quite determined to avenge their humiliating defeat at Austerlitz.

The Russians were slow marching. Their objective was to free Danzig and occupy Warsaw whilst at the same time protecting Konigsberg. The French troops' advance had to be blocked on the Vistula and pushed back. Tsar Alexander had no intention of letting a Polish buffer state with France as its ally be set up along his borders.

At the end of November, Benningsen's Russian army was concentrated on the Vistula, from Warsaw to Plock; Buxhœvden crossed the Niemen and moved forwards into East Prussia whilst Essen was moving up in the direction of Lublin and Warsaw. Lestocq was at Thorn with the 15 000 men who had escaped disaster. Prussian troops were shut up inside the Konigsberg, Danzig and Kolberg strongholds, others in those in Silesia.

Napoleon's Manoeuvre

Having left Berlin on the 25th, Napoleon reached Posen two days later. The French army was advancing along three axes.

To the north, Lannes left Stettin and advanced via Schneidemuhl and Thorn – where Lestocq had burned down the bridge when he withdrew – and moved on Warsaw along the left bank of the Vistula. He was followed by Augereau and soon by Bernadotte. Mortier had to cover the Baltic coast and invest the strongholds there.

In the centre, Davout passed through Posen and was ready to enter Warsaw, preceded by Murat's caval-

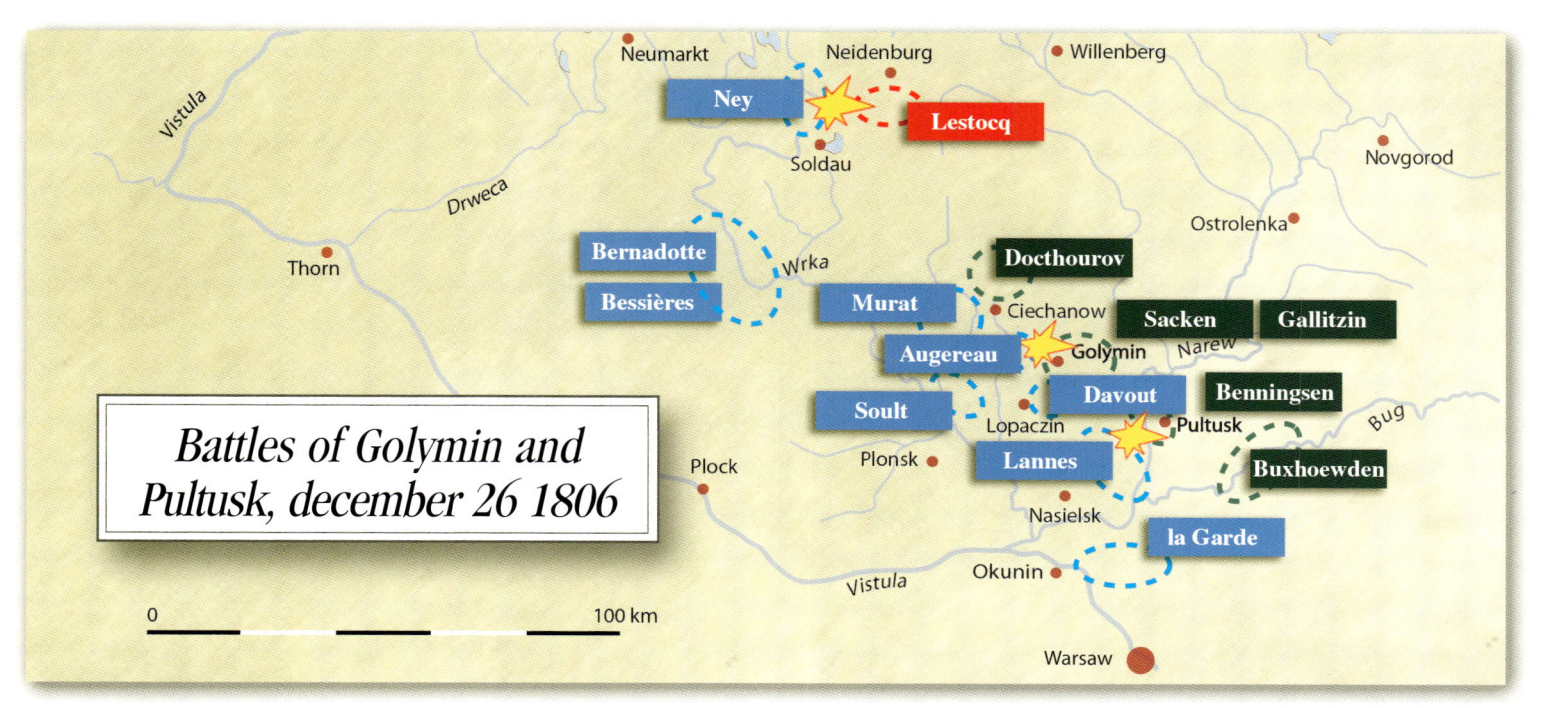

Battles of Golymin and Pultusk, december 26 1806

From left to right and top to bottom. **The Russian Generals Baggovut, Benningsen and Buxhœvden as well the Frenchman, Jérôme Bonaparte.** *(RR)*

ry reserve. The latter, acclaimed by the Prussians, already quite happily saw himself wearing the crown of the dismembered state. Napoleon put a quick end to that nonsense and the bubbly marshal was really "upset"; he was temporarily replaced by Nansouty. The Guard took the same route, as did Soult's corps and the Sahuc, Grouchy and d'Hautpoul Divisions. Ney, having advanced as far as Posen along the central road, turned off at an angle towards Thorn to link up with Bernadotte, thus forming the left of the future French deployment.

To the south, Jérôme and Vandamme started from Glogau, moved up along the Oder and took control of the Silesian strongholds, whilst still keeping an eye on those in Austria. From Parchwitz, they directed their march eastwards thus protecting the Grande Armée's flank.

The Emperor's objective was to stop the advancing Russians who had picked up Lestocq on the way and to take Warsaw so as to make it the pivot for his future outflanking movement on the right. On his side, Kamenski wanted to push the French troops back towards Plock beyond the Vistula. Without waiting for Buxhœvden, he concentrated Benningsen's army behind the Narev and the Wrka.

All these troop movements were carried out in terrible weather conditions. It was cold and rain followed upon snow. The roads were nothing but rivers of mud and progress was harassing. Supplies could not keep up and the troops were not able to live off the land. Whereas Murat and Davout had the support of the Polish people and passed through areas which were rich enough, the same could not be said for Lannes and Augereau. They had to advance through poorer regions where marau-

At Pultusk, Lannes fought one of the fiercest battles of his military career. His army corps, backed up by only Daultane's division, faced an enemy far outnumbering and outgunning him.
(RR)

ding was quite insufficient. The *Armée* was cold and hungry. The Russians met with the same problems but their soldiers seemed to be breathtakingly resistant to the harsh conditions of a Polish winter.

The French at Warsaw

Following on Murat's heels, Davout entered Warsaw on 29 November. He had to cross the Vistula and set himself up in position in the Praga suburbs, establishing a bridgehead for the troops who were to follow. But when he retreated, Benningsen had had the bridge destroyed and blocks of ice floated on the river which was formidable only with difficulty. However, the Russian general made the mistake of falling back behind the Narev and Davout took advantage of the protection afforded by the distance to build a new bridge and set up his 3rd Corps on the right bank before moving up north. At the same time, Soult crossed the Vistula at Plock, followed by the cavalry reserve under Bessières; Ney did likewise at Thorn, helped by Polish civilians.

Buxhœvden advanced along the left bank of the Narev, getting closer to Benningsen. Lestocq, with Ney and Bernadotte on his heels, was moving up the Drweca to Strasburg and trying to get closer to the main part of the army. But Ney caught up with him and defeated his rearguard at Soldau, forcing him to fall back near Neidenburg, thus separating him from his allies.

So when on 19 December, the Emperor entered Warsaw and met up with his Guard, his various corps were positioned on the left bank of the Wrka. Lannes, on the south of the arrangement, was placed between the Narev and the Vistula. Davout had had a bridge made at Okunin over the Narev and had crossed it, following on Gauthier's brigade; he fought a hard battle on the 23rd at Tzarnovo. Right to the north of the deployment Bernadotte, who had invested Graudenz, and Bessières both held the Upper Wrka whilst Ney pursued Lestocq towards Neidenburg. The arrival of the French had sparked off a revolt by the Poles who made up units to help Napoleon. Contingents from Bavaria and other states in the Rhine Confederation were on their way to reinforce Lefebvre who had laid siege to Danzig.

The Russians continued their concentration and Buxhœvden joined up with Benningsen who organised his defence around Pultusk and Tzarnovo. Thus Galitzin was at Pultusk, Sodmoradtsky and Ostermann at Tzarnovo and Sacken more to the west. Barclay de Tolly and Dokhtorov were staggered towards the Wrka with Pahlen.

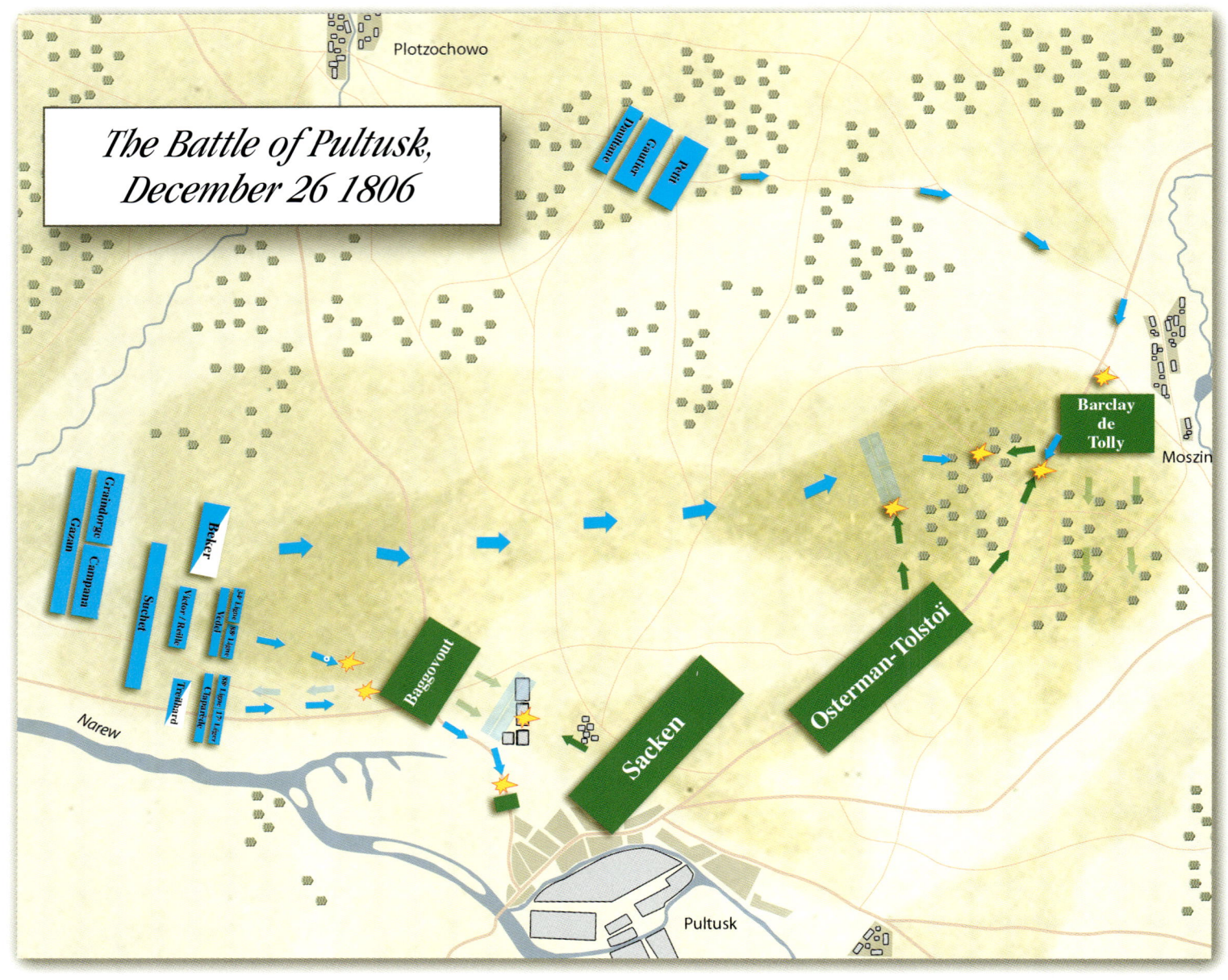

Napoleon could thus launch his attack. He wanted to strike where he thought the very centre of the enemy disposition was located. His corps set off. On the 24th Davout and Murat came across and beat a corps at Nasielsk whilst Augereau forced his way across the Wrka followed by Soult. Meanwhile Ney and Bessières pursued Lestocq and covered the left flank of the formations. However, the Emperor could only get a limited idea of the Russian situation. Indeed the thaw made the land and the roads impracticable; the light cavalry could not scout out the army's advance and bring their chief reliable information. So it was in these conditions that the French right wing met and engaged the enemy in two battles about twelve miles apart: Lannes at Pultusk and Davout, Augereau and Nansouty – temporarily replacing Murat who was ill – at Golymin. Further north, Ney confronted the Prussians at Soldau.

Pultusk, 26 December 1806

Benningsen had gathered together a force of between forty to forty-five thousand men on the plateau overlooking the town and in Pultusk. They were divided up into sixty-six battalions and one hundred squadrons. The left of this army – the Vilna and Stary-Oskol regiments, the Kiev Dragoons, the Polish Tartars and a regiment of Cossacks – under the command of Sacken backed onto the town of Pultusk and held the bridge across the Narev. It was covered en *grand garde* by General Baggovut and his force of ten battalions and twenty squadrons. The three-line centre was astride the Golymin road. The right, under the command of Ostermann-Tolstoi was deployed up to the little village of Moshin, covered by a detachment under Barclay de Tolly made up of the 1st, 3rd and 20th Chasseurs, the Tenga Regiment, five squadrons of Polish lancers and six artillery pieces. The whole front was covered by artillery batteries. Benningsen was counting on using the first troops from Buxhoevden's army as reinforcements. They were moving up from Ostrolenka together with the divisions coming back from Nasielsk. They were being pursued by the third division of Davout's corps, commanded temporarily by Daultane but the whole of this force was nevertheless formidable.

Lannes had been marching since morning with his 5th Corps. Unfortunately the weather was terrible – a mixture of snow and rain – and these and the mud made the roads unusable; the Marshall had to leave to his artillery and a number of his caissons behind, all stuck in the mud. When he arrived at Pultusk, his light cavalry had not been able to scout around out in front and all he had was Napoleon's information that there was only a Russian corps up in front.

Lannes attacks

Lannes had the southern tip of the plateau taken by the 17th Light which was marching at the head of the column, and then deployed his troops in two lines. Suchet was in front, placing the 17th Light, the Elite companies of the 88th and Treilhard's cavalry on the right under Claparède. He placed the 64th of the Line and a battalion of the 88th in the centre under Vedel. The right commanded by Victor and Reille was formed with the 2nd Battalion of the 88th, the 34th of the Line and Becker's Dragoon division. Gazan's division together with the Graindorge and Campana divisions formed the second line. The Russian position then revealed itself to be very solid but Lannes attacked the whole line.

On the right, Claparède attacked Baggovut and drove him back. But Benningsen threw six battalions from his reserve into the fray, supported by a cavalry charge, and in turn pushed back the French who were blinded by the whirling wind. Vedel in the centre made his troops march at an angle in order to support the right; but the battalion of the 88th was driven in by a further cavalry charge. The Russian column was

Some Frenchmen swum across the Vistula.
(RR)

From left to right and top to bottom. Maréchal Bessières, Generals Suchet, Gazan and Claparède. (RR)

then able to fall back without being worried. At the same time Reille, on the left, had Moshin and the wood next to the village attacked by the 34th of the Line. The fighting there was very fierce and the wood changed hands several times without the French being able to really to hold onto it in spite of support from the second battalion of the 88th.

At that moment, the fifth corps was at a halt when the division under General Daultane appeared on the left. He immediately formed up his battalions into attack columns and went over to the offensive on the Russian right wing at Moshin. Ostermann-Tolstoi's troops retreated in disorder but were saved from being routed by a counter-attack by the Russian reserve.

To every man his victory

With night falling, Lannes made a last attempt at cutting Benningsen off from his line of retreat and throwing him into the river. The Russian launched a powerful counter-attack against the French right, which was only just stopped by Suchet's tenacity and the stubbornness of the 34th and 85th of the Line.

Benningsen cried victory but because he thought he had all the French army in front of him, he feared he would be turned; so he took advantage of the darkness to fall back on Ostrolenka, abandoning the field littered with the dead and wounded. Entering the town of Pultusk, Lannes made 600 prisoners and found 1 200 wounded.

In a letter to the Emperor dated 27 December 1806, Lannes gave an account of that terrible day:

As soon as they were drawn up I had them attack this vanguard with the 17th Light Infantry and the 88th. After a few charges which were taken with a lot of cool-headedness, this cavalry fell back onto the army corps which was fighting, the right supported by the bridge at the other end of the town, the left on another bridge at the entrance of the town. General Victor was ordered to attack the bridge on the left with the 34th and a battalion of the 88th supported by Becker's division.

Meantime, the enemy had moved up about eight thousand infantry and three regiments of cavalry on my right, trying to turn me. I got the rest of the 88th and all the 64th to march against the bridge to cut the enemy's line of retreat to the bridge; and I got the 17th to attack this corps at the same time.

After intense firing, the enemy was overwhelmed and returned to the bridge in the greatest disorder. If a battalion of the 88th under severe pressure from enemy cavalry had not given way, the whole column might well have been taken prisoner.

The left held out against the firing from about fifteen thousand men. Had it not been for a formidable artillery barrage at the bridgehead which halted us with grapeshot when we moved too far forward, the enemy would have been driven into the river.

General Victor is full of praise for the 34th; it withstood the attacks from the infantry and the cavalry with extraordinary cool-headedness.

Seeing itself forced away from the left at around three in the afternoon, the enemy detached a column from its right in order to try and turn us on our right, but the presence of the Gazan division was enough to force them back in the line. We fought from ten o'clock in the morning until six in the evening, in mid-thigh high mud; it took our soldiers all their courage and strength to resist. Your Majesty saw what the day was like; the wind and the hail knocked our soldiers about. All the artillery got stuck in the mud and was practically of no use to us.

General Boussard was wounded, his horse killed. Colonel Barthélémi had his horse killed. The Dragoon division had 22 men killed including two officers; and 34 wounded including two officers, 88 horses killed and 22 wounded. General Treilhard had his horse killed and the Light Cavalry suffered a lot of casualties.

General Claparède had his horse killed, one of his aide de camps was wounded and the other killed. General Vedel was wounded as were the two battalion commanders of the 100th. I reckon the number of casualties for this army corps to be at least one thousand men. The enemy left behind more than three thousand casualties and several cannon and caissons. We found from one thousand to twelve hundred wounded at Pultusk. I can promise Your Majesty that since I have been fighting I have never experienced such fierce fighting as I did yesterday; we crossed bayonets with the enemy several times.

I can only praise the conduct of my aides de camp one of whom, M. Voisin, was killed. The Commander-in-Chief himself was in command personally. With him was General Balkson. We made about six hundred prisoners. We found several distinguished officers on the battlefield; among the wounded who are in the town the-

From left to right and top to bottom.
The Russian Generals Dokhtorov and Sacken. General Lasalle and Maréchal Augereau. *(RR)*

Below.
The Cossacks were a permanent thorn in the side of the French army. *(RR)*

"Sire,
I arrived yesterday with my army corps in front of Pultusk at about ten o'clock. I found the enemy on the plain in front of the town: about four to five thousand cavalry and some Cossacks formed the vanguard. General Suchet's division was ready for battle in two lines; General Gazan's was also in two lines but further back.

10

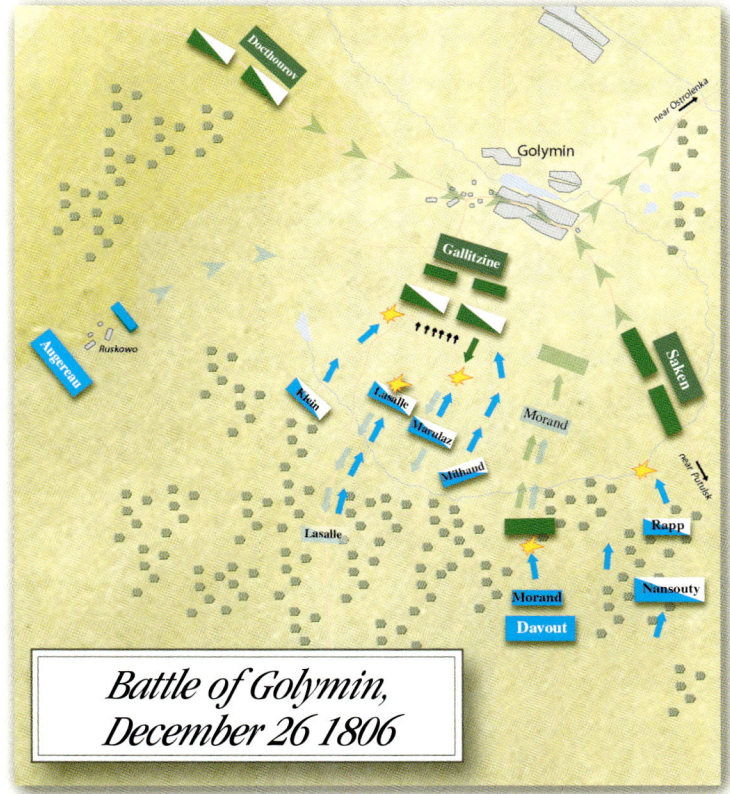

At Golymin, Lasalle "punished" his brigade by keeping his men within range of the enemy artillery. He lost two horses killed under him.
(A composition by Jack Girbal, Author's Collection.)

re are some remarkable people.

I reckon the Russian army which fought here yesterday was forty to sixty thousand strong in infantry and five to six thousand cavalry with at least fifty artillery pieces placed in batteries. Having been harassed all night, the enemy was only able to get part of his army over onto the left bank. The other is getting away to Rozau. I have ordered General Becker and the Light Cavalry to pursue them; he will be supported by General Gazan's brigade. The bridge has been burnt and is now being repaired. There are no resources in the countryside; it has been laid waste by the Russians. If a bridge could be set up at Sierock this would enable us to receive supplies from Warsaw."

In this letter, Lannes completely forgot to mention how d'Aultane's division intervened decisively and, as was the custom, he inflated the strength of Russians. However on that particular day he did face enemy forces outnumbering him two or three to one, supported by formidable artillery; he took the plateau overlooking Pultusk and forced Benningsen to retreat. This hellish day was one of the *Maréchal*'s greatest feats of arms. But he had had enough. He was ill and was shivering with fever. He had been wounded by a bullet. He had to rest and be cared for. He handed over command of the 5th Corps to the very competent Suchet. Napoleon rejected this choice and nominated Savary in place of the future Marshall. Moreover, the ever-susceptible Lannes held it against Napoleon for not including him in the honours list. But the Emperor made it up to him later when he entrusted him with the Elite Reserve Corps.

Battle of Golymin, December 26 1806

Golymin, 26 December 1806

Riding in front of the cavalry reserve, Lasalle and his light brigade discovered a large concentration of horsemen at Golymin – almost four thousand cuirassiers and dragoons, and a strong fifteen gun artillery position covering the advance of three infantry divisions heading towards Ostrolenka. These were the troops belonging to Generals Galitzin, Sacken and Dokhtorov, in all about fifteen thousand men. With Galitzin were the Dniepr Regiment, the St-Georges and Little Russia Cuirassiers, and the Tauride Grenadiers. Dokhtorov was bringing the Moscow and Ingermanland Dragoons, the Pavlograd Hussars and the Malachov Cossacks from Ciechanow. They were accompanied by Pahlen who had the 21st Chasseurs, the Sourny Hussars who had been split in two at Lopaczyn by the Chasseurs à cheval of the Guard led by Dahlmann who also took two cannon off them.

Thinking he had found the larger part of the Russian army, Napoleon deployed his corps. On the left, Augereau attacked along the Gollaczyn road across a wet plain scattered with lakes and little woods. His artillery was behind him, bogged down in the mud. The 16th Light took the little village of Ruskovo with a bayonet charge, enabling d'Heudelet's then Desjardins' divisions to deploy and march on Golymin. The fighting was very fierce. On the right, without either Gudin's division which was engaged at Pultusk under the command of d'Aultane, or Friant's which had still to come up, Davout launched Morand off towards the town through the woods. The Russians were driven out of them with bayonet charges and all their counter-attacks were driven off. Davout now attacked the Russian divisions passing along the road in the direction of Ostrolenka. In order to protect his left flank he ordered Marulaz to join up with Lasalle's brigade and to prevent the enemy attacking across the plain. The two brigades lined up. The horses got stuck in the mud and this caused a certain amount of alarm. Murat suddenly appeared and ordered Marulaz to attack the Russian cavalry and Lasalle to take the batteries.

Marulaz launched his Chasseurs but was very quickly stopped by the enemy cavalry. His men were saved by Klein's Dragoons who charged at the enemy, and by Milhaud who took the flank. The enemy Dragoons and the Cuirassiers were brought back to the village and reformed, sheltering behind the infantry which held the French off.

In order to take the batteries, Lasalle had no choice but to launch his brigade across the thousand yards separating his cavalry from the batteries, without giving the enemy gunners time to fire a second round of grapeshot and thus cause heavy casualties. Lasalle got his troops moving, but after only a few yards, the word *"Halt!"* was shouted and repeated along the line of cavalry. The two regiments, except for the Elite Company of the 7th Hussars, turned round and fled. Lasalle only managed to catch up with them several miles further back. He was furious. The General rallied his men then led them back to where they had come from and left them there, at the halt, until midnight under fire from the Russian guns. The casualties were relatively high. Lasalle, imperturbable in front of his horsemen, had two horses killed under him and ended up borrowing the horse of a trumpeter from the 7th Hussars. He had settled the Golymin Panic in his own way.

Marching in the mud became a terrible ordeal. Polish tracks were knee-deep in it and the troops advanced slowly, with great difficulty. The cold weather, cold as it was, was not cold enough to freeze the mud and some men, exhausted and despairing preferred to commit suicide including some in the ranks of the Old Guard. (RR)

Meanwhile on the right, Rapp took the heavy cavalry from the reserve and swept across the plain. His right arm was shattered in this fighting.

At nightfall, after resisting brilliantly, Galitzin preferred to break off and fall back on Ostrolenka, abandoning the artillery which had caused the French so much suffering. Napoleon started the pursuit but men and horses got bogged down in the mud which made pursuing anything impossible.

Soldau, 26 December 1806

Forty-five miles to the northwest of Golymin, Ney caught up with Lestocq's Prussians, strongly dug in the village of Soldau. To dislodge them, the troops of the 6th Corps had to pass along a raised road which crossed just over a mile of marshland, covered by two artillery batteries. The bridges along this road had been destroyed. Ney's cavalry under Colbert was too far away to play any part so he got Rouguet's Brigade to charge. The artillery was taken and the Prussian infantry which had come out in a column was pushed back into Soldau. The French then had to take the town house by house, each fiercely defended by the Prussians.

Finally at nightfall, they were driven out; but Lestocq rallied them further back. They resumed their attack four times. Each time they were beaten off. At midnight, Lestocq finally ordered his men to retreat, leaving behind several hundred dead and wounded, together with six cannon.

All during 26 December 1806, the French fought against the Russians along all the line to the east of the Wrka. The Russians lost almost twenty thousand men and eighty cannon. Quite a few caissons were also captured and pillaged. Coming up from Ciechanov which he reached on the 25th, Soult was unable to advance because of the terrible state of the roads. His 4th Corps was well and truly bogged down, blind and powerless. Bernadotte and Bessières did not meet any opposition but neither did they advance. The pursuit ordered by Napoleon was impossible. The army was immobilised, frozen, hungry and bogged down. The horses disappeared up to their bellies in the mud and the infantry had to make a superhuman effort for each step. Some of them in despair committed suicide, even among the Guard - what a scandal!

The Prussian General Kalckreuth. (RR)

The Winter Quarters

Napoleon had beaten the Russians, but the Polish winter had checked him. So the Emperor decided to call a halt, set up his winter quarters and wait for the weather to let him to resume operations later.

He spread his various corps out along a line going from the Baltic to the Bug along which Bernadotte, Ney, Soult and Davout established their quarters. The second line was made up of Murat who attached his dragoon division to the corps in the front line, together with those of Lasalle and Milhaud which were positioned between Soult and Davout, Augereau and Lannes. The Guard was with Napoleon in Warsaw, accompanied by the Nansouty, Suchet and Reille Divisions.

Rouyer and his Hessians blockaded Graudenz. Lefebvre was busy besieging Danzig where Kalkreuth and 10 000 men had sought refuge. All the corps commanders were ordered not to undertake any offensive operations. To the south, the Bavarians under Jérôme and the Wurtemburgers under Vandamme continued to occupy Silesia, both protecting the right flank of the Grande Armée and keeping an eye on nearby Austria.

Ney and especially Bernadotte both occupied vast wastes of land where it was difficult to find any supplies. Berthier severely reprimanded Ney for sending out foraging parties further north and ordered him back within the perimeter assigned to him.

Whilst the French were settling into their new positions, the Russians withdrew, moving up along the Narev with Benningsen proclaiming to everybody, and particularly the Tsar, that he had beaten Napoleon, and that victory would have been complete had he been supported by Buxhœvden. The main result of all this publicity was that Benningsen was given overall command of all the Russian troops on the front, thus brushing aside Buxhœvden and Kamenski. The Russian troops withdrew in weather conditions which were just as difficult for them as they were for the French, through Grodno, Novgorod and Biala. Lestocq fell back on Königsberg.

The two armies lost contact with each other by withdrawing and resting up. Everything seemed to indicate a winter truce which would allow wounds to be licked and things to be reorganised.

THE PRUSSIAN ARMY

LESTOCQ'S PRUSSIAN ARMY

Lestocq: Born of a French father in Hanover, he fought during the Seven Year War, then in Bavaria and Holland against the French during the Revolutionary Wars. Appointed Lieutenant-General in 1806, he was in command of the debris of the Prussian Army in 1806 and 1807. Under Kalkreuth, he contributed to the defence of Danzig and was made a Feldmarschall. He died on 1 January 1818.

The strength as at 3 June 1807 was as follows (24 000 combatants).

VON DIERECKE'S DIVISION
Fabrecky and Schliessen Grenadier Battalions
Rüchel, Prince Henry (ex-Schönig) and Piötz Regiments
Schlebowski and Besser 1 Battalions
Esebeck Dragoons
Stulpnagel and Wagenfeld Cuirassiers, and Bodyguards
2 Batteries of 6-pounders (Arent and Klapperbein)
2 12-pounder batteries (Kulke and Gunther)

VON REMBOW'S DIVISION
The Russian Sievsk, Azov, Perm and Kaluga Regiments
The Zieten and Baczko Dragoons
The Prittwitz Hussars
One Horse Artillery battery under Wedekin and one under Rentzel

KAMENSKI'S RESERVE DIVISION *(sent up as reinforcements)*
Kamenski? He was the General in command at the beginning of the campaign and was ousted by Benningsen, because he was too old. He spent two years in France. He fought against the Turks.

He was assassinated later. His son fought at Eylau and at Heilsberg. He was in command in Moldavia in 1810, but died in 1811 at Odessa.
The Russian Arkangel, Navaga and Mohilev Regiments
The 22nd Chasseurs
The Towarzysze Regiment and Battalion
(?) Russian Battery

ARNIM's DETACHMENT *(troops spread out along the Passarge consisting of mixed regiments)*

Wisibitzky's Brigade
The Bergen Fusiliers
The Prittwitz and Kohler (Russian) Hussars

Top. **After the great disaster of the Battle of Jena, the Prussian Army retreats.** *(RR)*

Centre. **After being captured by the Schill partisans, General Victor was exchanged for Blucher.** *(RR)*

Left to right. **Generals Blucher and Lestocq.** *(RR)*

LIEUTENANT-GENERAL LESTOCQ'S CORPS

Von Rüchel's Infantry Regiment IR N°2 from General von Blöz's First Division. The soldier is wearing full dress and on his right, the regimental flag and below that, the Colonel's flag.

Von Rüts' Infantry Regiment N°8 from General von Dieride's Second Division.

Von Schöning's N°11 Infantry Regiment from General von Blöz's First Division.

Von Besser's N°14 Infantry Division from General von Blöz's First Division.

André Jouineau © Histoire & Collections 2006

Opposite.
The Prussian Generals Lestocq and Zieten.

Bottom.
Prussia discovered with terror that its army was not invincible and that French bumpkins dressed in tatters could beat it and humiliate it.
(RR)

Zieten's Brigade
Zieten. He commanded the 1st Mixed Brigade at Friedland and protected Lestocq's retreat at Kœnigsberg.

He was mentioned at Laon in 1814 and then at Waterloo, He was made a Count in 1817. He retired with the rank of Feldmarschall in 1839.

The Wakenitz Fusiliers
The Wurtemberg Hussars
Horse Battery
The Russian Viborg Regiment
The Wedel Dragoons
The Pless Hussars
Sowinsky battery

Anhalt-Bernburg's Brigade
3 Russian Viborg Companies

Stutterheim's Brigade
Stutterheim's Fusiliers
The Russian Viborg Regiment
Wedel's Dragoons
Pless'Hussars (Russian)
One regiment of Cossacks
Bredow's Horse battery
Two pontoon crews (24 pontoons)

Von Schuler's Brigade
This brigade operated on the Nehrung.
The Russian Tobolsk and Poltosk Regiments
The Korff Battalion with the remainder of Bulow's and Pullet's battalions
Neumarkt Battalion
Heyking's Russian Dragoons
Cossacks and partisans

The Blücher Detachment
These troops operated in Swedish Pomerania.
Schill's Irregulars captured General Victor who was later exchanged for Blücher.
The Ruits Regiment
Schachtmeyer's Fusilier Battalion
Braun's Grenadier Battalion
One Chasseur Company
Schill's and Marwitz's Irregulars
The Queen's Hussars and Blücher's Hussars.

LIEUTENANT-GENERAL LESTOCQ'S CORPS

Von Plötz's Infantry Regiment N°42 from General von Dieride's First Division.

Battalion of Maffow Grenadiers, IR N°8 and IR N°42 from General von Blötz's First Division.

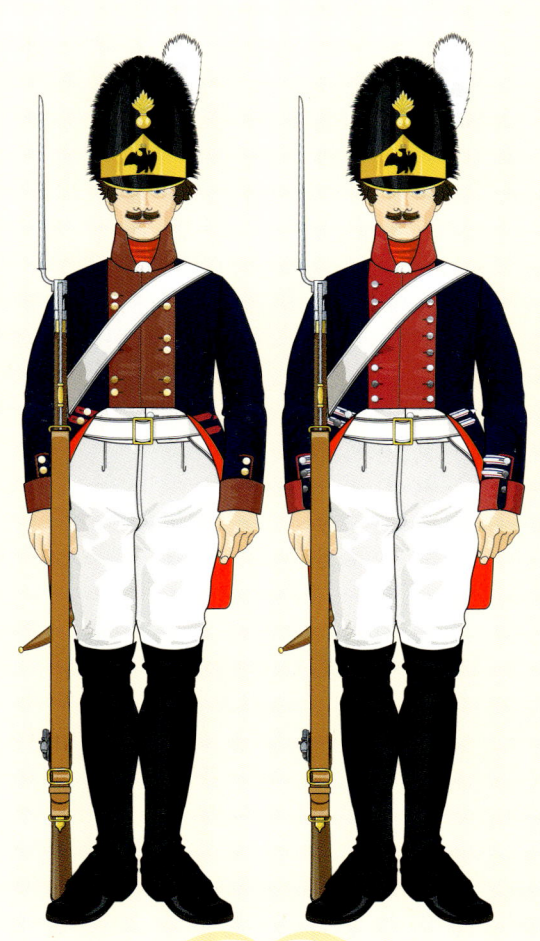

Battalion of Schieffen Grenadiers, IR N° 2 and N° 11, from General von Blöz's First Division.

Battalion of Fabedy Grenadiers, IR N°14 and N°16, from General von Blöz's First Division.

17

LIEUTENANT-GENERAL LESTOCQ'S CORPS

Battalion of Alt Braun Grenadiers IR N°3 and N°16, from General von Dieride's Second Division.

Soldier from von Rüchel's regiment IR N°2 in campaign dress.

Officer wearing a frock coat.

Cornet from von Schöning's Regiment IR N° 11.

Chasseur from von Plötz's Regiment IR N°42 wearing campaign dress.

Fife-player and NCO from von Besser's Regiment IR N°14.

LIEUTENANT-GENERAL LESTOCQ'S CORPS

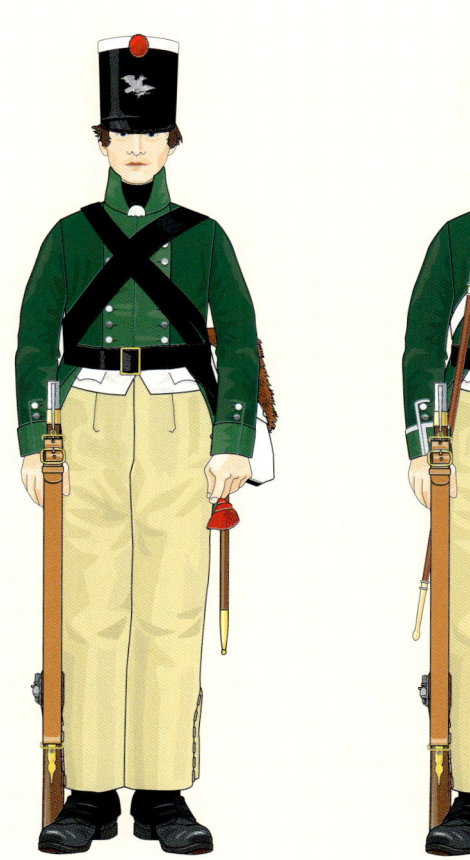

1st Brigade from East Prussia, the Corps' vanguard, General von Rembow, Fusilier Battalion von Bergen N°11.
From left to right: Fusiliers, NCO and cornet.

Fusilier Subaltern.

2nd Brigade from East Prussia.
From left to right
Fusilier from the Stuuterheim Battalion N°21.

NCO from the same battalion.

Fusilier from the Schlachtmeyer Battalion N°23.

Fusilier from the von Bulow Battalion.

LIEUTENANT-GENERAL LESTOCQ'S CORPS

Dragoons

Standard-bearer from the Auer Dragoons from General von Kall's Cavalry Division N°6.

Trooper from the von Auer Dragoons N°6.

Trooper from the von Baczko Dragoons, Division from General von Rhöler's Cavalry Division N°7.

Trooper from the von Esebeck Dragoons from General von Rhöler's Cavalry Division N°8.

LIEUTENANT-GENERAL LESTOCQ'S CORPS

Cavalry

Trooper in the von Rouquette Dragoons from General von Rhöler's Cavalry Division N° 13.

Trooper in the von Wagenfeld Cuirassiers from General von Rhöler's Cavalry Division N°4.

Trooper from the von Pritwitz Hussars from General von Kall's Cavalry Division N°5.

Towarczys Trooper, General von Kall's cavalry. The Towarczys wore the number 9 in the subdivision of the Hussar arm.

Trooper from the von Rouquette Dragoons from General von Rhöler's Cavalry Division N°13.

André Jouineau © Histoire & Collections 2006

LIEUTENANT-GENERAL LESTOCQ'S CORPS

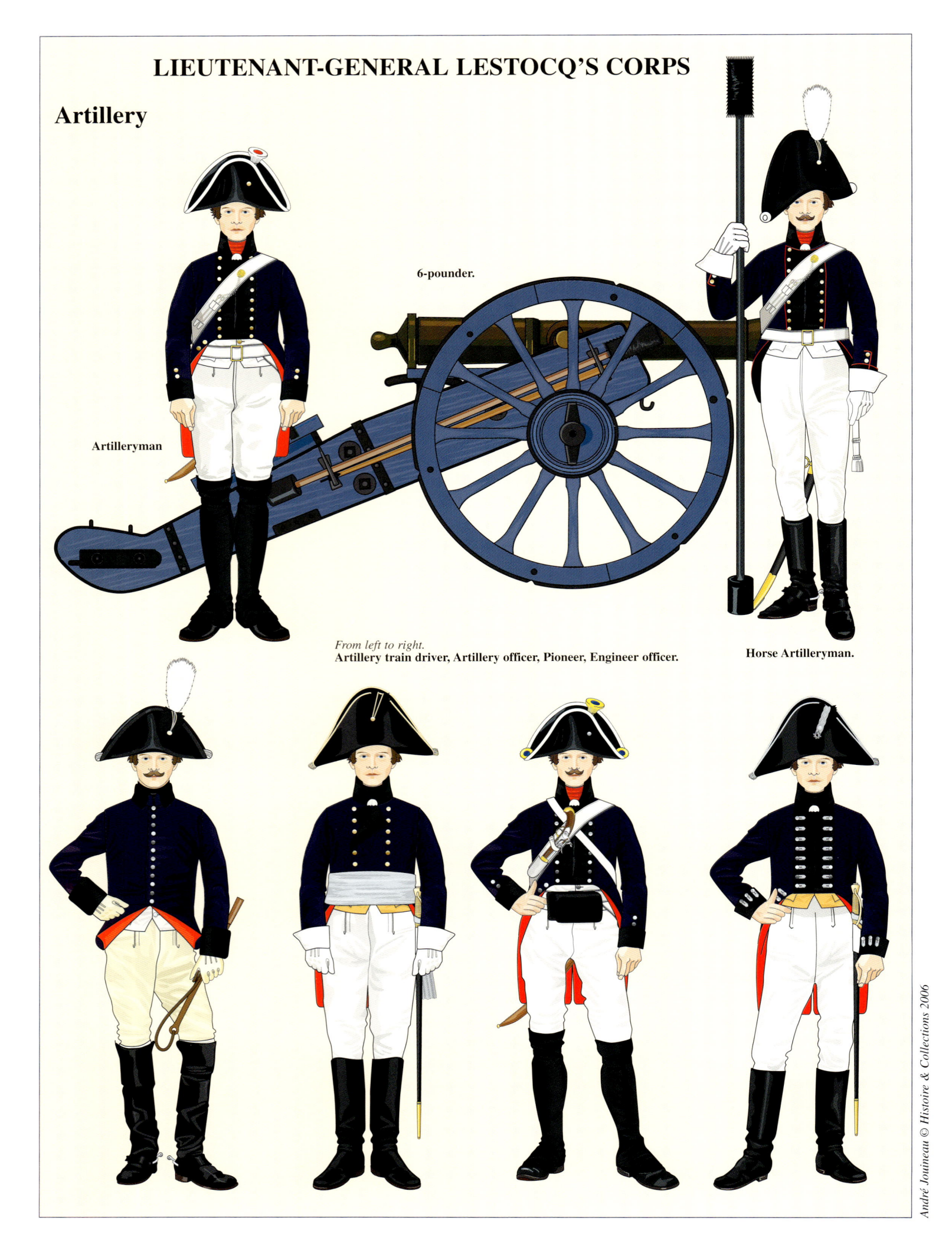

Artillery

6-pounder.

Artilleryman

Horse Artilleryman.

From left to right.
Artillery train driver, Artillery officer, Pioneer, Engineer officer.

GARRISON INFANTRY IN SILESIA

Von Alvensleben Infantry Regiment IR N°33.

Von Pelchrzim Infantry Regiment IR N° 38.

Von Grawert Infantry Regiment IR N°47.

From left to right.
Von Losthin Grenadier, Fusilier from von Moeller's Provisional Battalion, Von Schell Grenadier-Chasseur.

RUSSIAN INFANTRY

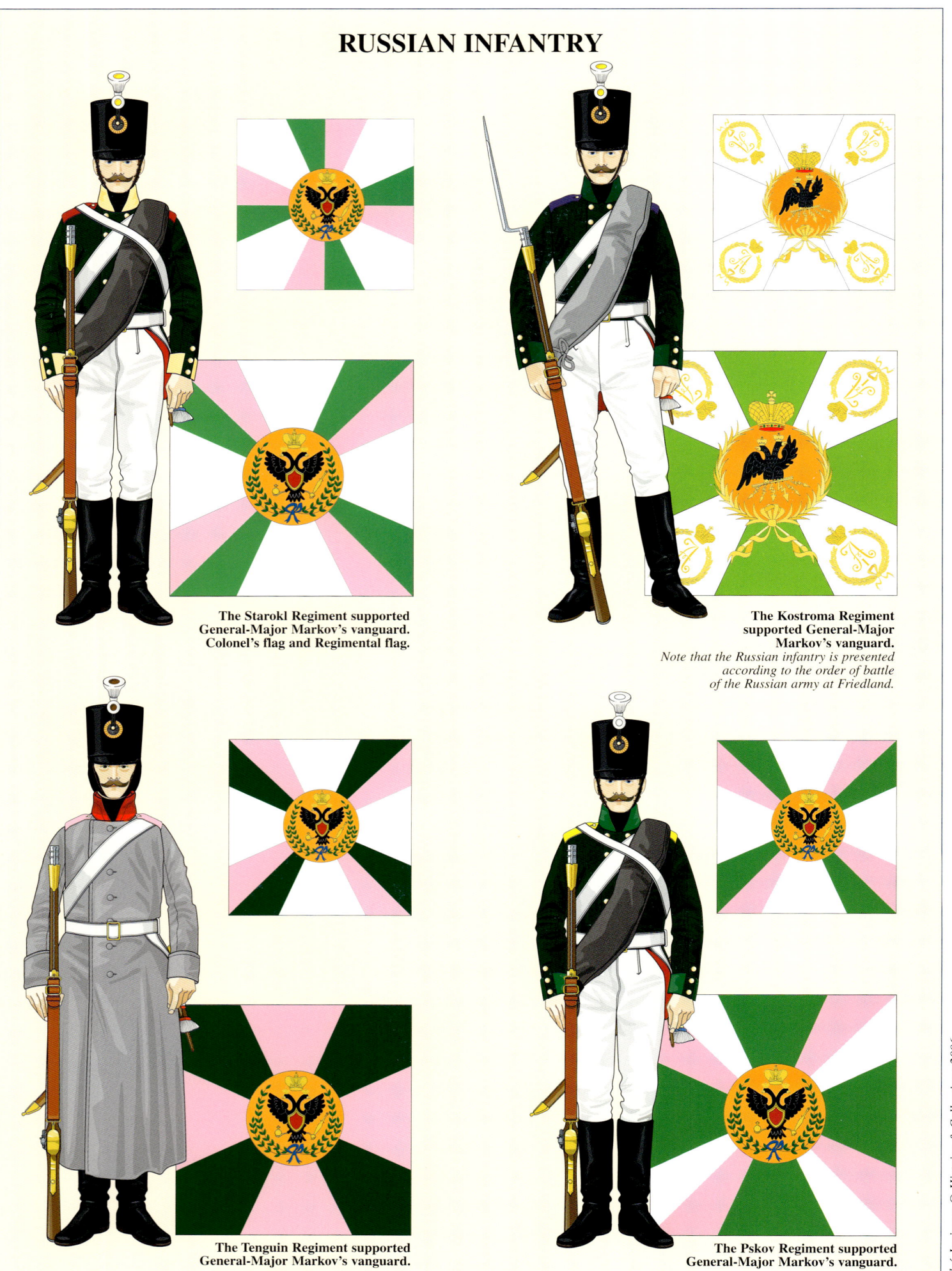

The Starokl Regiment supported General-Major Markov's vanguard. Colonel's flag and Regimental flag.

The Kostroma Regiment supported General-Major Markov's vanguard.
Note that the Russian infantry is presented according to the order of battle of the Russian army at Friedland.

The Tenguin Regiment supported General-Major Markov's vanguard.

The Pskov Regiment supported General-Major Markov's vanguard.

RUSSIAN INFANTRY

The Moscow Grenadiers supported General-Major Markov's vanguard.

The Rostov Regiment. 2nd Division, General-Lieutenant Count Ostermann.

Pavlovski Grenadier NCO. 2nd Division, General-Lieutenant Count Ostermann.

Jelest Regiment. 2nd Division, General-Lieutenant Count Ostermann.

St. Petersburg Grenadier. 2nd Division, General-Lieutenant Count Ostermann.

RUSSIAN INFANTRY

Litov Regiment.
3rd Division, General Baron Sacken.

Kopor Regiment.
3rd Division, General Baron Sacken.

Tchernigov Regiment.
3rd Division, General Baron Sacken.

Tauride Grenadier Regiment.
3rd Division, General Baron Sacken.

RUSSIAN INFANTRY

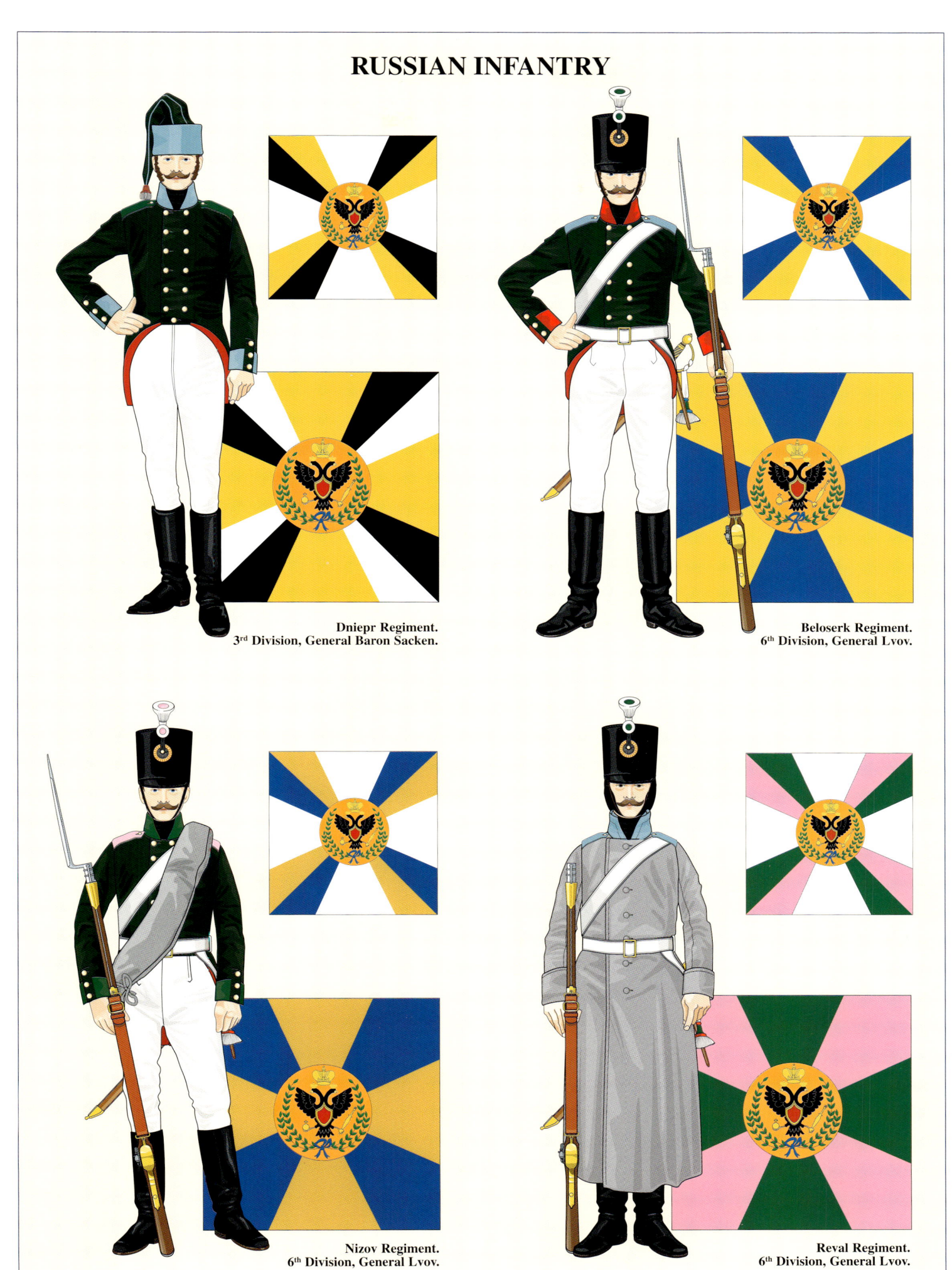

Dniepr Regiment.
3rd Division, General Baron Sacken.

Beloserk Regiment.
6th Division, General Lvov.

Nizov Regiment.
6th Division, General Lvov.

Reval Regiment.
6th Division, General Lvov.

THE RUSSIAN ARMY

THE RUSSIAN ARMY AT THE BEGINNING OF 1807

In his memoirs, Benningsen gives two versions of how the Russian army was made up. The first was made at the beginning of the campaign at the end of 1806 and gave a strength of 62 255 men. The second dates from the time of Friedland; the army had been reinforced after Eylau and numbered some 85 000 men.

The Russian army in existence at the end of 1806 was organised along the same lines as the one that was trounced at Austerlitz. It comprised two corps, the first under the command of Benningsen. It was made up of four inter-arm divisions, each having the strength of a French army corps, except for the cavalry which was shared out among the divisions, instead of being grouped together into a powerful reserve, like the one commanded by Murat. The second corps was commanded by Buxhœvden and also had a strength of four divisions. After the terrible bloodbath at Eylau, the army was reinforced but was also reorganised in a way that foreshadowed the army of 1812-14. Indeed the strength of the divisions was reduced and the cavalry and the infantry were sometimes endivisioned separately. The whole gained in flexibility.

BENNINGSEN'S CORPS

Benningsen. Born in Brunswick, he entered Russian service in 1773 but was disgraced by Paul I in whose murder (attempt) he took part. He commanded the Army of the North. He played an important part in the victory at Leipzig. He died in 1826. Benningsen's chief of staff was Count Steinhel and his artillery was commanded by Rezvoï.

LIEUTENANT-GENERAL OSTERMAN'S 2nd DIVISION
Makovski's Brigade
Pavlovsk Grenadiers
Rostov Musketeers
Sukin 2's Brigade
St-Petersburg Grenadiers
Eletz Musketeers
Lieven's Brigade
1st and 20th Chasseurs
Kochkin's Brigade
Corps Cuirassiers
Kargopol Dragoons
Isyum Hussars
Yefremov and Ilovayiski Cossacks
1 Company of Pioneers
5 Artillery batteries

LIEUTENANT-GENERAL SACKEN'S 3rd DIVISION
Ushakov Brigade
Tauride Grenadiers
Lithuanian Musketeers
Titov 2's Brigade
Koporski Grenadiers
Murom Musketeers
Briseman von Netting's Brigade
Dniepr and Chernigov Musketeers
21st Chasseurs à pied
Pahlen's Brigade
Little Russia Cuirassiers
Courland Dragoons
Sum Hussars
Papuzin Hussars
One company of Pioneers and Pontoneers
6 Artillery batteries

LIEUTENANT-GENERAL GALITZIN 5'S 4th DIVISION
Somov's Brigade
Tula and Tenguinsk Musketeers
Arsenyev's Brigade
Novoiginsk and Tobolsk Musketeers
Barclay de Tolly's Brigade
Polotsk and Kostroma
3rd Chasseurs à pied
Korf's Brigade
Korf was wounded at Eylau, he carried on throughout the whole campaign and was promoted to Lieutenant-General in 1811. He served during the following years and commanded the 21st Cavalry Division in 1815.
Cuirassiers of the Military Order
Pskov Dragoons
Polish Uhlans
Grekov Cossacks
One company of Pioneers and Pontoneers with 50 pontoons
Two 12-pdr batteries, three 6-pounder batteries and one 12-piece horse artillery battery

MAJOR-GENERAL SEDMORATSKI'S 6th DIVISION
Rachmanov's Brigade
Vilna and Nizov Musketeers
Bykov's Brigade
Volhynia and Revel Musketeers
Baggovut's Brigade
Staroskol Musketeers
4th Chasseurs à pied
Lvov's Brigade
Ekaterinoslav Cuirassiers
Kiev Dragoons
Alexandria Hussars
Tartary Hussars
One Popov V Cossack regiment

From left to right and top to bottom.
The Russian Generals Benningsen, Osterman-Tolstoi, Sacken and Pahlen.
(RR)

RUSSIAN INFANTRY

Volnyia Regiment.
6th Division General Lvov.

Ekaterinoslav Regiment.
7th Division,
General Essen.

Moscow Regiment.
7th Division, General Essen.

Vladimir Regiment.
7th Division, General Essen.

From left to right and top to bottom.
The Russian Generals Korf, Barclay de Tolly, Tutchkov, Dokhtorov, Volkonski and Bagration. *(RR)*

One company of Pioneers
Two 12-pounder batteries, three 6-pounder batteries and one 12-piece horse artillery battery

BUXHŒVDEN'S CORPS

Buxhœvden. Major-General against the Swedes in Poland. He commanded an army corps reinforcement. He succeeded Benningsen, pushed back the Swedes from Finland and left the army in 1800. He died in 1811.

LIEUTENANT-GENERAL TUCHOV I'S 5th DIVISION
Tuchov. Major-General then Lieutenant-General, he replaced Buxhœvden and was mentioned at Eylau. He commanded the 5th Division in Finland. He commanded the 5th Corps in 1812 and was killed near Utitza.

(?)'s Brigade
Kaluga and Sevsk Musketeers
24th Chasseurs à pied

Leontiev's Brigade
Perm and Mohilev Musketeers
25th Chasseurs à pied
Kazan and Riga Dragoons
Elizabetgrad Hussars
Lithuanian Uhlans
Gordeyev Cossacks
Two 6- and two 12-pounder batteries and one twelve-piece horse artillery battery

LIEUTENANT-GENERAL DOKHTOROV'S 7th DIVISION
X's Brigade
Ekaterinoslav Grenadiers
Moscow, Vladimir, Azov and Pskov Musketeers
5th Chasseurs à pied
Czaplitz Brigade
Moscow and Ingermanland Dragoons
Pavlograd Hussars
Malkhov and Andronov Cossacks
One company of Pioneers and one of Pontoneers

LIEUTENANT-GENERAL ESSEN III'S 8th DIVISION
Essen. A General since 1799, he was decorated at Eylau, served with Bagration at Heilsberg and was seriously wounded at Friedland. He commanded the 25th Division in 1815. He became Governor of St-Petersburg in 1830 and was made a Count the following year.

Prince Karl von Mecklenburg's Brigade
Moscow Grenadiers
Vyborg Musketeers
Engelhardt's Brigade
Schlisselburg and Old Ingermanland Musketeers
(?)'s Brigade
Podolia and Archangelsk Musketeers
7th Chasseurs à pied
Olviopol Hussars
Two Cossack regiments
One company of Pioneers
Five artillery batteries

LIEUTENANT-GENERAL SOMOV'S 14th DIVISION
At the beginning of the campaign, the division was commanded by Anerep, made up in a different manner, and responsible to Buxhœvden.

Alexeyev's Brigade
Belosersk and Riazan Musketeers
Gersdorff's Brigade
Sophia and Uglitsk Musketeers
23rd and 26th Chasseurs à pied
Finland and Mittau Dragoons
Grodno Hussars
One company of Pioneers and three artillery batteries.

ESSEN I'S RESERVE CORPS

PRINCE VOLKONSKI III'S 9th DIVISION
Volkonski. General and aide de camp to Tsar Alexander I, he was decorated at Austerlitz. He was promoted to Field-Marshal in 1830.
Astrakan Grenadiers
Galich, Ukraine, Crimea and Penzel Orel Musketeers
10th Chasseurs
Glukhov Cuirassiers
Novorossisk Dragoons
Mariopol Hussars
Two Cossack regiments

MELLER-ZAKOMELSKY'S 10th DIVISION
Kiev Grenadiers
Riask, Kura, Laroslav, Briansk and Viatka Musketeers
8th Chasseurs
Kharkov and Chernigov Dragoons
Akhtyrka Hussars
Two Cossack regiments
Two batteries of twelve-pounders and one horse artillery battery.

(Continued on page 34)

RUSSIAN INFANTRY

Voronej Regiment.
7th Division, General Essen.

NCO,
Schlisselburg Regiment.
8th Division General Engelhardt.

Podolia Regiment.
8th Division General Engelhardt.

Riazan Regiment.
14th Division General Somov.

RUSSIAN INFANTRY

Uglist Regiment.
14th Division General Somov.

Sophie Regiment.
14th Division General Somov.

Tula Regiment.
14th Division General Somov.

Vilna Regiment.
14th Division General Somov.

RUSSIAN "CHASSEURS À PIED"

3rd Regiment of Chasseurs à Pied. Vanguard, General Baggovut.

4th Regiment of Chasseurs à Pied. Vanguard, General Baggovut.

5th Regiment of Chasseurs à Pied. Vanguard, General Baggovut.

7th Regiment of Chasseurs à Pied. Vanguard, General Baggovut.

Drummer.

Officer.

2nd Regiment of Chasseurs à Pied. Grand Duke Constantine's Reserve.

Above. At Tilsit, the Tsar Alexander I showed his army to Napoleon. Cossacks and Bashkirs were not the least exotic elements in his army. At the time, the Russian army was being fully reorganised but this only bore its fruits in 1812. (RR)

(Continued from page 30)

RUSSIAN ORDER OF BATTLE, JUNE 1807

LIEUTENANT-GENERAL PRINCE BAGRATION'S VANGUARD

Bagration. Originally from Georgia, he served under Suvarov in Poland and Italy. He was promoted General in 1799, then Lieutenant-General in 1805. In 1807, he was either at the rearguard or in the vanguard, depending on the circumstances. He beat the Swedes in 1806, then the Turks. He was killed at Borodino while commanding the 2nd Army in the West.

Kutayissov commanded the artillery.

MAJOR-GENERAL BESTUSCHEV'S LEFT WING
20th, 23rd, 24th, 25th and 26th Chasseurs à pied
Grodno Hussars
One horse artillery battery

MAJOR-GENERAL BAGGOVUT'S RIGHT WING
3rd, 4th, 5th and 7th Chasseurs à pied
Pavlograd Hussars
One horse artillery battery

MAJOR-GENERAL MARKOV'S SUPPORTING INFANTRY
Moscow Grenadiers
Kostroma, Tenguinsk, Starokolsk and Pskov Musketeers

LIEUTENANT-GENERAL GORTCHAKOV'S FRONT-LINE CORPS

Gortchakov. A nephew of Suvarov, he was his aide de camp at Zurich. He was at Heilsberg and Friedland. He was Minister of War in 1812.

LIEUTENANT-GENERAL OSTERMAN-TOLSTOI'S 2nd DIVISION
Osterman-Tolstoi. Major-General in 1798, Osterman-Tolstoi was at Pultusk and at Eylau. He was wounded at Guttstadt and was awarded a golden sword. He subsequently replaced Tchkov who was ill, staying on the Narev to face Masséna. Wounded at Borodino, he lost his left hand at Kulm. Commanding officer of the Pavlovsk Regiment and of the Grenadiers in 1815, he died in 1857. Not to be confused with the writer Leo Tolstoi.

Makowski's Brigade
Pavlov Grenadiers and Rostov Musketeers

Sukin's Brigade
Saint-Petersburg Grenadiers
Jeletsk Musketeers
One company of Pioneers
Two 12- and two 6-pounder batteries, and one horse artillery battery

GENERAL SACKEN'S 3rd DIVISION
Sacken. Wounded and captured at Zurich, he was at the time Lieutenant-General. Benningsen's had him in his bad books and excluded him for five years and then reinstated him. He was mentioned in 1813, then at Brienne and la Rothière; he was nonetheless beaten at Montmirail. He was present at Laon and Craonne. King Louis XVIII and the inhabitants of Paris offered him gifts for his behaviour whilst Governor of that city. Field-Marshall in 1826, he was made a Prince of the Empire.

Ushakov's Brigade
Tauride Grenadiers
Lithuanian Musketeers

Titov II's Brigade
Murmansk and Koporsk Musketeers

Netting's Brigade
Chernigov and Dniepr Musketeers
One company of Pioneers and one of Pontoneers with 50 pontoons
Two 12- and three 6-pounder batteries and one horse artillery battery

LIEUTENANT-GENERAL UVAROV'S LEFT WING CAVALRY
Uvarov. Lieutenant-General in 1800 and commanded the Chevaliers-Gardes. He was mentioned in 1807. He commanded the cavalry at Leipzig and commanded the Imperial Guard in 1821.

(Continued on page 40)

RUSSIAN "CHASSEURS À PIED"

20th Regiment of Chasseurs à Pied. Vanguard, General Bestuschev.

23rd Regiment of Chasseurs à Pied. Vanguard, General Bestuschev.

24th Regiment of Chasseurs à Pied. Vanguard, General Bestuschev.

Officer. Chasseur. Drummer. Chasseur.

25th Regiment of Chasseurs à Pied. Vanguard, General Bestuschev.

26th Regiment of Chasseurs à Pied. Vanguard, General Bestuschev.

RUSSIAN CAVALRY

Kazan Dragoons. General Dolgorukov's Cavalry.

Riga Dragoons. General Dolgorukov's Cavalry.

Courland Dragoons. General Dolgorukov's Cavalry.

Ekaterinoslav Cuirassiers. 6th division Cavalry, General Lvov.

Kiev Dragoons. 6th Division Cavalry, General-Major Galitzin.

RUSSIAN CAVALRY
Dragoons

Pskov Dragoons.
6th Division Cavalry,
General-Major Galitzin.

Moscow Dragoons.
6th Division Cavalry,
General-Major Galitzin.

Mitau Dragoons.
7th Division Cavalry, General-Major Borozdin.

Finland Dragoons.
7th Division Cavalry,
General-Major Borozdin.

Livland Dragoons, 7th Division Cavalry,
General-Major Borozdin.

37

RUSSIAN CAVALRY

Trumpeter, Saint Petersburg Dragoons. 8th Division Cavalry, General-Major Zakomenski.

Kargopol Dragoons. 8th Division Cavalry, General-Major Zakomenski.

Ingermanland Dragoons. 8th Division Cavalry, General-Major Zakomenski.

Grodno Hussars. General-Major Bestuschev's Cavalry Vanguard.

Pavlograd Hussars. General-Major Baggovut's Cavalry Vanguard.

RUSSIAN CAVALRY

Hussars

Sum Hussars. Front-line Cavalry, General-Major Yurkovski.

Elisabethgrad Hussars. Front-line Cavalry, General-Major Yurkovski.

Alexandria Hussars. 6th Division Cavalry, General-Major Galitzin.

Isium Hussars. 6th Division Cavalry, General-Major Galitzin.

Olviopol Hussars. 6th Division Cavalry, General-Major Galitzin.

the left wing. He took part in the battles of 1807; he retired in 1809, offended. He was reinstated in 1812, 1813 and 1814 as commanding officer of the 2nd Corps, and Governor of Moscow.

Dolgorukov's Brigade (?)
Alexandria Hussars
Polish Uhlans
Yurkovski's Brigade (?)
Pskov and Moscow Dragoons
(?)'s Brigade
Izium and Olviopol Hussars

LIEUTENANT-GENERAL DOKHTOROV'S SECOND-LINE CORPS

MAJOR-GENERAL ESSEN III'S 7th DIVISION
Zapolski's Brigade
Ekaterinoslav and Moscow Musketeers
(?)'s Brigade
Vladimir and Voronchev Musketeers
Borozdin's Brigade
Borozdin. Colonel in the Guard in 1800, he commanded Gortchakov's vanguard at Guttstadt and drove Ney off towards Deppen and the Passarge. Promoted to Major-General, he was decorated at Heilsberg with a gold and diamond sword. The following year, he fought against Sweden. In 1812, he was at Borodino, the Beresina and Vilna. During the French Campaign, he was present at la Ferté, Fère-Champenoise and Paris. He was then Commander-in-Chief of the cavalry against the Turks.
Mittau, Livland and Finland Dragoons
One company of Pioneers and one of Pontoneers
Six artillery batteries

GENERAL ENGELHARDT'S 8th DIVISION
(?)'s Brigade
Schliesselburg, Old Ingermanland and Podolia Musketeers
Sakomelski's Brigade
Kargopol, St.-Petersburg and Ingermanland Dragoons
Two artillery batteries

GENERAL SOMOV'S 14th DIVISION
Olsufiev's Brigade
Riazan Musketeers
Gersdorff's Brigade
Uglitsk and Sophia Musketeers
Alexeyev's Brigade
Vilna and Tula Musketeers
One company of Pontoneers and three artillery batteries

ATAMAN PLATOV'S COSSACK CORPS
Platov. Ataman of the Don Cossacks in 1801, he was mentioned in the fighting against the Turks. He was made a Count in 1813. In 1814, he was given an ovation by the English as was Blücher. A monument to him was erected at Novo-Cherkask.
1st Chasseurs à pied
20 Cossack regiments
One 12-piece Don Cossack artillery battery

GRAND-DUKE CONSTANTINE'S RESERVES, THE IMPERIAL GUARD
Grand-Duke Constantine's Brigade (?)
Chasseurs à pied of the Guard
2nd Chasseurs à pied
Militia of the Guard
Cossacks of the Guard
Mallutin's Brigade
Preobrajenski, Semenovski and Ismailovski Guards Regiments
Velikolutsk, Pernau and Kexholm Musketeers
Kollogrivov's Brigade
Chevaliers-Gardes
Horse Guards
Uhlans of the Guard
Hussars of the Guard
Two heavy 12-piece artillery batteries and one horse artillery battery, also with twelve pieces.

From left to right and top to bottom. **The Russian Generals Gortchakov, Uvarov and Olsufiev. Grand Duke Constantine and the Ataman Platov.** *(RR)*

(continued from page 34)

Dolgorukov's Brigade (?)
Kazan, Riga and Courland Dragoons
Yurkovski's Brigade
Sum and Elizabetgrad Hussars
Lithuanian Uhlans
One battery of horse artillery

MAJOR-GENERAL GALITZIN'S RIGHT WING CAVALRY
Galitzin was Prince *Sérénisimme*. He spent six years in France in Strasbourg with his brother. Lieutenant-General in 1800, he was at Golymin then commanded the cavalry on

RUSSIAN CAVALRY

Lithuanian Uhlans.
Front-line Cavalry, General-Major Yurkovski.

Tartary Uhlans.
6th Division Cavalry, General-Major Kretov.

Polish Uhlans.
6th Division Cavalry, General-Major Galitzin.

Cossack Corps.
Ataman General-Lieutenant Platov.
This corps comprised 20 Cossack regiments and two companies of militia.

41

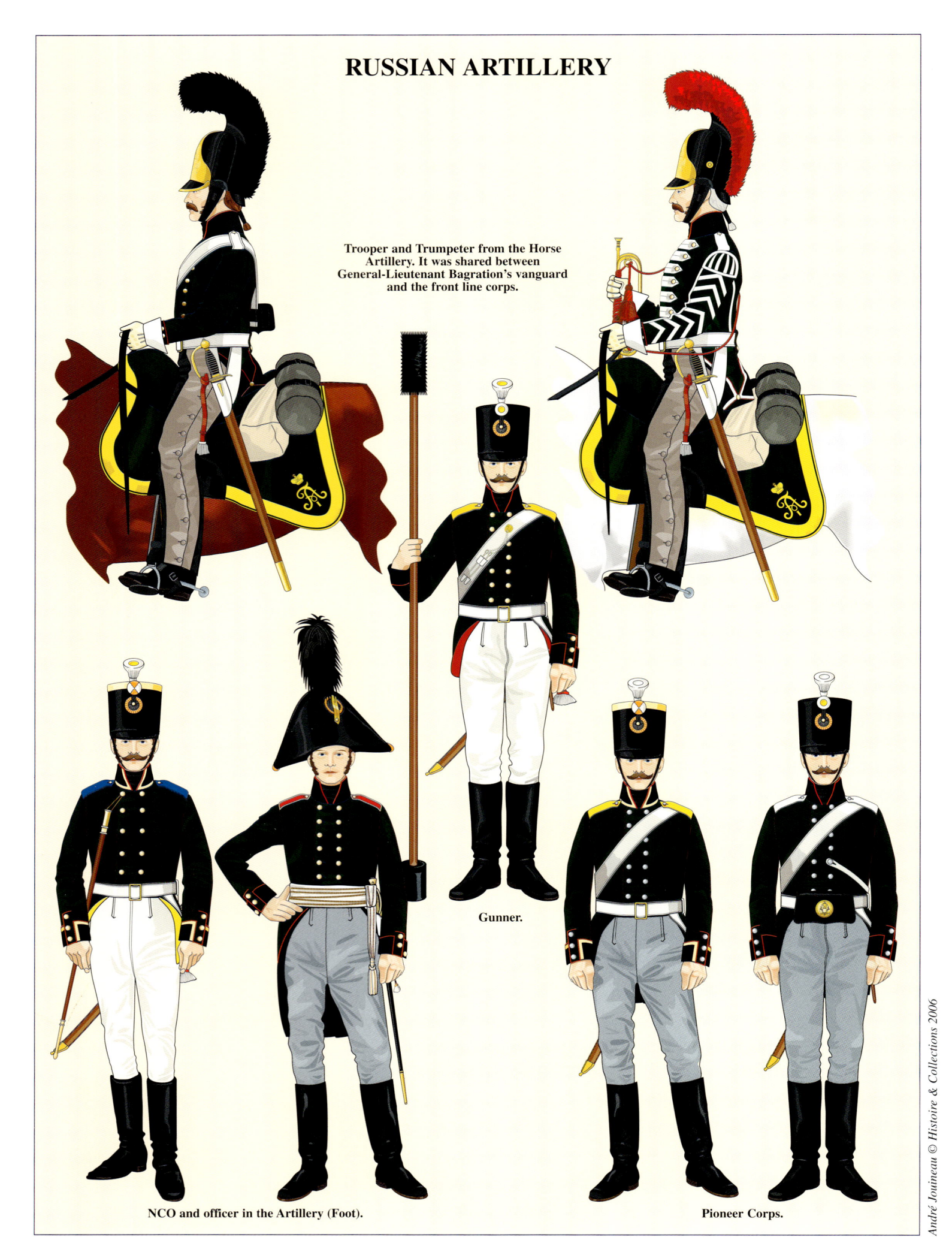

RUSSIAN ARTILLERY

Trooper and Trumpeter from the Horse Artillery. It was shared between General-Lieutenant Bagration's vanguard and the front line corps.

Gunner.

NCO and officer in the Artillery (Foot).

Pioneer Corps.

TSAR ALEXANDER'S FOOT GUARDS

Preobrajenski. NCO and Drummer.

Semenovski.

Ismailovski.

Chasseurs à Pied.

Foot Artillery Artilleryman and NCO.

TSAR ALEXANDER'S HORSE GUARDS

Chevalier-Garde.

Cuirassier of the Guard.

Hussar of the Guard.

Uhlan.

Horse Artillery.

THE BATTLE OF EYLAU

Above.
Baron Lepic at Eylau. "Heads high, grapeshot is not sh…" *(RMN)*

Tricking Napoleon into believing that the Russians were setting up their winter quarters, Benningsen continued his retreat then started a turning movement. For this, the Russian forces regrouped, moved towards Rhein then headed off towards Bischofstein. Lestocq flanked them on their left. Only Sedmoratzki and Essen, each at the head of about 18 000 men, remained east.

Benninsen's manoeuvre

This movement was intended to envelope the French army from the north, with the Russians then falling upon its rear, thus cutting off its lines of communications which were obviously vital, whilst at the same time themselves remaining close to Königsberg with its well-stocked stores and warehouses. The Russian army was aided in its move by the wintry conditions which froze the roads and the rivers solid. And so it was that with a mass of some 60 000 men and more than 400 cannon, Benningsen marched against Bernadotte's First Corps which had been spread out widely on account of the vast area of land it had to cover.

The Russian presence was nevertheless discovered thanks to Ney's disobedience. Indeed, realising that his sector was too poor to sustain his 18 000-men corps, he decided to send light columns out foraging – or marauding – towards the north: Bartstein, Guttstadt and even Heilsberg. Berthier in a letter dated 18 January reminded him icily where his duty lay. At the same time, one of the detachments from the 6th Corps discovered that the Russian army was marching west and heading straight towards Bernadotte's army. Ney fell back and immediately informed Soult and the Emperor on one hand, and Bernadotte on the other. The latter however had a lot of trouble concentrating his troops so he decided to regroup them in two places, Osterode and Mohrungen.

It was near this hamlet that the first real skirmish of the offensive took place. On 25 January, the Russian vanguard under Markov engaged Pachtod who resisted brilliantly then was reinforced first by Drouet's division under the direct command of Bernadotte, then finally by Dupont's division who arrived at the cost of a hard forced march. The Russians were stopped then pushed back.

The Eve of the year 1807

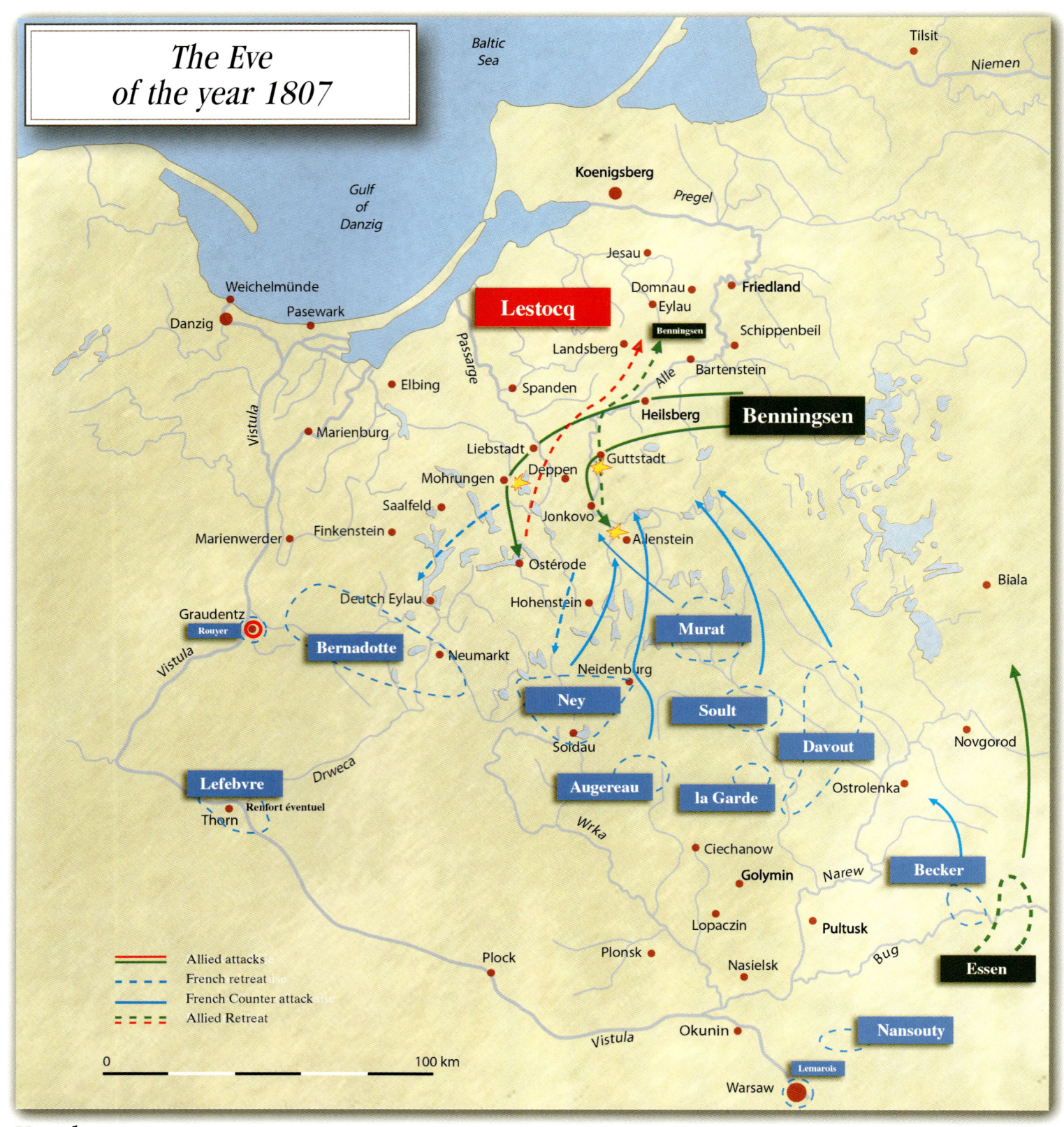

Napoleon reacts

Napoleon then saw clearly through Benningsen's plan. He reacted quickly and efficiently. Orders were given to the First Corps to withdraw slowly in the direction of Thorn in order to draw the Russians more towards the west. Lefebvre had to be ready to support Bernadotte if necessary. Savary, replacing Lannes who was ill, had to remain covering Warsaw which Oudinot, reinforced by Necker's Dragoons, was protecting against Essen. All the other corps – Ney, Soult, Murat, Davout, Augereau and the Guard – moved up towards Allenstein to cut off Benningsen's retreat, using Ney as the pivot for this movement. The line of the attack was due north, in the direction of Allenstein with, as objective, to outflank Benningsen's army and to cut it off from its rear if it crossed the Passarge. Once again, Napoleon asked his men to win the battle not with their bayonets but with their legs. The freezing weather made marching easier.

Unfortunately for the French army, on 1 February some Cossacks intercepted a courier from Berthier informing Bernadotte of all the Emperor's plans.

They reported to Benningsen who immediately grasped the danger of the situation. His army risked getting itself wiped out if he persisted with his manoeuvre. He reacted immediately ordering a forced march withdrawal. Napoleon who was not yet informed of the Russian reaction continued to moving up his corps in three columns: Murat and Soult in the van; Ney on the left – reinforced by Espagne's Cuirassiers, supported by Bernadotte and Nansouty's division covered by Thorn – with Liebstadt as his objective. Davout was moving up on the right. Augereau and the Guard formed the centre. When the Emperor learnt of the Russian withdrawal, he carried on with his move all the same, making sure he held all the crossings over the Alle and ordering his Marshals to get ready for the battle. He wrote to Davout: *"I think we will shortly have some work to do."* Likewise he ordered Bernadotte to move forward and follow Lestocq as closely as possible.

The fighting at Inkowo

On 3 February, Murat discovered the Russian army deployed in battle order on the Inkowo Plateau, protecting both the Liebstadt road and the bridges over the Alle. Kamenski was obliged to fight. Napoleon ordered the attack to begin. On the left, were Murat at the head of his cavalry corps and Ney's corps reinforced by St. Hilaire's division. Soult led the right. Milhaud's division and the Guard were kept in reserve. The attack only really started towards 3 p.m. when the St. Hilaire Division attacked with the 10th Light, the 36th and 43rd of the Line and Colonel Baron's 6th Dragoons. On the right, Soult started his turning movement, the fighting was hard and the French only advanced with heavy casualties. But night soon fell and interrupted the fighting. Seeing that his left was about to be turned, Benningsen decided to take advantage of the night to break off the engagement and withdraw, covered by a screen of light troops which the French cavalry soon dealt with the following day. 880 Russian dead lay on the field and 300 men were captured together with six cannon. The pursuit then started.

The Chase

On 4 February while Soult was advancing, Murat reached Deppen on the Passarge with Ney who forced Baggovut's rearguard to move back. The 5th and 7th Hussars were mentioned in dispatches with Colonel Céry, as were the 9th Dragoons. Sixteen cannon were captured.

On 5 February, Guyot reached Guttstadt and a number of prisoners were taken. Marulaz pushed on to Heilsberg where he was stopped and driven back. He was followed by Friant's 33rd. They took 1 200 prisoners with the support of Soult's 46th.

Benningsen withdrew towards Königsberg via Wolksdorf – where he set up his headquarters, sending his heavy artillery towards Eylau – leaving Lestocq to look after himself and catch up with the rest of the army. After passing through Osterode, Lestocq reached the Passarge but Ney caught up with him at Deppen and Liebstadt. To save his army corps, the Prussian chose to sacrifice his rearguard which then fought a very hard struggle with the men of the 6th Corps. The Prussian corps was nevertheless able to continue its march towards Benningsen, but Ney was close on its heels.

The following day the French continued the chase, skirmishing several times with the Russian rearguard. The advance was carried out in three columns.

On the left, Ney was still hard on Lestocq's heels; in the centre were Murat, Soult, Augereau and the Guard; Davout made up the right. The latter met stern resistance at Heilsberg in the form of a rearguard which the Morand and Friant Divisions despatched after a fierce but brief fight.

Above.
Maréchal Ney was in command of the 6th Corps. General Savary took command temporarily of the 5th Corps to replace Lannes.

Bottom from left to right.
**A Chasseur à Cheval and a Hussar from the 5th Regiment…
The beginning of the campaign was remarkable because the French Light Cavalry was unable to get any information due to the terrible weather conditions. When the weather started to freeze again they were able to start reconnoitering again.** *(RR)*

The Fighting at Hoff

On the evening of 6 February, the French were on the Russians' backs and Benningsen was worried that he might not be able to get all his army together before the big battle which was gradually becoming more and more inevitable. He therefore decided to create a bottleneck at Landsberg. At Hoff he placed a force of twelve battalions supported by artillery and cavalry astride the road, protected by a ravine which could only be crossed by means of a single bridge; this force was commanded by Barclay de Tolly. When Murat drew up with the vanguard, he decided to take the position immediately, without waiting and launched his light cavalry into a charge. The leading brigade was Colbert's with the 3rd Hussars and the 10th Chasseurs. Bowled over by the fire from the Russian infantry and artillery, then by a counter-attack by Russian cuirassiers, the brigade was forced to the edge of the ravine suffering hea-

The fighting of Hoff February 6, 1807

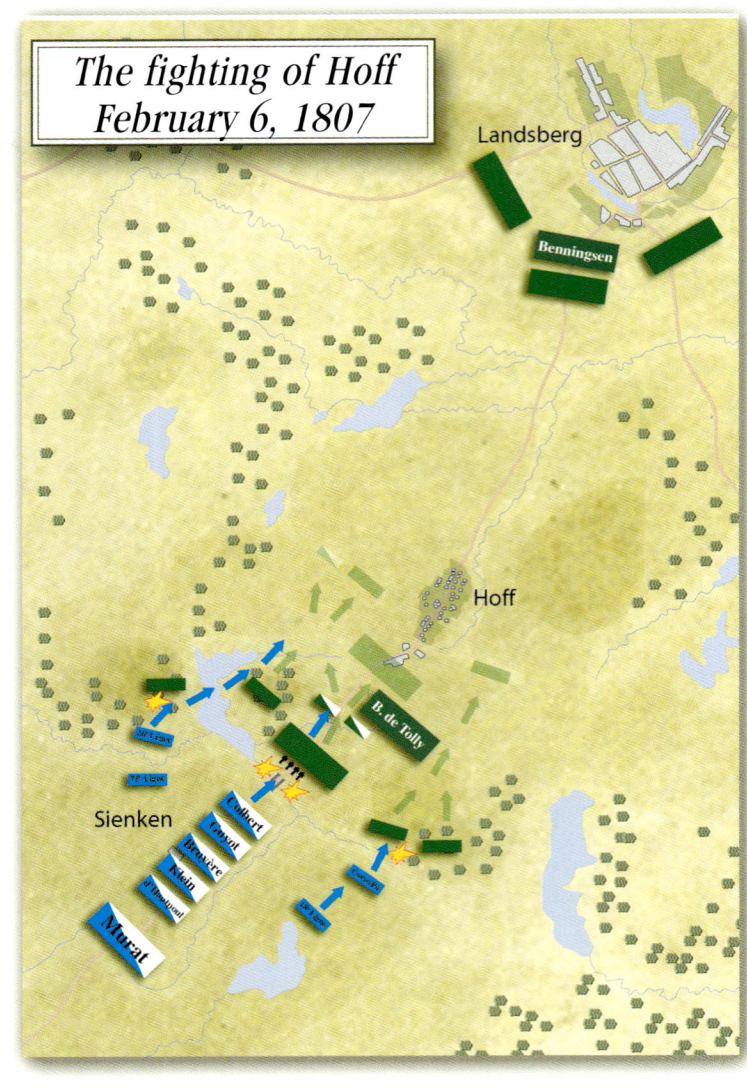

Above, from left to right. **General Klein, commanding the 1st Dragoon Division. The Russian Generals Barclay de Tolly, Bagration and Markov. The heavy cavalry General d'Hautpoul, the hero of Hoff.** *(RR)*

Below. **The Battle of Hoff. The weight and strength of the cuirassiers, led by Murat and d'Hautpoul, was finally able to break the Russian infantry's stubborn resistance.** *(RR)*

vy casualties. Klein's 1st Brigade of Dragoons set off in turn and got hold of a battery but was then also driven back. Confident that he could get hold of the position easily, Murat's pride was now hurt. When d'Hautpoul's Cuirassier division arrived, he rushed to their head and gave out an order a concise as it was brief: "Follow me!"

The *"Gros Talons"* (the Big Heels) of the 1st Regiment threw themselves into a charge following this God of battles, crossed the log bridge and bore down onto the Russian squares which were driven in and all cut up. The Russians were on the brink of being routed when their own Cuirassiers launched another counter-attack. Soult's infantry arrived however and Legrand, who got his troops across the ravine, managed to contain the enemy's attempts. Barclay de Tolly finally decided to withdraw, leaving 3 000 dead, 1 500 prisoners and 11 cannon behind him nevertheless. Four flags had been captured, one of which by Lieutenant Cade of the 1st Cuirassiers. When he arrived later in the evening, Napoleon congratulated d'Hautpoul and kissed him on the forehead in front of his assembled division. Moved and proud, the General said to his chief: *"To be worthy of such an honour, I'll have to get myself killed for your Majesty"*.

His wish would soon be granted.

The Eylau Preliminaries

It was now clear to Benningsen that battle was inevitable. He called Lestocq back and concentrated his army on the Königsberg road, beyond the little village of Eylau, between the villages of Serpalen and Schloditten. He nonetheless left Bagration with a strong rearguard on the Ziegelhof plateau to the west of the town; he was supported by Barclay de Tolly and Baggovut with a total of 15 000 men whose mission was to delay the French advance, giving Benningsen time to get the main part of his army into battle order. Benningsen's report gives the disposition of the Russian forces.

The right wing under the command of Tchukov was backed onto Schloditten behind a frozen marsh which would prevent artillery and cavalry passing. He was reinforced by Markov who fell back after the fight at Ziegelhof.

The left wing occupying Serpallen was made up of Osterman-Tolstoi with Kamenski and the 14th Division in reserve.

Sacken was placed in the centre with a lot of artillery and was supported by Dokhtorov who made up two columns one of which was commanded by Somov.

The front line was made up of the first two battalions of the regiments, deployed in three ranks. The second line, one hundred paces further back, comprised the third battalions all deployed. A third line was formed of elements of the 4th and 14th Divisions and the cavalry which was spread out between the lines and on the wings.

Benningsen had a large artillery force at his disposal, in all between 450 and 500 pieces. He made up three large batteries and placed them on his army's front. There were therefore 60 pieces on the right, 70 facing Eylau and 40 in front of Rothenen. Several smaller batteries were spread out all along the line. An artillery reserve numbering 80 pieces was also formed.

The Fighting at Ziegelhof

Realising he had the French hard on his heels, Benningsen placed a strong rearguard in front of Eylau under Bagration.

On top of his own troops, Benningsen gave him reinforcements by detaching the Sofia Regiment, the Moscow Grenadiers, the 21st Chasseurs, the Saint-Petersburg and Ingermanland Dragoons and the Elisabethgrad Hussars to him. Benningsen placed Markov on the Ziegelhof Plateau, putting the reinforcements behind him. The cannon were disposed on the plateau supported by the Pskov and Sofia Regiments.

On 7 February, Soult reached Grünhöfchen on the Landsberg road and developed his attack. The 24th Light, and the 4th and 28th of the Line from Leval's division all moved up on the right. On the left was the 57th of the Line with Férey's and Guyot's cavalry. Legrand advanced in the centre with the 18th of the Line followed by the 46th of the Line from Leval's division under the command of General Levavasseur with the cavalry reserve. The Saint-Hilaire Division and the rest of Legrand's remained in reserve.

At three o'clock, the 18th of the Line attacked the plateau with its 1st Battalion where it was greeted by artillery fire and sustained firing from the Russian infantry. It was then charged by the Saint-Petersburg Dragoons which dislocated it before it had the time to form into squares. The fleeing soldiers sought refuge in Pelleport's 2nd

Opposite.
The attack on the cemetery.
There was very bitter fighting for this position. *(RR)*

Below. **The beginning of the Battle of Eylau on 7 February 1807.** *(RR)*

Bottom. **The attack on the cemetery at Eylau on 6 February.**
(Jean-Charles Langlois, Musée des beaux Arts de Caen)

Following page Bottom.
The Cossacks and the Tartars from the Russian army roamed at will across the battlefield at Eylau making sending messages very difficult.
(RR)

Battalion's square which halted the charge. The regimental eagle was nonetheless captured by the Russians in rather doubtful circumstances. The 13th Chasseurs and Milhaud's Dragoons finally managed to push the Russian dragoons back and get the survivors away. Pelleport was wounded and lay buried under the snow and the corpses: he had had thirty sabre blows and five bayonet thrusts. He was found the following day by a soldier under a pile of corpses frozen by the snow and the cold. The 18th of the Line eventually rallied but it had been reduced by half and could only muster 700 men who nevertheless resumed fighting and took part in capturing the town, commanded by their Colonel Ravier, who was made a General in 1809. The 46th of the Line under Colonel Latrille de Lorencez which was following the 18th continued the attack, drove back the Russians, entered the village and resisted the charges from the enemy cavalry. The French Dragoons also got into the village, followed by the 24th Light.

Inside Eylau on the night of 7-8 February

Barclay de Tolly was in command of the forces defending Eylau. Viviès led the 4th and 28th of the Line and took the cemetery. The Russians engaged the reinforcements coming from the 4th Division and attacked the 24th light which had to fall back.

The village was almost recaptured by the Russians but Napoleon ordered the village to be taken again. Legrand's division came up and the Corse and Pô Chasseurs entered the village preceded by Commandant Hulot who was then wounded. The 4th and the 28th of the Line were resisting extremely well when the 26th in turn entered the terrible fray. The village was littered with corpses and wounded. Nevertheless, Legrand finished taking Eylau with the 26th of the Line. Leval was seriously wounded and was evacuated. Michel, his Chief-of-Staff was killed. The French had lost almost 4 000 men in this fighting and Soult's soldiers were exhausted.

On the other side, the Russian defenders fell back behind their main battle line and Markov placed himself behind Tchukov, probably with the cavalry.

In his memoirs, Marbot who was aide de camp to Augereau at the time relates how Augereau came up behind Soult on the Landsberg road and met Napoleon after the capture of Ziegelhof. Marbot heard the Emperor say that he did not want to push on too far forward because he did not like night fighting and that he was waiting for Davout and Ney before engaging the battle. He was going to bivouac beyond Ziegelhof, surrounded by his Guard. But since the town had been captured, he installed his quarters in the Eylau post office because the Palace Fourriers had got as far as there, having moved up beyond the Imperial bivouac. They chose the building without realising that the Russians were just nearby. They were then attacked by an enemy patrol and were only got out of that tight spot by the Guard escort and Soult's troops. They then finished getting things ready and Napoleon joined them there. The Guard settled down in the town surrounded by Murat's cavalry.

Soult's corps was then put into position. Legrand's division was placed in front of Eylau with Leval's on its left. The artillery from these divisions was placed near the cemetery. Saint-Hilaire covered the right, in front of the village of Rothenen, himself covered on the right by Milhaud's cavalry. Augereau placed himself in between Saint-Hilaire and Legrand, in front of the cemetery.

The Guard and the cavalry reserve were behind him and the light cavalry was on the left flank of this disposition. Napoleon sent a message to Davout to march towards Serpelen and Klein-Sausgarten, but the brilliant Maréchal had already given his orders and had got his 3rd Corps marching. Ney still in pursuit of Lestocq was also called back but the message only reached him during the morning. Moreover, the Prussian managed to hoodwink him and reached the battlefield before him. The 6th Corps nevertheless had to march on Schmoditten.

On the morning of 8 February 1806, Napoleon had 45 000 men to confront Benningsen's 80 000 Russians.

Opposite and from left to right and top to bottom.
General Milbaud, General Legrand, Marbot and General Soult commanding the 4th Corps. *(RR)*

Bottom, following pages and pages 62 and 63.
The panorama of the Battle of Eylau painted by Jean-Charles Langlois only exists as a series of Daguerreotypes. It does however perfectly reflect the violence of the fighting, as it does here with the charge of the Grenadiers à Cheval under Lepic *(Collection ARDI, Caen).*

"The Russians greeted us early that morning with a terrible cannonade…" There were casualties everywhere immediately. The French gunners, certainly the best in Europe, made up for lack of numbers by their formidable precision, removing entire ranks from the opposite lines: *"The Russian army in columns was within half-range of the cannon: every shot took its toll…"* Although the Russian cannonballs had less of a destructive effect on the thin French lines, which were partly protected by the village buildings and walls, Eylau and Rothenen soon caught fire.

At nine o'clock, Benningsen ordered his right wing to attack. Tchukov launched his columns against Viviès and Ferey in Leval's division. The Russians advanced towards Windmill Hill. After a moment of wavering, they were driven off with heavy losses but they were not pursued; this was so that the weak French left wing would not be destabilised.

Davout arrives

At the same time, Davout's corps started to invest the left wing of the Russian line. Indeed, Friant's division appeared in front of the village of Serpallen from which it chased elements of Baggovut's corps after a brief struggle. The Russians launched a counter-attack with cavalry, but Friant's men were protected by the village, and the gates and the walls surrounding it. The Russian cavalry was driven off. A second counter-attack was launched supported this time by two infantry columns. The infantry was repulsed by Friant's regiments and the cavalry charging the 33rd of the Line from Lochet's brigade which had formed up into a square, broke up against it. Morand's division then appeared. Bonnet-d'Hornières' brigade remained to support Friant while the rest of the division – Guiot's and Brouard's brigades – deployed between Serpallen and Saint-Hilaire's division. Marulaz's cavalry arrived and positioned itself on the right of the 3rd Corps, followed by Gudin. Davout was then able to launch his attack on the Russian left which he drove back, gradually forcing it to fallback on Klein-Sausgarten. This village was on the point of being taken when Benningsen ordered Ostermann and Sacken to intervene, thus weakening the Russian centre.

The 7th Corps Calvary

Seeing the Russian movement, Napoleon decided to break the enemy front by launching the 7th Corps held in reserve until that moment against the left of its centre. General Corbineau, Napoleon's aide de camp carried the Imperial order to attack. As he was giving the order to Augereau, he was killed by a cannonball. Not a good omen… According to the 63rd Bulletin of the Grande Armée, Augereau was *"riddled with rheumatism, ill, barely aware of what was going on around him"*. He had to be attached to his horse.

THE TERRIBLE BATTLE OF EYLAU

After the sunny days, the weather was now grey with low clouds and soon the snow started to fall.

At half – past five, Benningsen opened fire with all his batteries. Napoleon, who had set up his forty guns belonging to the Guard in a battery alongside those of the Line, also opened fire. The firing was terrible. In his memoirs Coignet mentions this terrible opening to the fighting.

He formed up his divisions for the attack: Desjardin on the left, Heudelet on the right. The first brigade of each division was deployed; the second was formed into a square. The 7th Corps occupied the line between Eylau and Rothenen. Saint-Hilaire covered the right flank and had to link up with Morand. The aim of this attack was, on one hand, to relieve the 3rd Corps which was getting ready to fight - outnumbered three to one - and on the other, to make a feint from right to left, with Eylau as the lynchpin and with the intention of driving Benningsen's left wing from the field and throwing it back onto the rest of the line which was held in a pincer movement by Ney's corps whose arrival was imminent.

The attack got under way at shortly after ten. Although the initial deployment took place under a heavy artillery barrage, all the Russian artillery in the sector was firing at the 7th Corps which nevertheless carried on with its attack. Unfortunately a sudden flurry of snow rose up and with the wind blowing straight at them, the French were very quickly blinded and disorientated by this gale. The Russian gunners had the snow behind them so were not bothered by it. The 7th Corps column, disorientated went off slightly to the left and marched within short range of the big Russian 72-gun battery which started spewing out its grapeshot. The casualties were immediately very heavy. Maréchal Augereau was wounded and all the senior officers and generals were either killed or wounded. 5 200 men were out of action within several minutes.

Marbot relates: *"The Maréchal passing between Eylau and Rothenen with his two divisions advanced proudly against the enemy's centre and the 14th of the Line had already overrun the position which the Emperor had ordered to be taken and kept at all costs, when a number of heavy calibre cannon which formed a semi-circle around Augereau started firing balls and grapeshot such as had not been seen in living memory."* He continues: *"In an instant our two divisions had been ground down by this rain of steel. General Desjardins was killed and General Heudelet seriously wounded. They held fast however until the army corps was almost entirely destroyed; they were obliged to gather up what remained and get back to the cemetery at Eylau, except for the 14th of the Line which was totally surrounded by the enemy and remained on the hill which it occupied."*

Taking advantage of this event, Benningsen decided to counter-attack. He launched Dokhtorov's corps, supported by the Moscow Grenadiers and several cavalry regiments. The remnants of the 7th Corps fell back slowly despite the Russian attacks and rallied at the foot of the cemetery at Eylau. Only the 14th of the Line, encircled, was unable to get back. It was formed up into a circle and resisted without flinching all the attacks by the Russian dragoons. Marbot explains that *"the 14th remained isolated, surrounded by Russians. It was in a square and bombarded and attacked from all sides."* He then goes on to tell his own story of how he was the third to be sent in after the failure of the two previous messengers to get through and give the order to fall back to the beleaguered regiment. He managed to get through with *"Lisette"*, his formidable mare, across to the square surrounded by dead horses; he managed to get in and to give his orders to the battalion commander, leading the remnants of this heroic unit. The latter, knowing that his regiment was inevitably doomed entrusted Marbot with the Eagle. Once he had left, the

Above.
The Artilleryman of the Guard. *(RR)*

Above, from left to right. **Maréchal Davout commanding the 3rd Corps together with his divisionaires, Generals Friant, Morand, and Gudin de la Sablonnière.** *(RR)*

Opposite, left. **Two other participants in the battle: the Russian General Tutchkov and the Frenchman Augereau.** *(RR)*

Opposite, right. **The 14th of the Line from Augereau's 7th Corps about to fold up. Just before the fatal moment, Marbot was entrusted with the eagle which he brought back to the safety of the French lines.** *(RR)*

last survivors were overwhelmed and annihilated by a last attack led by the Pavlov Grenadier Regiment. The following day on the very spot where this sacrifice was made, one could read *"Here rest the 28 officers and 590 soldiers of the 14th of the Line."* Augereau's corps was so depleted that it was disbanded after the battle.

Meanwhile, Davout continued to advance driving back the Russians who were desperately trying to prevent the *"Three Immortals"* – the three infantry divisions of the 3rd Corps – from advancing. The village of Klein Sausgarten was taken. The rout of the 7th Corps however did leave Davout's left dangerously exposed.

The weather brightened very slightly and Napoleon, who was in the cemetery at Eylau, was able to realise how dangerous the situation was becoming for his army. A huge hole had been opened up on his right, isolating Davout and Saint-Hilaire's division from the rest of the army. Benningsen sent the 14th Division and the 20 cavalry squadrons from Korf's corps against this wing. Davout risked being overwhelmed and a battalion of the 10th Light was cut down. The 3rd Corps withdrew beyond Klein Sausgarten and started retreating in the direction of Serpallen.

Even more serious for the French army were the Russian 4th and 7th Divisions who were advancing towards Eylau where there was no infantry able to counter this attack. All there were were the debris of Augereau's corps gathered together in front of Eylau church, next to Leval; their artillery commanded by Captain Chopin was showering the Russians with grapeshot. This meagre force was not up to stopping this Russian offensive.

Furia Francese

Napoleon saw the danger and grasped the risks: there was a risk of the army being cut in two and its right crushed despite the efforts of the 7th Corps which had managed to relieve it a little. He made his famous remark to Murat: *"Well, are you going to let us be*

devoured by these people?" Before the Imperial Guard was brought in, the cavalry was the only intact force which the Emperor still had at his disposal.

The Grand Duke of Berg rushed to the head of his cavalry and gave the order, just as concise as it was brief: *"Follow me!"* All the determination of this legendary cavalryman is contained in those two words. But Murat did have the benefit of commanding competent and experienced officers who could judge the importance of the situation for themselves and knew where and how to position their squadrons in order to get the best out of them. Thus the eighty squadrons of the reserve followed their chief in what was probably the greatest cavalry charge during the Empire. At the head, Grouchy took his dragoons from the 1st Brigade, the 3rd and 6th Regiments, and drove off the Russian cavalry which was beginning to invest the terrain between the cemetery and Saint-Hilaire. The General's horse was wounded and his aide de camp Georges Lafayette saved him by giving him his own mount. Grouchy returned with the 2nd Brigade, made up of the 10th and 11th Dragoons and engaged the first line of the enemy infantry but without success.

The battle of Eylau
February 1807

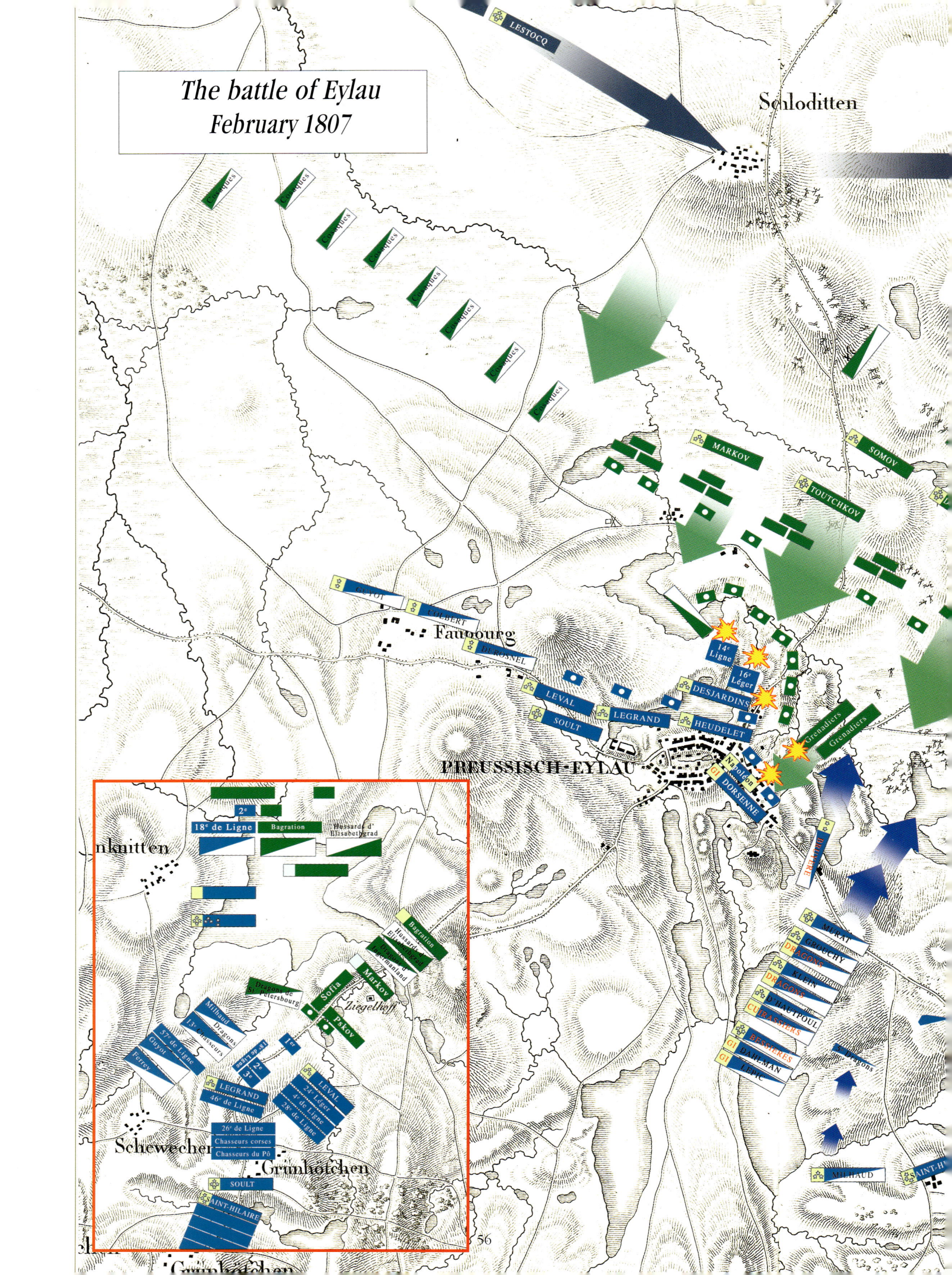

Kutschitten

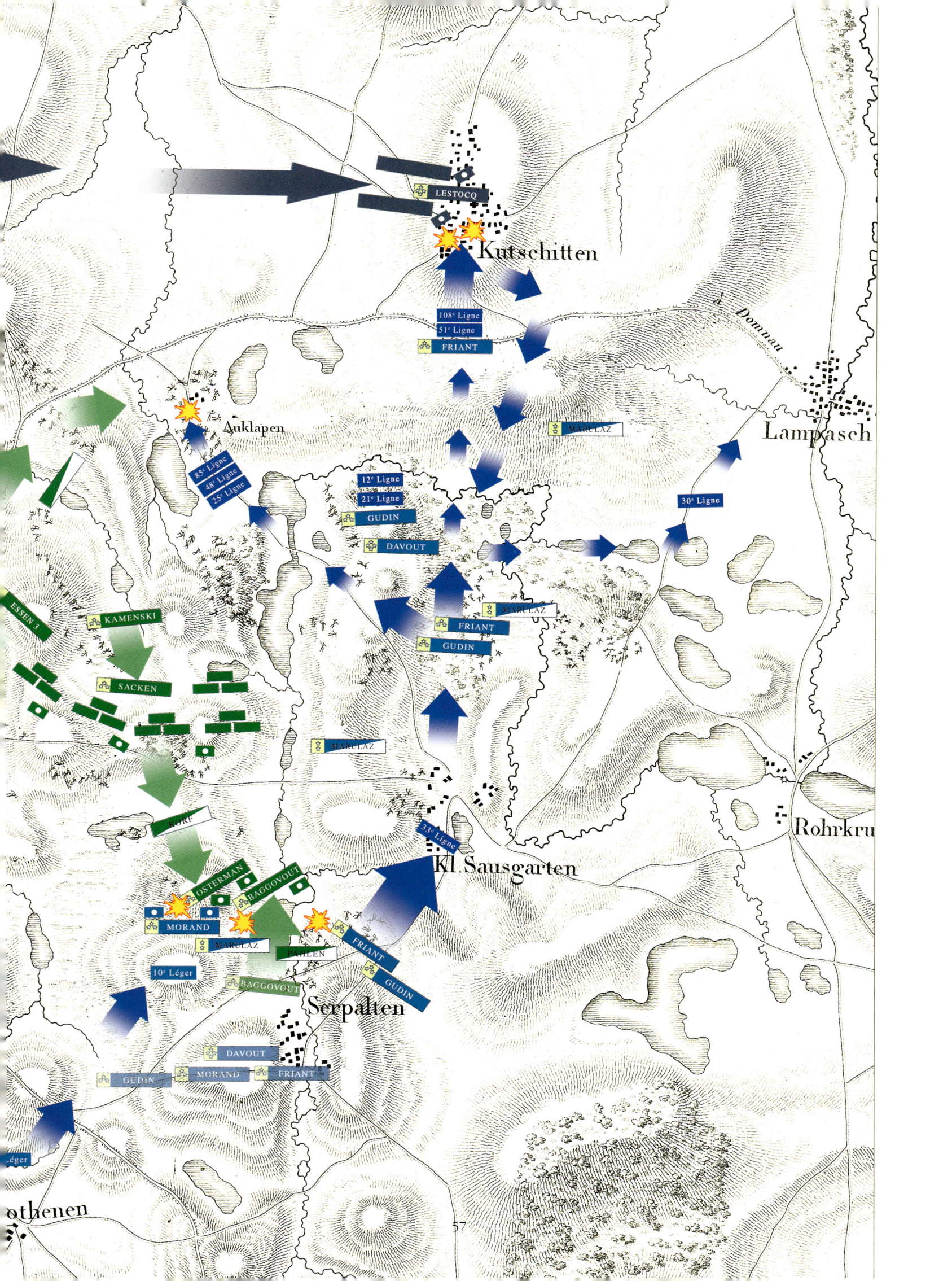

LESTOCQ

108e Ligne
51e Ligne
FRIANT

Auklapen

85e Ligne
48e Ligne
25e Ligne

MARULAZ

Lampasch

12e Ligne
21e Ligne
GUDIN
DAVOUT

30e Ligne

ESSEN 3

KAMENSKI

FRIANT
GUDIN

SACKEN

MARULAZ

Rohrkru

33e Ligne

Kl. Sausgarten

KORF

OSTERMAN
BAGGOVUT
MORAND
MARULAZ
PAHLEN
FRIANT
GUDIN

10e Léger
BAGGOVUT

Serpalten

DAVOUT
GUDIN MORAND FRIANT

othenen

The 14th of the Line on the point of being overwhelmed by the Russian Grenadiers. Marbot, riding Lisette, his mare, was wounded by a cannonball but managed to save the regiment's emblem. (RR)

Opposite top.
Having just received the order from Napoleon to break through the Russian Centre, Murat passes on the order to his subordinates. In reality, his orders were as brief as they were concise: "Follow me!"

Bottom.
At the head of almost 9 000 troopers, Murat accomplished his mission, breaking through the first two Russian lines stopping their advance. This charge was really a bloodbath for all these elite regiments.
(Composition by Job, RR)

Opposite: Marbot, aide de camp to Augereau and General Grouchy commanding the 2nd Division of Dragoons. (RR)

Behind them followed the 24 Elite Squadrons of the d'Hautpoul's Cuirassier Regiments. They fiercely attacked the Russian infantry which although formed up in lines and not squares withstood the attack and repelled this charge. The second attempt met with more success and drove in the enemy lines before running up against the second line; this was despite the support of Grouchy's Dragoons which had rallied, together with Klein's. During this assault, General d'Hautpoul was wounded by a biscayen bullet which shattered his right thigh; refusing to be amputated, he died in terrible pain a week later. The French cavalry was now dispersed and cutting down the Russian ranks which had broken up. The regiments and the squadrons no longer formed coherent units but groups of horsemen were worried more about saving their own skins rather than seeking glory.

The Russian infantry in the front ranks, who had lain down on the ground to avoid being trampled and cut down, now started to get up and to encircle the French cavalry. Despite its initial successes, the cavalry risked getting itself into a very tricky situation indeed. Seeing the danger, Napoleon decided to commit the cavalry of the Guard, commanded by Maréchal Bessières.

The Chasseurs à Cheval of the Guard, with Bessières, then charged and widened the breach through which d'Hautpoul's horsemen had poured. They fought into the middle of the enemy forcing their way through the first Russian ranks like demons. They were brought round, rallied and taken back into the fray. Dahlmann was killed as were a number of Chasseurs. Langlois recalls: *"The horse belonging to Lieutenant Rabusson from the Chasseurs got killed and he received seventeen bayonet wounds. He managed to get rid of five or six Russians, got hold of a horse off a dead chasseur, but during the retreat he received a sixth blow which floored him. Captured at night, he was taken to Anklappen where he was freed by soldiers from Friant's 48th."*

It was Guyot who then rallied the Chasseurs. The Grenadiers à Cheval in turn entered this gigantic fray. Napoleon was reassured and said: *"Lepic is with them, they will return."* The 5th Cuirassiers also took part in this charge. Lepic was indeed outstanding: with two squadrons, he forced his way through the enemy lines but got stopped in front of the Russian reserves made up of the third line and the artillery reserve, all backing up against the Anklappen wood. It was at this very moment that the famous episode occurred when a Russian officer asked Lepic and the handful of Grenadiers à Cheval, who had managed to get through the whole of the enemy army with him, to surrender. The Frenchman retor-

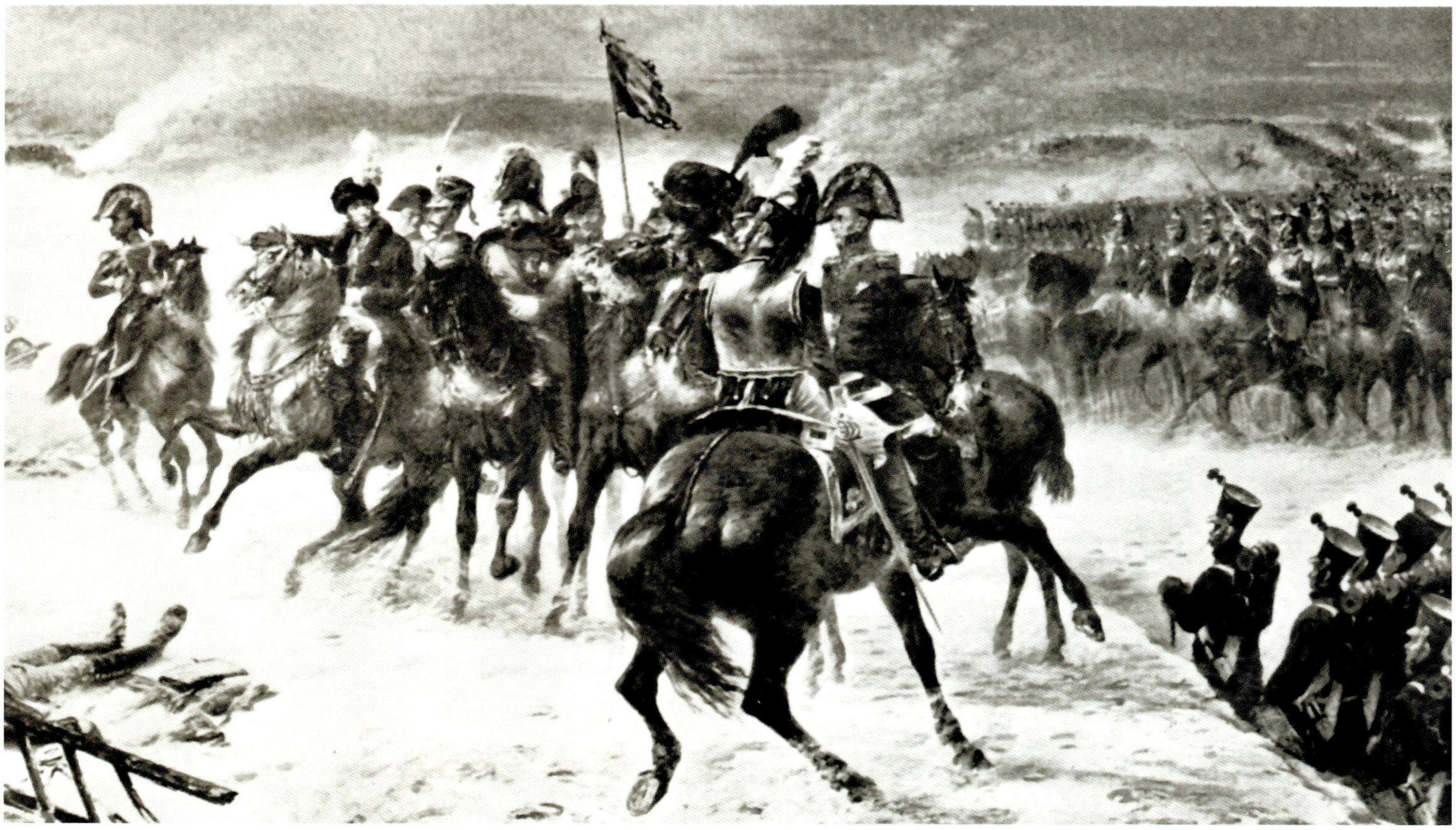

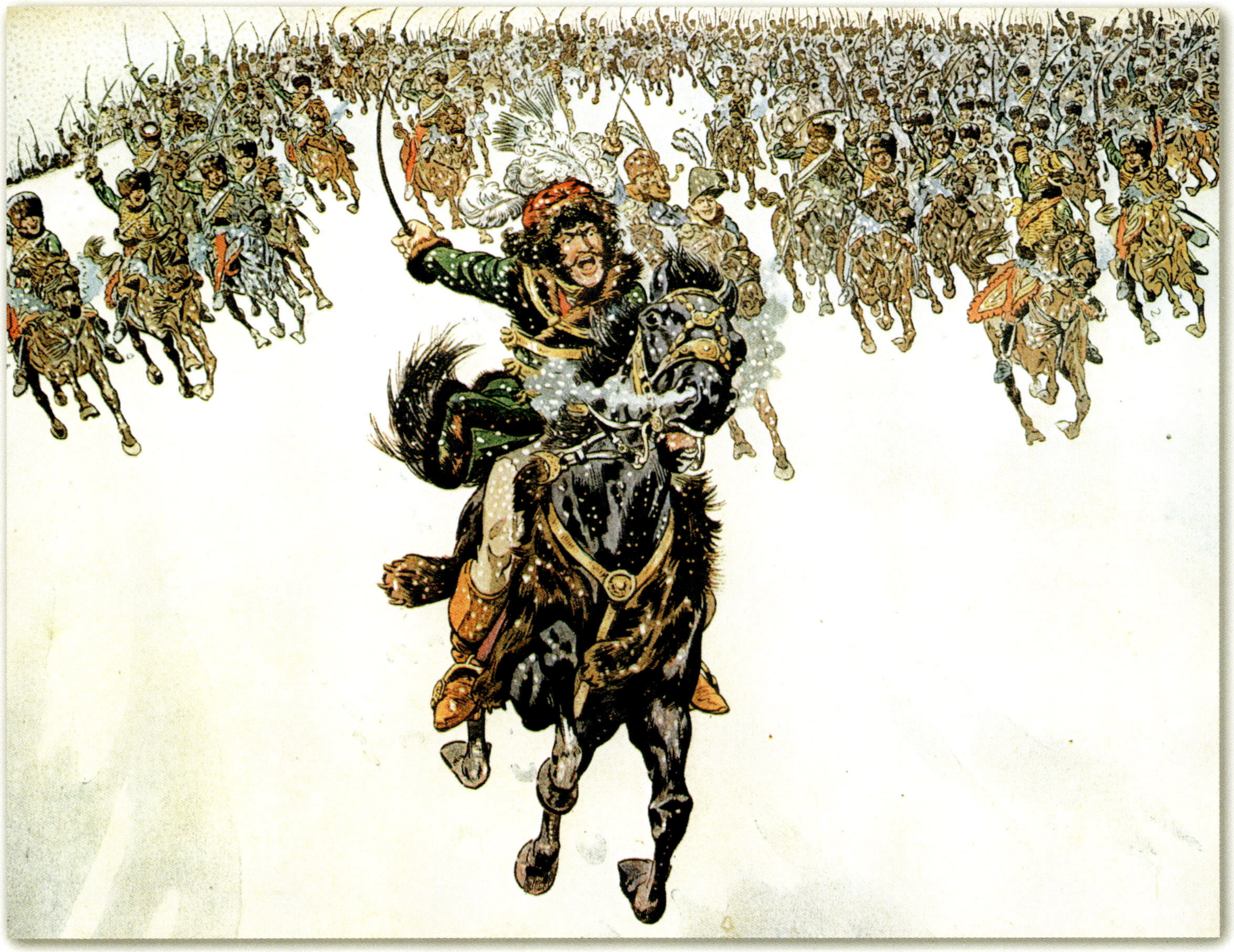

ted pointing at his men with the tip of his sabre: *"Look at those mugs there, tell me honestly, sir, do they look as though they want to surrender?"* Having said that, he took his men and they all cut a path through to the French lines with their sabres. Lepic was hit twice by sabres and twice by bayonets.

This terrible charge by the Cavalry of the Guard enabled Murat's squadrons to rally their starting points. The Russian attack was halted and driven off; more than 8 000 were left dead on the battlefield. The French also deplored the loss of some 3 500 men. During the gigantic fray, the Russian artillery continuously fired "into the heap", cutting huge swathes through the units on both sides.

The Attack on the Cemetery

While the French cavalry was throwing itself into its legendary charge, a column of some 4 000 Russian Grenadiers continued its advance on the Eylau cemetery where Napoleon was positioned.

Above. **Like Epamonidas' column, the cavalry under Murat broke through the Russian lines.** *(RMN)*

Below.
General d'Hautpoul's cuirassiers and the Chasseurs à Cheval of the Guard charged the Russian infantry and bowled them over where they stood. *(RR)*

In order to bolster up this corner of the French disposition which was caving in and threatening to break the army into two, the Emperor sent the service squadrons to attack the enemy there and slow them down. At the same time, he ordered Dorsenne at the head of a battalion of Grenadiers of the Guard to repulse the attack. The French general formed the battalion into a column and marched to meet the Russians. When they got into range, it was suggested that he should order his men to fire, but he cried: *"Grenadiers! Hold arms. The Guard only fights with its bayonets!"* and with that they charged the Russians head on.

Even though he had committed himself fully in the great cavalry charge, Murat also saw the danger which the enemy column represented. He therefore ordered the Light Cavalry Brigade under Bruyères to charge it. The 1st Hussars and the 13th and 24th Chasseurs threw themselves on its rear. Attacked in the front by the Old Guard, in the rear by the Light Cavalry and on the flanks by the service squadrons, the 4 000 Russian Grenadiers were wiped out.

First Tally

The French were engaged at one o'clock: Soult was defending Eylau; after a struggle, Davout – whose Morand Division had been worried for a moment until it was supported by Klein's Dragoons – had taken Anklappen now occupied by Gauthier and the 25th of the Line, had elements at Kuschitten and was now continuing his advance; the cavalry reserve and the Cavalry of the Guard had driven off the Russian attacks; and Augereau's corps had ceased to exist as a unit. Napoleon's only reserve was the Infantry of the Guard.

He could launch this elite unit against the Russian centre and commit his cavalry again which was rallying behind Eylau. Napoleon however did not want to risk doing anything until Ney appeared on his left; he also knew that Lestocq was marching towards the battle. The Russians did not have any reserves either. Neither side seemed able to force the issue and the arrival of the corps on the march was going to be the only solution, as much for Napoleon as for Benningsen.

By three p.m., Napoleon was even envisaging a withdrawal from the battlefield at dusk behind a protective screen provided by Grouchy's Dragoons in order to hide this movement from the Russians. Benningsen tried to push back Davout who was getting too close; he too was considering a withdrawal.

The arrival of Ney and Lestocq

Ney was chasing Lestocq's corps. Whereas the Prussian had been informed of the battle and knew the others were expecting him, Ney knew nothing at all. He had only received the message brought by de Fezensac at 2 p.m. In order to get well ahead, Lestocq placed a *"stopper"* consisting of two infantry companies supported by cavalry and four artillery pieces on the Kreutzburg road. He led the rest of his corps towards the battle through Althof and Schmoditten.

Ney reached Wackern where this rearguard was set up; he ordered it to be attacked immediately and after a brief fight, the Prussians were pushed back, retreating towards Kreutzburg and chased by the French who were thus moving further away from Eylau.

A short time before 6 p.m., the Prussian corps reached the battlefield at Schmoditten. It had a strength of 8 battalions, 28 squadrons and 16 artillery pieces, i.e. more than 10 000 men. Passing behind the Russian army where it rallied several regiments, it advanced towards Kuschitten and attacked immediately, driving Davout's corps back toward Klein Sausgarten. The French were also chased out of Anklappen. Davout organised his exhaus-

Above. **The Russian regiments in the Line stood up to the charges of the French cavalry.** *(F. Flameng/RR)*

Below. **Napoleon on the left watching the great charge as it unrolled.** *(RR)*

ted divisions superbly into forming a defence, telling them that *"the cowards would go and die in Siberia but that the brave would die here as honourable men."* The 3rd Corps retreated as far back as Serpalen, where it started to resist then push the Russians and the Prussians gradually back to Klein Sausgarten.

Ney was going in the wrong direction when he received the message ordering him to move towards Eylau; the guards on the flanks informed him of the battle taking place. He immediately directed his march towards Schlodditten which he reached at 7 p.m. The right flank of the Russian army was turned. Benningsen therefore launched Sacken's corps against the village of Schlodditten; the Russians were however repelled with heavy casualties by the 6th Light and the 39th of the Line from Bellair's brigade which, after keeping up sustained and deadly fire, made a bayonet charge. Ney had arrived in the nick of time! It had now been dark for two hours and the fighting gradually ceased.

The arrival of the *"Rougeaud"* ("old ruddy face") had changed everything. By 10 p.m.,

Opposite. **The death of Dahlmann. The Chasseurs à Cheval of the Guard paid a heavy tribute for this victory.** *(RR)*

Opposite. **After luring Ney away, Lestocq's Prussians crossed the battlefield and threw themselves at the 3rd Corps under Davout which they pushed back.** *(RR)*

Bottom. **This other fragment of the Langlois panorama shows the confrontation between the Prussians under Lestocq and the French under Davout in the direction of Anklappen.** *(Collection ARDI, Caen)*

Benningsen was very much aware that he could by trapped and encircled by Ney on his right and Davout on his left. He knew that half of his army was either dead, wounded or in disorder and that the position he was holding would not enable him to take up the fight again the following day. As a result he gave the order to retreat in the direction of Friedland and Königsberg.

The French also ceased fighting, literally collapsing from exhaustion where they stood. This grandiose battle lasted from 3 a.m. on the 7th to almost 10 p.m. on 8 February. The combatants were fantastically courageous. Here, just as on the day they fought at Jena-Auerstadt, Davout's 3rd Corps had played a determining role. 16 flags had been captured.

The Losses at Eylau

The losses suffered during the day were enormous.
Langlois gives the following figures for the French corps.
- **Soult's 4th Corps:** 370 killed and 7 880 wounded out of 14 500 present.
- **Augereau's 7th Corps:** 929 killed and 4 271 wounded out of 6 500 present.
- **Davout's 3rd Corps:** 584 killed and 4 107 wounded out of 15 000 present.
- **For the cavalry reserve:** 100 killed and 1 000 wounded out of 5 000 present.
- For the Guard: 60 killed and 500 wounded out of 4 000 present.

A grand total of 2 043 killed and 17 758 wounded out of 45 100 present. This represented about 20 000 men out of action to which must be added the 10 000 to 20 000 men who were slightly wounded and who continued to follow the army, but not the 6 000 seriously wounded who remained in the field hospitals.

A note from Berthier gives a different tally: 2 124 killed and 17 555 wounded with 1 152 prisoners.

Augereau's corps was disbanded and the wounded Maréchal left to recuperate. His remnants of his corps were divided up and shared out among the others. It is worth men-

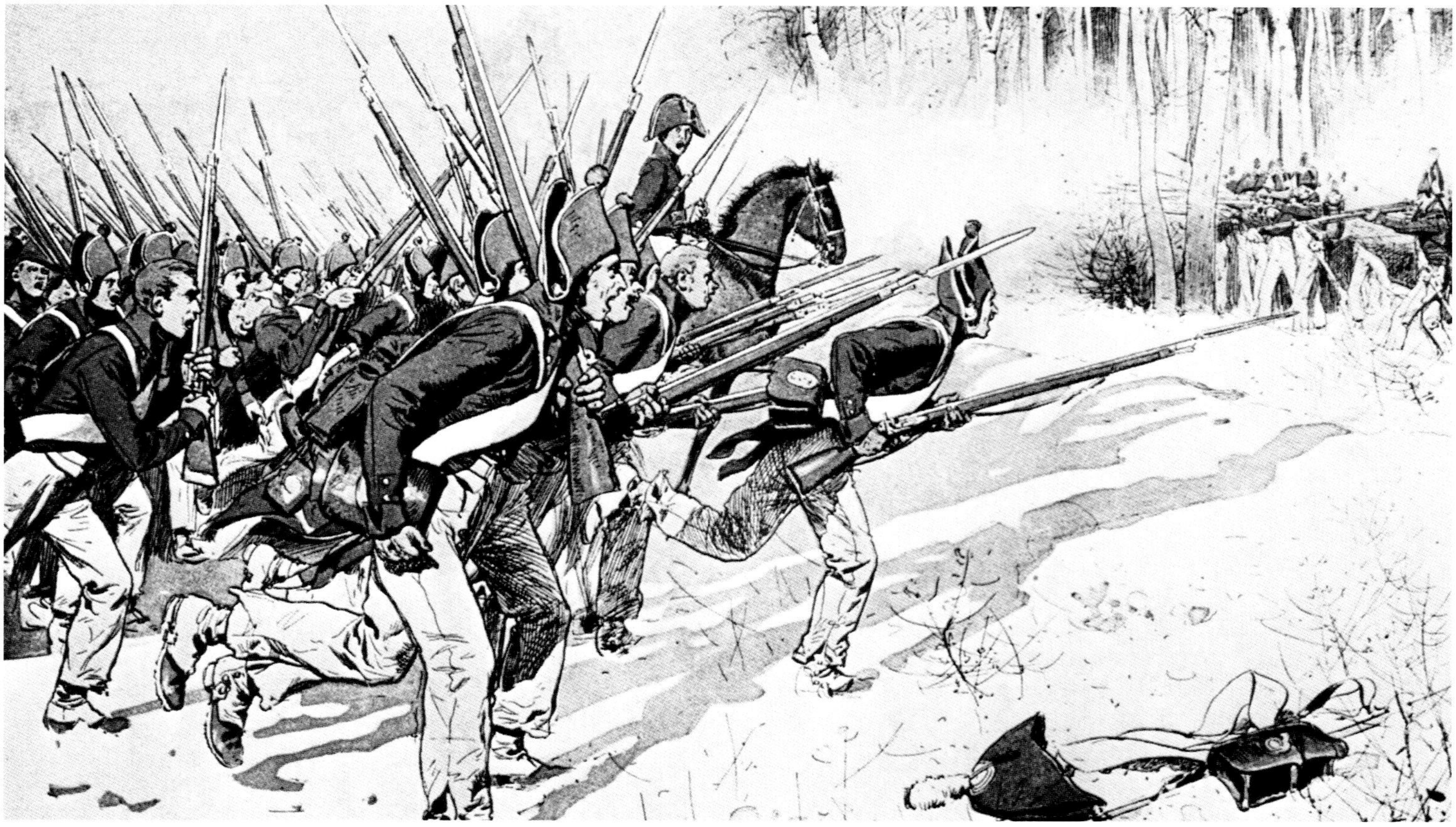

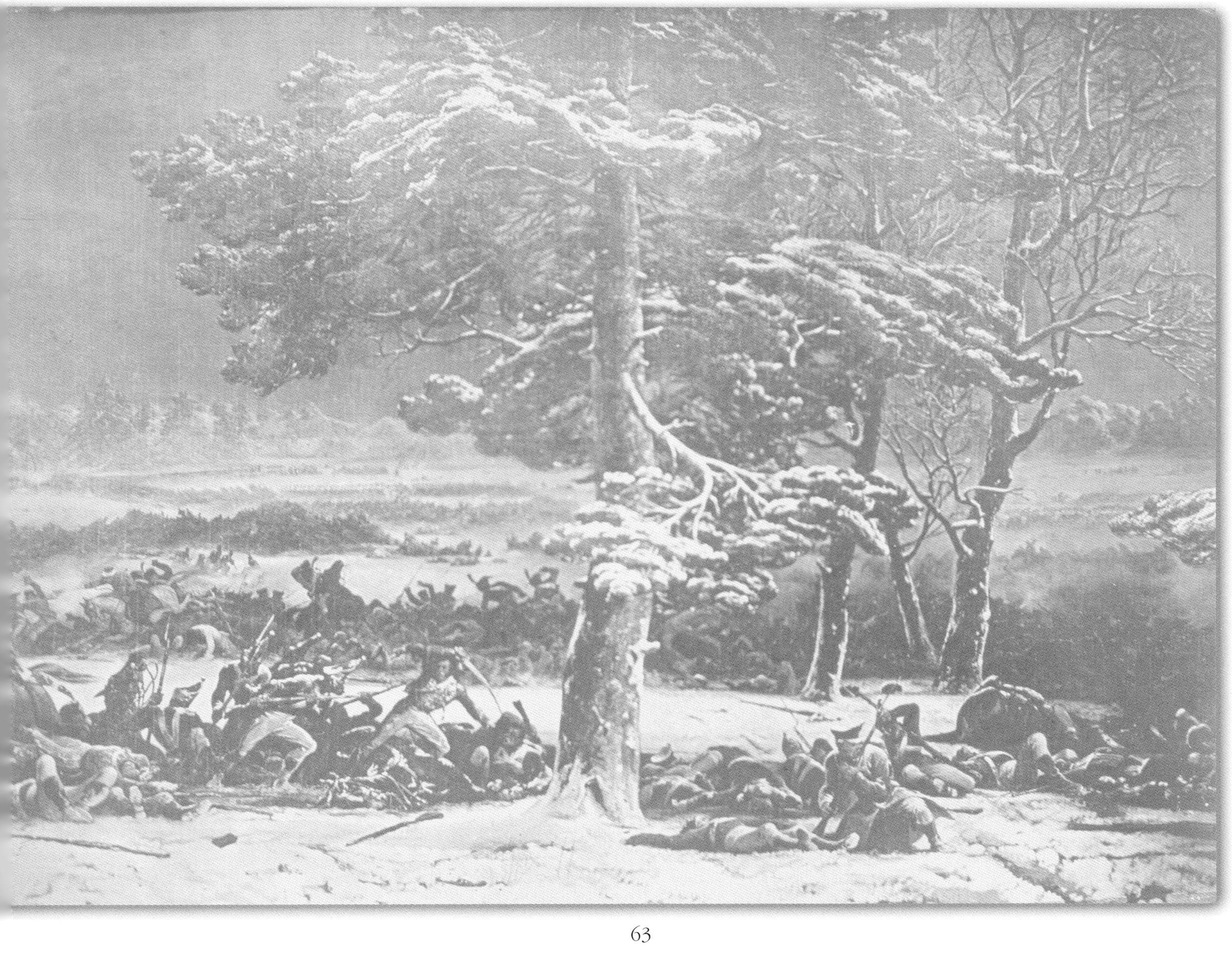

tioning that on the evening of Eylau, the 7th was commanded by a Lieutenant-Colonel, all the colonels, generals or major-generals and even the Maréchal himself having been killed or wounded.

Percy and Larrey were both very quickly overwhelmed and the Emperor was forced to consider improving his medical service units.

The battlefield strewn with corpses and seriously wounded soldiers, not forgetting the huge numbers of horses killed, was depicted in the great painting showing Napoleon riding around the battlefield on the day after the battle and on the following days. The various debris littering the field increased the horror inspired by the scene.

According to Both, the Allies left behind them 7 000 killed and 5 000 wounded, evacuating 14 000 seriously wounded, most of whom would eventually die. This meant a total of 26 800 men out of action plus the slightly wounded. The wounded that were left on the field were obviously taken prisoner. For most authors, the Allied losses were estimated at 26 000 men whereas Benningsen only declared 14 000 casualties. Lestocq lost 900 men. With both armies counted together, the casualties at Eylau totalled 70 000.

Report by General Saint-Hilaire of the 4th Corps

On 7 February at 7 o'clock, the division was joined by the other two from Soult's corps. It was given the order to move over to the right, backing on the village of Rothenen from which Cossacks and enemy forward positions were dislodged.

The following morning at daybreak, the division was gathered on the plateau with one battalion deployed and the other in a column ready to march forward. The oblique march which was used united my right with the left of Morand's division. The 1st Battalion of the 10th formed the tip of my right with Morand's two regiments on the left and carried out its attack on the rear of Klein-Sausgarten by turning the plateau on its right.

Preceding page and above:
The Grenadiers à Cheval of the Guard commanded by the famous Baron Lepic broke through three Russian lines and when commanded to surrender, knocked the enemy troops over again, fought their way out and rejoined their lines. *(RR and Patrice Courcelle)*

Below.
As for the Grenadiers à Pied of the Guard commanded by General Dorsenne (medallion), they made a bayonet charge and bowled over a column of 4 000 Russian Grenadiers. *(RR)*

A 3 000-strong Russian corps with eight artillery pieces was enveloped by this manoeuvre and was on the point of being beaten when a cavalry charge on the 10th's flank by Guards' regiments and Cuirassiers caused some disorder among the first three regiments which had to withdraw from the plateau. The division managed to set itself up there once again and our artillery made the Russians pull back, evacuate Klein-Sausgarten, and occupy the nearby wood on the left of the plateau.

Still linked to the 3rd Corps, the division had lost 3 200 men out of action but got hold of 6 artillery pieces during the second attack. Marulaz's light cavalry and Milhaud's dragoons were weakened in this fighting but the guns were taken to Schloditten. The Legrand and Leval divisions lost 5 050 men wounded or killed and most of the officers were out of action.

Report by General Pannetier, Chief-of-Staff of the 7th Corps

An order from Napoleon asked us to move up towards the Chapel at Eylau at daybreak, place ourselves on the right and then advance. This movement was carried out under fire from the numerous cannon in the enemy centre. The corps was charged by an impetuous enemy cavalry forcing us to pull back.

Maréchal Augereau, being wounded, was replaced by Major-General Compans. General Lecamus came and took over command of the 1st Division and General Amey the second.

Above. **Murat ordering General Bruyère and his brigade of light cavalry to charge a 4 000-strong column of Russian grenadiers rushing at Eylau.** *(RR)*

Below, left. **Some French wounded being treated in a lazaret. Several thousands of others however froze to death on the battlefield, demonstrating the desperate lack of, and need for, a proper medical service.** *(RR)*

The two divisions took up their positions backing up against the town with the artillery to the front.

There were 929 killed and 4 271 wounded this day. General Desjardins was wounded in the head and died three days later. General Heudelet was wounded. General Binet was killed as was Adjudant-Commandant Mac Sheeby and Colonel Lacuée. Generals Sarrut and Albert were wounded as was Adjudant-Commandant Rouyer and Colonel Sicard, Maréchal Augereau's aide-de-camp. General Amey had two horses killed under him and General Pannetier one.

The officers and men showed constant devotion to duty and bravery beyond what words can describe.

The Maréchal was ill that morning and was not able to ride, but he returned in a sled and in the end managed to get on his horse with a lot of difficulty. He had been given permission to go to Warsaw and had to leave the battlefield at four p.m.

This report was taken up by General de la Chasse de Vérigny in 1824.

Concerning the 3rd Corps

The 3rd Corps committed itself fully during the whole day and suffered heavy casualties.
- Friant's Division
General Lochet was killed at the head of the 33rd and 48th of the Line during the capture of Klein-Sausgarten, as was General d'Honnières with the 13th light. Colonel Faure of the 61st was killed as were 28 officers and 247 men in his regiment. Colonel Walthert of the 30th of the Line was seriously wounded. In all the division lost 177 officers and 2 486 men. Friant mentioned Colonel Barbanègre, his Captains Croux and Armand of the 48th, Rottembourg of the 108th, the artillerymen Villeneuve and Legrand, and Captain Chemin

who had had his pieces dismantled and went and got himself killed with his ordnance.

- Gudin's division

The division only lost 4 officers and 83 men killed, 1 officer and 250 men wounded.

- The Light Cavalry

Marulaz's Brigade with its 1st, 2nd and 12th Chasseurs lost 3 officers and 7 troopers killed.

The eyewitness account from General Berthézène is enlightening. It says: *"The battlefield was a hideous sight; there were 9 000 dead and about 20 or 25 000 wounded among which 16 000 enemy. Until Davout's corps arrived, the fighting was indecisive and thus the successful outcome of the day was due to his patriotism. What would have happened if the Maréchal had stuck only to the normal procedures and waited to be given the order to go into battle? The battle would not only have been lost but the future safety of the army would have been compromised. Occasionally, a general has to rise above principles and risk his head for the good of the undertaking."*

Berthézène also alludes to Grouchy, and Ney who made a mess of his arrival.

Note concerning Milhaud

He was ordered to support Saint-Hilaire, but one of his biographers does not mention the Battle of Eylau which is surprising. Likewise the history of the 5th Dragoons deals with this particular day very discreetly and it is not known whether he stayed with Saint-Hilaire or whether he took part in the big charge with Murat. Did he support Davout towards Kuschitten?

In his memoirs, the Captain of Engineers Paulin tells an amusing anecdote: *"I was on my way to try and join the Engineers HQ and General Chasseloup. On the way, I met the Engineer Captain Lesecq from Desjardins' division. His horse had just been killed and like me he was trying to join up with General Chasseloup. He was carrying his harness on his back hoping to find a horse to finish the day with. We entered Eylau together.*

"There was a terrible fight going on there. Russian and French soldiers were lying all over the place, as far as the eye could see on that snowy and foggy day. Marshals Soult and Davout were struggling but apparently retaining the advantage. Maréchal Ney was expected at any moment. He was busy pushing back the Prussian corps.

"Suddenly the snow stopped falling and the sky brightened slightly.

"The Emperor, surrounded by his Guard, was on the hillock where the Eylau church and cemetery were situated… Although you could see daylight through the battered belfry thanks to the enemy, it still had its staircase, less a few steps of course. I climbed to the top where I had a grandstand view of everything that was going on below.

"I was totally absorbed by the drama unfolding in front of me when General Chasseloup arrived on the platform beside me where, it is true, he did not remain for very long because the place was too often peppered for comfort by salvoes from the Russian artillery.

"With an experienced eye, he saw all he needed to see and without delay in the face of the danger, he set off down to report to the Emperor.

"In spite of the gravity of the situation, I was shaken by an uncontrollable desire to laugh when the general left the belfry. Imagine my venerable general, impatient because of the cannonballs which were grazing our heads, hurrying to get to the bottom of the twisting staircase, going through the exit, hampered by his sword (even though it was a short one) which got caught on the walls all torn apart by the projectiles; it hit every step with a sound of old metal and I, following close on his heels, kept stepping on the sword nearly causing him to tumble down the stairs."

This being said, Paulin was just as much in a hurry to leave the belfry as his General was.

A debatable victory

Napoleon wanted to erect a statue dedicated to General d'Hautpoul as a Cuirassier made from melted down cannonballs taken from the battlefield. On the final map attached to the Grande Armée bulletin, it seems he was the author of small drawings of corpses scattered all over the map in different places.

With his usual lack of objectivity, Benningsen passed himself off as the winner of the battle when in fact he could very easily have been surrounded and wiped out had Ney arrived earlier or been able to neutralise the Prussians.

At any rate, although Napoleon had clearly managed to beat his badly-mauled adversary into retreating, the combatants on both sides had shown marvellous and exceptional courage. As the French were wont to repeat: *"Killing a Russian is not enough. You have to push him so that he falls over."*

The French army was exhausted and it had to rest and reorganise and get itself back into condition. Napoleon had his troops bivouac for a week on the battlefield to mark the victory which had been so dearly won. Benningsen did not return to the attack – he had toyed with idea - and the Emperor decided to pull his army back beyond the Passarge and the Upper All to refit and to get reinforcements.

Eylau was a terrible carnage. (Job/RR)

Above.
The grand parade at Elbing, the French cavalry in all its splendour.
(Drawing by Jack Girbal, Author's collection)

FROM EYLAU TO FRIEDLAND

"Soldiers, we were beginning to get a bit of rest in our winter quarters when the enemy attacked our 1st Corps and reached the Lower Vistula. We marched to meet them, we chased them very closely for eighty leagues then they sought refuge under the ramparts of their strongholds and crossed back over the Pregel. In the fighting at Bergfried, Deppen, Hoff and at the battle of Eylau, we captured sixty-five artillery pieces, sixteen flags off them and killed and wounded forty thousand men.

The brave men on our side, who remained on the field of honour, died a glorious death: it was the death of true soldiers. Their families will get full rights to our solicitude and our good deeds. Having thus thwarted all the enemy's projects, we are going to go closer to the Vistula and enter our billets. Whoever dares to trouble our rest will live to regret it. For beyond the Vistula as it was beyond the Danube, in the middle of the wintry weather just like at the beginning of the autumn, we will always be the French soldiers of the Grande Armée."

The Emperor handled his pen just as mightily as his sword. The glory of the latest fighting was to the benefit his soldiers and he promised them rest.

Winter Quarters

On 21 February, General Headquarters were moved up, near to Osterode, at the Ordenschloss, as was the Guard who set up headquarters in no time in keeping with the standing of their Emperor. Oudinot's Grenadiers, from the 5th Corps joined them shortly afterwards.

The different Marshals' corps marched back and settled down behind the Passarge: Murat and the cavalry reserve were between Elbing and Osterode. Bernadotte was covered by the Lower Passarge, billeted between Braunsberg and Spanden. On his right, Soult set himself up between Liebstadt and Mohrungen whereas Davout was between Allenstein and Hohenstein. Ney was slightly ahead of this disposition between the Upper Passarge and the Upper Alle, between Guttstadt and Allenstein, with a strong vanguard at Heilsberg.

After having brilliantly beaten Essen at Ostrolenka, Savary was brought back to Warsaw with the 5th Corps which was reinforced by Polish troops, but he was replaced by Masséna who had returned from Naples.

The winter campaign was over and everybody was waiting for the weather to clear up and for the terrain to improve. Napoleon used this respite to mould the army into a tool in keeping with his ambitions and his military genius. The regiments were allowed to rest, their strength being made up with the arrival of the laggards, the depot troops and the 1808 conscripts, who had been called up earlier in spite of Cambacérès' warnings. The Allied countries were also made to contribute, and thus the numbers were reinforced. However, this winter campaign and especially the Battle of Eylau had cut bloody swathes through this army of experienced soldiers. Although the regiments' strength was made up numerically, nothing could replace the value of the battle-hardened veterans of the various campaigns who had fallen in the snow and the mud of East Prussia. For the first time since the half-brigades were amalgamated during the winter of 1793-1794 by Carnot, the quality of the French army had dropped, although it was still the best in all Europe.

A reserve corps was made up and entrusted to Lannes who had recovered. It comprised the Verdier Division which came from the 5th Corps and the Grenadier division under Oudinot which had been formed in Berlin. A mixed Saxon division comprising an infantry and a cavalry brigade completed this elite corps.

Supplying the troops was also improved. The weeks spent marching through a poor country in sometimes quite unimaginable conditions had revealed the extent to which an army was limited when trying to feed itself off the land. Moreover the cartage was carried out by private companies. Following Napoleon's orders, Daru made sure that supplies were sent and depots set up in the various captured strongholds once the horses' and soldiers' needs had been met. He had up to three pairs of shoes issued to all soldiers and had bread ovens built. The Emperor wrote to Talleyrand "…If I've got bread, beating the Russians is child's play." To transport the

Above, from left to right.
The canteen women and the administration, the team crews. *(RR)*

Below, Centre. **General Deroy commanded a Bavarian division.** *(RR)*

Bottom. **The taking of Breslau by Prince Jérôme's 9th Corps.** *(RR)*

supplies, equipment and ammunition, Napoleon created the transport train consisting of ten battalions with 120 caissons each drawn by four horses. Everything had to be ready for when hostilities resumed, which the Emperor estimated would be on 10 June. Each army corps had to have ten days' supplies. Thus for his Dragoon division, General Milhaud received twenty thousand rations of biscuits, rice, brandy and eight thousand horseshoes.

On 1 April Napoleon transferred his headquarters to Finkerstein from where he directed everything.

But no matter how well prepared the French army was, it could not launch its summer campaign without having solid bases; thus the strongholds which had been left behind had to be reduced and the threat of the English all along the coast and of the Swedes in Pomerania averted.

A War of Sieges

During their advance from Berlin and the heart of Prussia, the French had by-passed a number of strongholds and citadels, being content with investing them and leaving them to be watched over by second line troops. Thus it was with the towns in Silesia, those along the Vistula or along the Baltic coast.

Prince Jérôme with his 9th Corps comprising mainly the Wurtemburgers under Vandamme and the Bavarians under Deroy was left in charge in Silesia. He had already reduced Globau on 3 December and Breslau a month later. Once captured, these two towns yielded large quantities of ammunition, weapons and supplies. Some towns did in turn fall before the end of hos-

THE SIEGE OF DANZIG

Danzig was one of the biggest strongholds on the Baltic coast, 60 miles to the west of Königsberg. Situated in the estuary of the Vistula, two miles from the sea, it was protected to the north by the river and to the east and south by marshy ground which made the approaches difficult. The fort of Weichselsmünde had been built at the mouth of the Vistula, on the right bank, covering the north of Danzig which as well as having plentiful supplies, was a grave threat to the French army's flank and lines of communications. It could also be used as a base for English or Russian forces to land and thus compromise all Napoleon's plans. In short, Danzig was a thorn in the side of the Grande Armée.

Kalkreuth, the old Russian general, was in command there. He was seventy one years old and was himself fiercely determined to resist and expected the same of all the other defenders. He had the suburbs burnt down and the fortifications consolidated. He had at his disposal a garrison of 14 000 Prussians and 4 000 Russians, vast warehouses and depots of supplies, weapons and ammunition. Kalkreuth was ready and waiting.

To carry out the mission he was entrusted with, Lefebvre at first only had 18 700 men: 3 000 Frenchmen of whom 600 Sappers, 2 200 men from Baden, 6 000 recently-recruited Poles, 2 500 men from the Northern Legion – made up mainly of Poles and Russian deserters - and 5 000 Saxons. The siege artillery arrived on 23 April.

Danzig is invested

The investing of Danzig started on 16 March and on the 19th General Schramm finished isolating the town when he cut it off from the Weichselmünde Fort and from the

Top. **Danzig seen from the west.** *(RMN)*

Bottom.
Prussian wounded helped by the civilian population. *(RR)*

Opposite. **The Baden contingent under the command of the Crown-Prince got its baptism of fire under the walls of the Prussian town.**
(Composition by Jack Girbal, Author's Collection)

Nehrung, a strip of sandy land linking Danzig to Königsberg. This attack was carried out with 3 000 men among whom were the 2nd Battalion of the 2nd Light, and Grenadiers from various French, Saxon, Baden and Polish contingents. During this attack, the troops bowled over all the Prussian units they met and chased them to the glacis of Weichselmünde Fort, causing heavy casualties.

During the following two weeks the besieged made a number of sallies in order to destabilise the Imperial troops and to destroy the siege works which had been undertaken.

On 1 April the French Sappers opened a first sap and were able to start approaching the town. But during the night of the 2-3 April, the defenders made a vigorous sally and recaptured the Kalke-Schanze redoubt which was occupied by Baden and Polish troops from the Northern Legion. Knowing nothing about siege work, Lefebvre was exasperated by the slowness with which the work was progressing; he complained to the Emperor and took advantage of the situation to complain also about the Allied troops: *"The Germans are inclined to desert; they have to be fed better than the French soldiers to stop them marauding through the villages… The only thing they are good at is devouring the supplies and are not much interested in climbing over walls…*

*Above, from left to right and top to bottom. **The Prussian General Kalkreuth, Maréchal Lefebvre and the French Generals Lariboisière and Chasseloup-Laubat.** (RR)*

*Right. **The French drive back an attempted sally from the town by the defenders. The defences were gradually worn down causing the garrison to surrender.** (RR)*

Although the Saxons fight well, they are less inclined to work; the Baden units are neither good at working nor at fighting… You'll have to get rid of all these people…" Somebody had to take the blame! Napoleon told him to be patient and to give the Allied troops the time to get war-hardened: they could not become like the French overnight!

"Make a hole in it and I'll get through!"

To help the Maréchal handle the siege, Napoleon sent him two very talented men in their domain, Lariboisière from the Artillery and Chasseloup-Laubat from the Sappers. Lefebvre had no option but to respect the rigorous discipline of the laying a siege and capturing a town. He nevertheless pressed Chasseloup-Laubat not to waste time. *"I don't understand anything about all this but make a hole in it and I'll get through."* He also said that he was ready to push the walls of Danzig down with his Grenadiers' chests if needs be. Once a fighting cock always a fighting cock.

On 13 April, a sally by the Prussians drove out the Saxons occupying a redoubt and reached the head of the saps. Lefebvre immediately took command of a battalion of the 44th of the Line and led a vigorous counter-attack pushing the attackers back to the Hagelsberg glacis.

On 12 May a corps of 8 000 Russians under Kamenski was landed at Weichselmünde to break the siege and 2 000 men also advanced up the Nehrung in reinforcement. Napoleon directed Lannes who had come up to reinforce the 10th Corps together with Mortier who was now available due to the armistice signed with the Swedes. The Russians under Kamenski sallied forth from the fort and, supported by English corvettes, marched against the French positions. They ran into the 2nd Light, reinforced by a detachment of the Paris Guard under the command of General Schramm. The 10 000 attackers were driven off leaving 2 000 dead and wounded on the field. During this fight, an English corvette, which had run aground on the sandbanks, was captured by the French infantry. It was the last time any attempt was made to force the siege of Danzig.

The final assault on the town was decided for 21 May. Kalkreuth was discouraged and considered that further resistance was useless. He asked to capitulate. On the 24th the capitulation was signed and the garrison was accorded the honours of war. By taking control of Danzig, the French also got hold of the richly stocked warehouses which enabled all the corps to be resupplied; and it also took the thorn out of the Grande Armée's side.

Napoleon congratulated Lefebvre and rewarded him by making him Duke of Danzig. ❏

Bottom.
***The capture and surrender of Danzig earned Lefebvre his Duke's title.** (RR)*

campaign.

The first was Danzig which was an important strategic and logistic town. The second was Kolberg which although not as important as Danzig, it did have a considerable impact on the Prussian people and on future German "patriotism".

Watching the Coast

Whilst it was reducing the strongholds, the French army was also keeping an eye on the North Sea coast and the Baltic to prevent the English from trying to open up another front. This task was entrusted to the corps of Junot, Brune and Mortier, thus immobilising several tens of thousand men. A fictitious landing in Ireland was imagined which obliged the English also to mobilise a certain number of troops. Mortier invaded Swedish Pomerania in January 1807 with his 8th Corps. He was then replaced by Dutch troops who marched on Straslund. This period was marked by a number of attacks by Swedish light troops during which the Hussars and the Jägers in particular distinguished themselves. An armistice was signed at Schatkow leading to operations being halted in this sector.

Hostilities are resumed

Benningsen had withdrawn northwards after the battle of Eylau and had profited from these hundred days to reinforce his decimated troops. He ordered Kamenski to join Lestocq and recalled Olsufiev's division. He had the sick of whom there were many and the wounded evacuated towards Friedland. Bagration was rested at Lanau. The 14th division and the artillery were sent to Heilsberg where Constantine and the Guard concentrated as a reserve, forming a formidable obstacle indeed.

The Guttstadt Preliminaries

On 2 June, Benningsen's headquarters were in Heilsberg which he fortified; he transformed the right bank of the Alle into a fortified camp. He was expecting the

The siege of Kolberg. (RR)

tilities – such as Brieg, Schweidnitz and Neisse – but others held out until the armistice.

Invested in November, Graudentz, on the Vistula was commanded by the Prussian General, Courbières. It was relieved during Benningsen's offensive in January 1807, but was besieged again by the Hessians under General Victor.

Two other sieges also marked the campaign. Each had a different influence on the

THE SIEGE OF KOLBERG, OR THE FORCE OF WILL

Situated on the Baltic, 125 miles to the west of Danzig, Kolberg was not a very important stronghold. But it was a place where Russian or English troops could be landed to threaten the Grande Armée's rear. Its fortress had not been kept up and its warehouses held nothing of any significance. Its 1000-men garrison had however been reinforced with 5 000 soldiers before the town was invested at the beginning of March 1807. It had 90 cannon.

Napoleon had entrusted the 8th Corps with protecting the coast between the estuaries of the Oder and the Vistula. In a letter to Maréchal Mortier, Napoleon placed the divisions as follows: "…Dupas' division will remain billeted in Stettin and Kolberg, Grandjean's division between Kolberg and Danzig, and Loison's division will besiege Kolberg…"

The Mayor, Joachim Nettlebeck, took charge of the town's defence with the firm intention of yielding nothing to the French. Given the lack of troops, he encouraged the population to take part and work on the fortifications and the defence of the town, so as to relieve the soldiers.

When faced with his fellow citizens' discouragement, he retorted with suitably forceful answers like *"Citizens, the moment has come to show them what we're made of!"* or *"I'll kill the first man who talks of surrender."* The 8 000 French could not make much progress against such determination so they started work on the siege.

On 29 April, Gneisenau arrived to take command of the town and organised sallies intended to hinder the French with their approach work and to tire them out by forcing them to be on the qui-vive all the time.

On 25 June 1807, Napoleon and Frederick-William signed a cease-fire; the town still held out and Loison still attacked it. Ignoring the Imperial agreements, the French general continued attacking and bombarding the town.

On 3 July when a truce was agreed, almost all the town's houses had been damaged and 2 000 out of the 6 000 defenders were out of action. Kolberg, however, had not fallen.

This episode from the Napoleonic wars was put to good use by the IIIrd Reich in its death throes. In 1945, Goebbels had a film made. It was called *"Kolberg"* and highlighted the bravery and the will of the German people in the face of the invaders. ❑

Opposite.
General Gneisenau.
(RR)

Above, from left to right.
Maréchal Mortier and the Governor of Kolberg, N. Nettlebeck. *(RR)*

Below.
Defending the town was also the townspeople's business… *(RR)*

Benningsen attacks, 1st of June, 1807

The Russian General Kamenski reinforced Lestocq's Prussian corps.
(RR)

2nd, 3rd and 14th Divisions. His 100 000-men army was now concentrated at Heilsberg, flanked on the left by Ostermann-Tolstoy's 18 000 men who were on the Narev, and on the right by Lestocq and Kamenski's 20 000 men. The latter had in fact fled from Danzig with 2 551 men under General Schuler together with the Tobolsk and Polotsk Regiments, 16 cannon and two squadrons of Heyking Dragoons.

The French meanwhile left their billets and according to the Emperor's instructions concentrated on the left bank of the Passarge from its estuary in the north up to Holenstein.

Soult was between Mohrungen and Lomitten; he had Bernadotte on his left and Davout on his right. Lannes who was joined by Mortier's troops was at Marienburg with Lasalle's division. The heavy cavalry reserve – the Nansouty, Espagne and Saint-Sulpice Divisions – under Murat was at Elbing whilst the Dragoon Divisions were supporting various corps, Latour-Maubourg at Bischofswerder, Grouchy at Strasburg, Milhaud at Soldau and Lorge at Willenberg. The Imperial Guard, commanded by Bessières was round Finkerstein.

To the south of this disposition, Masséna was keeping an eye on Ostermann. His corps was deployed from Willenberg to Warsaw. He was reinforced by the Poles under Poniatowski whose Zajonczek Division was at Neidenburg.

Napoleon planned to go over to the attack on 10 June by striking the Russians and separating them from Königsberg before chasing them and destroying them on the Niemen. It was Benningsen however who took the initiative of the attack, strongly encouraged to do this by his entourage and the Tsar himself.

The aim of the Russian offensive was to chase the French from the Lower Passarge then with a feint to push them far from their base towards the Narev by cutting their lines of communication. Benningsen's plan was just a repeat of the winter's manoeuvre and the Russian General was convinced that it would work.

Benningsen Attacks

The Hessian Corps at the siege of Graudentz

Musketeer, Erbprinz Regiment

2nd light Infantry Regiment

3rd light Infantry Regiment

The siege was directed by General Victor and the Hessian Corps was commanded by General Rouyer de Saint-Victor.
Three battalions of Light Infantry
— 2nd Hessian Infantry Regiment (two battalions)
— Berg Regiment (two battalions)
— A detachment of Berg Chevau-Légers
— 2nd and 4th Polish Regiments of the Line
— The Württzburg Regiment
The 3rd Hessian Regiment of the Line which was part of the division was acting as garrison in Thorn. This corps formed a mixed force of 7 000 men. ❑

Above. **Poniatowski was already a Prince but not yet Maréchal de France.** *(RR)*

Opposite, from left to right.
Maréchal Soult and General Guyot-Etienne, commanding the Light Cavalry from the 4th Corps, who was killed in a Cossack ambush. *(RR)*

Bottom, left.
To General Savary who offered to accept the capitulation of Graudentz, General Courbières replied that "if there was no longer a King in Prussia, then he was still the King of Graudentz!" The stronghold nonetheless ended up falling into French hands. *(RR)*

The offensive started on 4 June along three axes of which two were diversions. Along the Lower Passarge, Lestocq attacked Soult at Braunsberg but was pushed back. Up river, the 1st Corps stood up to a violent attack from Kamenski and Rembow towards Spanden. The Russians were repulsed but Bernadotte was wounded in the neck by a bullet and had to be replaced the following day by Victor, who had just been swapped for Blucher. On the 5th, the Russians attacked again and were again repulsed. During this successful engagement, General Frère and his 27th Light were mentioned in despatches as were la Houssaye and the 17th Dragoons. The aim of these assaults on the Passarge was to divert and thus to isolate Ney. It was in fact the 6th Corps which was to receive the brunt of Benningsen's attack. Ney was at Guttsadt but called Davout over as cover to Deppen. The Russians attacked towards Wolfsdorf with Sacken on the right, Uvarov and Olsufiev and the 3rd Division in the centre and on the left, Galitzin V and Ostermann. Dokhtorov supported this attack with Essen III at the Lomitten bridgehead where the 57th distinguished itself with the 46th and the 24th under Maréchal Soult. The Chasseurs of the Russian Imperial Guard were repulsed, two officers were killed and 10 wounded, as were 150 Guardsmen.

Platov had to cross the Alle and join up with Gortchakov and his Cossacks. On the way, he attacked and captured a convoy in which he found all Maréchal Davout's papers and luggage together with his Maréchal's baton which is now on display in the Hermitage Museum in Saint-Petersburg. The Englishmen, Wilson and Hutchinson, were accompanying Platov. A bridge over the Alle was built at Bergfried.

Ney defended himself against Bagration with the 50th, 59th and 31st Light in front, and Marconet's brigade: the 39th under Colonel Soyer and the 76th reinforced by the 6th and the 69th.

Ney had to fall back on Ankerdorf and Deppen drawing Benningsen further west and thus enabling Napoleon to set up the same manoeuvre as in February in order to take the Russians on their flank.

On 6 June Ney was attacked by a large force and had to fall back on Deppen where there was some very heavy fighting. The position was lost and retaken six times but Ney managed to hold on to the bridge over the Passarge. Dutaillis lost an arm. A boat bridge enabled Ney to get his men beyond the Passarge. He had run out of ammunition and bread because his convoys had been captured by the Cossacks and Grodno's Hussars. Bagration had reached the river. Ney had Davout on his right and Soult on his left and the line was reformed. He had managed to escape from the Russians. He had 16 596 men left with 1 681 cavalry, and had made a model retreat.

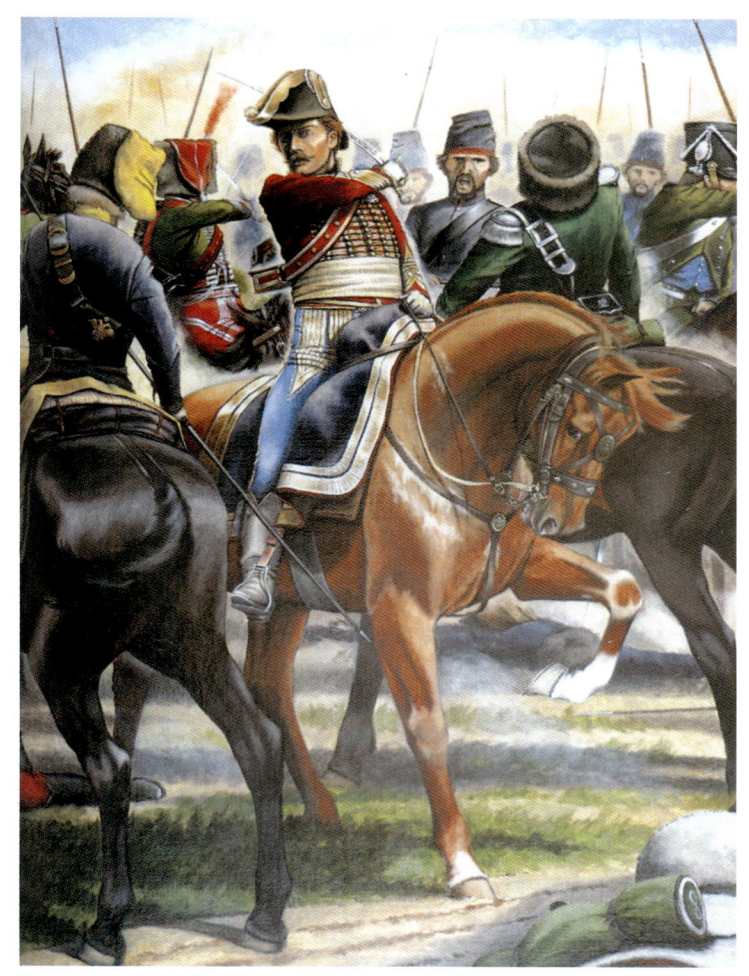

Benningsen complained about Sacken, his scapegoat with the Tsar who believed him and had Sacken withdrawn. He was reinstated in 1813. The General had nevertheless seen through the Emperor's manoeuvre and ordered a hurried retreat towards Heilsberg and the entrenched camp.

The Preliminary Fighting on the Passarge

On 7 June, Soult crossed the Passarge at Elditten and advanced towards Wolfsdorf against Uvarov. Some Cossacks who had ventured forwards were driven back by the 8th Hussars. The Tirailleurs Corses distinguished themselves on this occasion. Victor, who had replaced Bernadotte, still faced Lestocq. On 8 June Maucune attacked from Deppen.

Benningsen sent Gortchakov and Kamenski - who had reached Lestocq - to Heilsberg. Grand-Duke Constantine was at Lanau with his Guard. Bagration was in the rearguard, leaving Baggovut at Ankerdorf, covered by the Cossacks, as well Markov who was with Platov. Galitzin was up in support on the left at Guttstadt. The Ilovaisky II and IV, and Grekov IV Cossacks met Guyot's light cavalry at Kleinfeld. In this ambush, the brigade lost its General. 30 men were killed, 9 seriously wounded and 116 taken prisoner.

On 9 June, Ney retook Guttstadt and 200 prisoners. He forced Kamenski to fall back towards Heilsberg but Platov destroyed the bridges across the Alle. To the north, Victor repulsed Lestocq at Zagern. Tolstoi and Essen had remained on the Narev and the Omulev in front of Masséna. Murat, leading the five divisions of the cavalry reserve, was close on the Russians' heels. He was slowed down by Bagration's strong rearguard action but he knocked these 20 000 men aside and entered Guttstadt. Benningsen withdrew into Heilsberg.

The Battle of Heilsberg

Benningsen had put two boat bridges across the Alle at Amt-Heilsberg and had disposed his troops in the following way:

Bagration who had fallen back with Lvov and Borodin,

The battle of Heilsberg, the first round

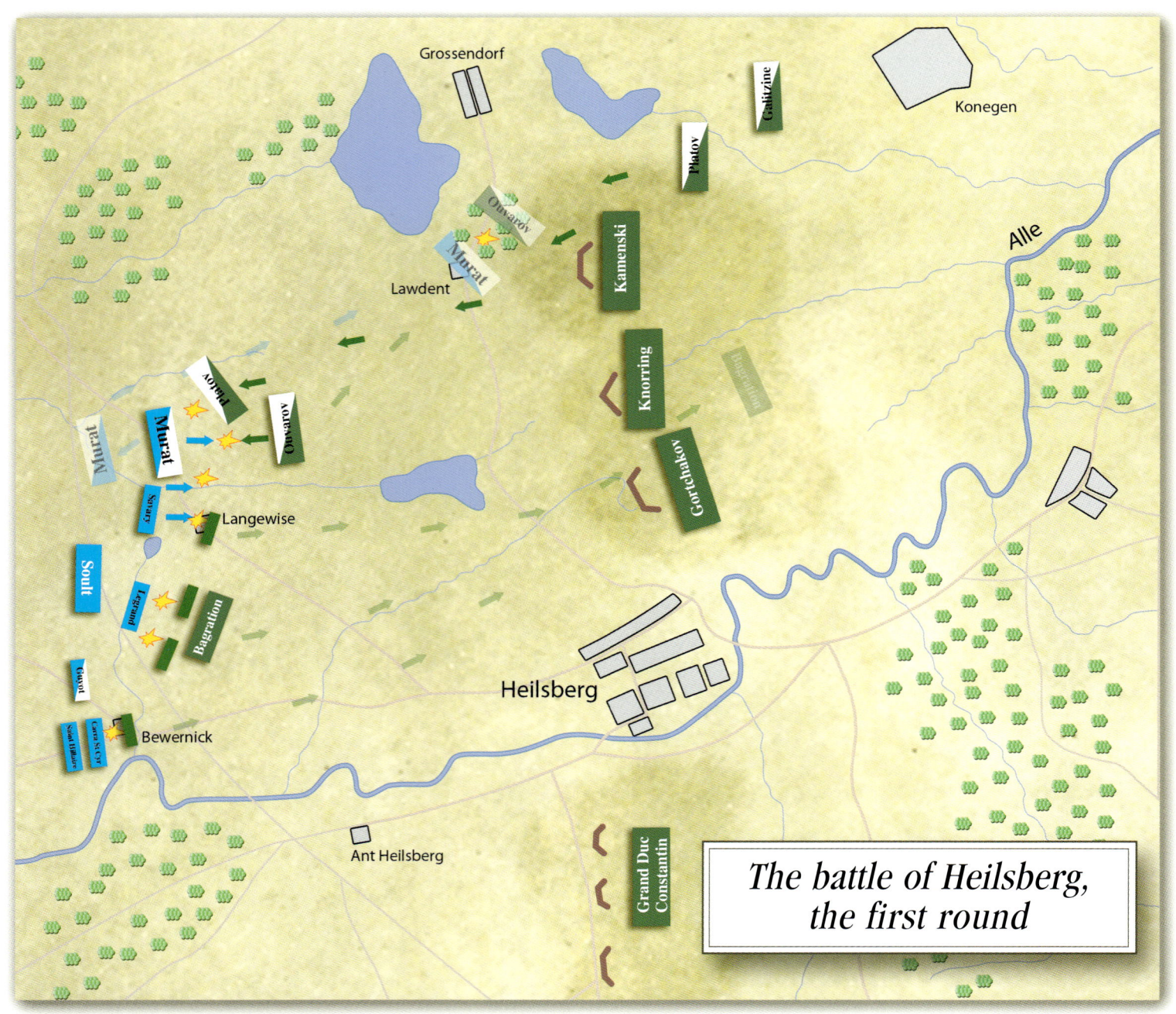

*Opposite. **The Prussian Hussars from Prittwitz's Regiment get hold of the Eagle of the 55th of the Line during the Battle of Heilsberg.** (RR)*

Opposite.
Maréchal Murat at Heilsberg. When his horse was killed beneath him, Murat managed to get out from under it and immediately mounted another horse. One of his boots however remained buried under the first horse, but the fastidious Maréchal nevertheless went back into battle just in his stockings!
(Drawing by Job, RR)

occupied Bewernick and Landwiese as well as the space separating these two villages with two battalions, fifteen dragoon squadrons and eight artillery pieces. Uvarov and his cavalry covered Bagration's right flank.

On the heights behind him there were four redoubts and between them, a number of batteries and fortifications. Redoubts N° 4 and 5 were on the right bank of the Alle; 6 and 7 were on the left bank.

Redoubts N° 4 and 5 were on the right bank of the Alle and behind them Grand-Duke Constantine's Guard was astride the Guttstadt road; an attack in this area was what Benningsen dreaded most.

On the left bank behind the fortified zone, Benningsen had placed (from left to right) Kamenski with the 5th Division and the Archangel, Mohilev and Naviginsky Regiments together with the 21st Chasseurs and a Prussian half-battery; Knorring with the Bielosersk, Volhynia and Pernau Regiments in the front line and the Nizowsky and Reval Regiments – which were in fact with Borodin at first at Bewernick but which then fell back into the second line here; Gortchakov and the 2nd, 4th and 6th Divisions were deployed between Redoubt N°6 and the Alle.

The Fusilier-Grenadiers of the Guard distinguished themselves at the Battle of Heilsberg.
(Drawing by Jack Girbal, Author's Collection)

Benningsen had placed his cavalry with Platov and Galitzin backing up against Konegen and in front of Grossendorf.

The French arrive

Murat and his cavalry, i.e. the Lasalle, Latour-Maubourg and Espagne Divisions arrived in front of Bewernick. They were followed by Soult and the Carra-Saint-Cyr and Saint-Hilaire Divisions and their large artillery contingent, the Fusiliers and a battery from the Guard. Lannes was following with Verdier.

Ney, Davout and Mortier were kept in reserve with the Guard at Guttstadt, but Davout then followed to the left of Heilsberg in order to turn the town.

The Battle on 10 June

Arriving in front of the Russian positions, Murat forgot the Emperor's orders. He had been ordered in fact to feint a frontal attack in order to fix the enemy; Napoleon would then turn them and cut them off from Königsberg. The only thing the Grand-Duke of Berg could see was the glory which would be his if he could, with only his 9 000 horsemen, chase the Russians from such a formidable position. So he applied the only strategy which he thought suitable, the only one that had always been successful for him: he charged. Without giving any precise orders to anyone in particular, he immediately led his divisions in a mad charge. Lasalle - from whom Murat had removed Colonel Déry's 5th Hussars and thrown them into the fray - saw the madness of such action, but could not allow his Light Cavalry to sit there doing nothing, so he launched them into the fight as well.

Above and following page.
Maréchal Murat and General Lasalle at Heilsberg. They saved each other's lives during this battle where the French cavalry suffered very heavy losses for rather insignificant results.
(Drawing by Jack Girbal, Author's Collection and All Rights Reserved)

Bagration fell back chessboard-fashion towards the redoubts covered by Baggovut, and by Kogin who led the Emperor's Cuirassiers away but who got himself killed. He was also supported by the Ingermanland, Pskov and Courland Dragoons, They were driven off and two cannon were lost and recaptured.

The cavalry divisions came and threw themselves at the Russian positions but were met by grapeshot from 400 artillery pieces. There was total chaos among the French squadrons immediately. Benningsen in turn launched his own cavalry reserve: 15 000 horses set off and counter-attacked; there followed such a compacted fray as had scarcely ever been seen before.

Very heavy cavalry fighting took place near Langewiese and it was this action which was used to describe Murat's and Lasalle's courage when they managed to disengage themselves from the fray and seek refuge in a square with Soult. Aubier from the 20th Chasseurs relates how Murat had his horse killed by a cannonball. "I immediately jumped to the ground and holding the horse's bridle under my arm I helped the Prince to get himself out from under his horse. 'It's nothing, it's nothing,' said the Prince, 'get me a horse!' " Aubier therefore gave him his. The Maréchal had left one of his boots in the stirrup; it was a magnificent boot made of red morocco all braided with gold, part of Murat's uniform. His men described him as dressed up as a Drum-Major. Brigadier Henri of the 8th Cuirassiers threw himself into the middle of the Russians and brought back the boot. He was awarded the Legion d'Honneur.

Carra-Saint-Cyr, arriving with the 4th and the 24th Light, drove back the Russians towards their entrenchments. Saint-Hilaire supported the attack by moving up front and went as far as the lines of fortifications; but he was attacked on both flanks. The 10th Light and the 57th of the Line were mentioned in this very hard fighting.

Legrand and the Fusiliers of the Guard formed up into squares on the plain and resisted. The French stopped and started a march so as to turn the town. Legrand got hold of the wood in front of Grossendorf. On the left, they got the Russians out. An attack by the Fusiliers of the Guard was driven off but that by the 26th Light against the 7th Redoubt was more effective, supported as it was by the 55th whose Eagle was captured by some Prussian Hussars.

Davout's arrival later enabled the right of the position to be turned towards Grossendorf with Legrand in support, thus posing a threat to the Königsberg road.

Colonel de Gonneville relates in his memoirs that with the Russian cavalry falling back, they set off in pursuit, reinforced by the 50th Chasseurs and the Saxon Cuirassiers. The latter gave way but tried to rally around young sixteen-year-old officers. General Espagne was wounded.

The Losses at Heilsberg

The losses during this very harsh battle were variously estimated and the Russians were not at all objective on this matter.

The following figures were given for the French:
- For Soult, the 4th Corps lost 35 officers and 630 men killed, 215 officers and 5 613 men wounded and 5 officers and 25 men taken prisoner.
- Lannes had 15 officers killed, 63 wounded and 3 missing, 249 men killed, 1607 men wounded and 215 missing.
- The Fusiliers of the Guard lost 2 officers killed and 18 wounded. 25 men were killed and 323 wounded.

- Among the generals, Roussel was killed, Espagne, Ferey, Lorencez, Fouler and Viviès wounded.

The casualties among the cavalry were not counted. The 6th Cuirassiers however lost 17 officers and on the evening of the battle, the 150 surviving Cuirassiers were commanded by a simple Lieutenant.

For the Allies, Hoptner and von Lettow give 12 321 killed or wounded of which 864 prisoners. Percy found 600 wounded in Heilsberg and many others were found on the road to Heilsberg.

Soult gives the Russians losses at 17 000 men.

All during 11 June after the battle, Benningsen wondered what to do next; the battle had now developed into a defeat and he discussed the matter with Constantine. He managed to convince him that the best solution was to get the army back beyond the Pregel so that the expected reinforcements could be brought up and so that they could try and reach Königsberg.

The Imperial Guard deploying behind the French lines and Davout's corps getting into position towards Grossendorf ended what doubts the Russians still may have had about what to do the following day: they had to withdraw.

Murat wanted to start the chase and took Saint-Sulpice, Milhaud and Lasalle with him; but Napoleon called him back towards Friedland together with Davout.

What the Emperor wanted was not just to chase the Russian army but to outmarch it on its way to Könisgberg, destroy it and put an end to the war.

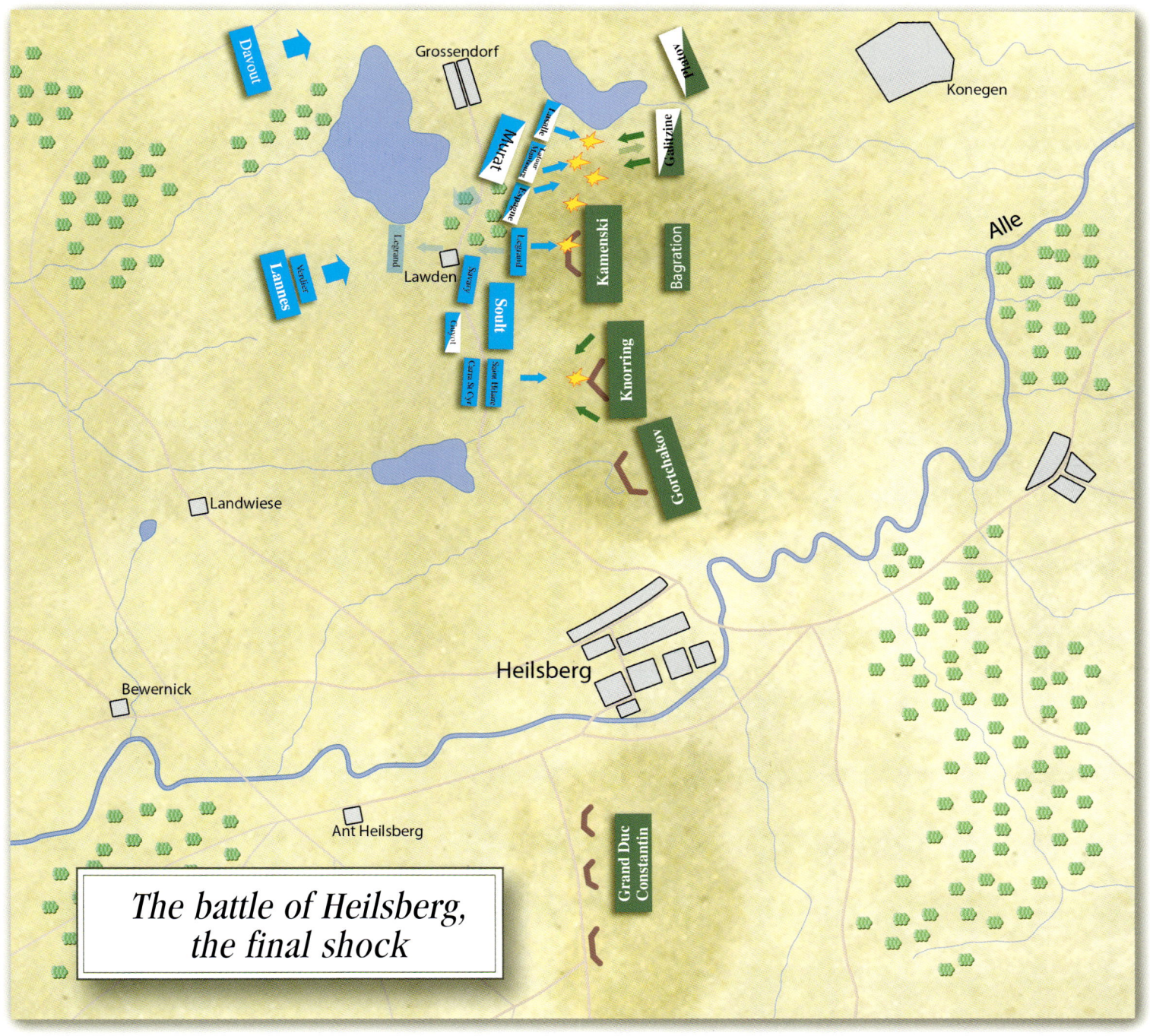

The battle of Heilsberg, the final shock

THE BATTLE OF FRIEDLAND

Above.
The Cuirassiers from the 12th Regiment saluting the Emperor before taking up their positions facing the Russian lines.
(Meissonier, Metropolitan Museum of Art, New York)

Opposite. **General Kollogriboff facing General Oudinot.** *(RR)*

Napoleon had understood Benningsen's move and how he wanted to move up along the right bank of the Alle via Bartenstein, Schippenbell and Friedland. During this march the Russians had to follow a bend in the river which took longer. The Emperor decided to outmarch them and set off towards Königsberg by the most direct route.

The March on Friedland

Murat, followed by Soult and Davout, set off via Landsberg, Eylau and Kreuzberg. Lannes and Mortier also headed for Eylau but from there they marched towards Friedland which was only a short distance away, accompanied by Grouchy's Dragoons. Ney, Victor, the heavy cavalry and the Guard remained at Eylau ready to head off along both axes. Latour-Maubourg and his Dragoons, together with the Durosnel and Wathier Divisions, followed the Russians along the right bank of the Alle; they captured a number of wounded who confirmed that the enemy was moving in that direction.

After the Battle of Heilsberg, Benningsen sent Dokhtorov to protect the Königsberg road since he wanted to hold on to the town. However on the 12th he received confirmation that the French were now heading towards that stronghold and decided to attack them on their flank. In order to do this he had to cross the Alle at Friedland, then advance on either Eylau or on Kreutzburg.

On 13 June, Galitzin was sent forward with 20 squadrons, among whom the Uhlans of the Guard and the Cuirassiers of the Order. In Friedland he found some French cavalry whom Lannes had sent out reconnoitering and among whom were the 9th Hussars who were then driven back to Heinrichsdorf. Behind this cavalry vanguard were Bagration, Dokhtorov, Uvarov and Kollogriboff.

Lannes' Fight

Lannes was perhaps the best vanguard leader among the French; he sent the Cuirassiers and the Saxon Chevau-Légers up in support. Moreover he got his corps marching faster so as to reach the town and close up the gap through which the Russian army seemed to be wanting to pass. He reached Posthenen at about one a.m. and drove out the enemy elements there with Ruffin's brigade from Oudinot's Grenadiers, the only troops available. In the feeble moonlight, he managed to see the enemy masses and came to the conclusion that he could not drive them back by himself. He nonetheless sent the Voltigeurs into Sortlack Wood which was already occupied by Russian Chasseurs. The musketry fire picked up quickly and the Russians fell back, but returned to the attack several times. The Russian Chasseurs were never able to get through the wood. When they approached, Pils remembers: *"Towards nine o'clock, a Russian regiment had occupied the forest of fir trees on the right of the Grenadiers so Oudinot dislodged them with two battalions from Ruffin's brigade; then taking advantage of the disorder caused by their retreat, he ordered Colonel Gauthrin of the 9th Hussars to sweep across the plain with his regiment and the Saxon Cuirassiers to have a go at the infantry protecting the village of Friedland."*

At three o'clock in the morning, the sun rose and Lannes was able to take in the serious situation he was in. He only had Oudinot's elite division, Grouchy's Dragoons, the cavalry brigade from his reserve corps, the 9th Hussars, the Chevau-Légers and the Saxon Cuirassiers. He sent Marbot, his aide de camp, to the Emperor to make a report on the situation.

In order to get his army across the river and deployed faster, Benningsen had had three boat bridges built across the Alle and three footbridges across the Moulin/Watermill stream. They were in use early in the morning. Once the troops had crossed over onto the left bank, the Russian General got them into position. On the left, between Sortlack wood and the Moulin/Watermill stream, Bagration commanded the 2nd and 6th Divisions with Grand-Duke Constantine's Imperial Guard in reserve. In the centre under Gortchakov and facing Heinrichsdorf, he placed the 8th, 7th and 3rd Divisions in the front line supported by the 1st Division in the second line. Kollogriboff's and Uvarov's cavalry corps made up the right wing of this disposition. The artillery was spread out all along the front line with two heavy batteries remaining in place on the right bank of the Alle where the 14th division was also positioned.

Lannes had the infantry and Oudinot's artillery deploy completely along the ravine behind Posthenen. The idea was to give the impression that they were stronger than they really were; as it was they were probably out-numbered three or four to

Right.
The 18th Dragoons were not with Grouchy, but with the Laboussaye Division, Margaron's Brigade.
(Drawing by Jack Girbal, Author's collection)

June 1807, from 11 to 14, The March on Friedland

Maréchal Mortier. (RR)

one. The artillery of the reserve corps held the enemy at a distance whilst the Tirailleurs fought it out in Sortlack Wood. On the subject of Oudinot's defence, Thiers wrote that *"he in turn hid or revealed his soldiers, spread them out as Tirailleurs or countered all the Russians' efforts like a porcupine, with a mass of bayonets."*

Reinforcements reach the French

Towards 7 a.m., the slowness with which Benningsen's troops deployed enabled the reinforcements to reach Lannes. First to arrive were Nansouty's Cuirassiers, the Dupas division from Mortier's corps, then Verdier with the 2nd Division from the reserve corps. Lannes had held all by himself until then; after 9 a.m., he had 26 000 men at his disposal with which to fight the 70 000 Russians. He held out again until midday. He then occupied Posthenen and placed his troops in front of the village supported on the right by Sortlack Wood and on the left by Heinrichsdorf, which Grouchy had orders to take.

Supported by the Dupas Division and the Albert Brigade, Grouchy rushed off with his 2nd Dragoon Division and sent the Carrié Brigade, the 10th and 11th Dragoons, to turn the enemy position. They captured all the troops who tried to get out of the village, taking

Above.
Violent fighting took place on the edge of the Sortlack Wood. *(Rugendas, RR)*

Opposite, from left to right.
General d'Ornano and Maréchal Victor. *(RR)*

Below. ***The Friedland church is still standing to-day.*** *(RR)*

Colonel Balbois. This artillery cut down the Russian centre where Essen I and Steinel, who was Quartermaster-General, were wounded and withdrew.

Gortchakov was with the Ismailovski and Semenovski Regiments of the Russian Guard on the left of the Russian army. Sutine II lost a foot, blown off by a cannonball. Bagration therefore sent Markov with the Moscow Grenadiers, the Pskov Regiment and the 3rd and 7th Chasseurs to Sortlack. The Chasseurs of the Guard and the 20th Chasseurs were pulled back, as was Rayevski. Sortlack Wood was occupied by the French, but the Russian 5th Chasseurs à Pied remained on the edge of the wood.

Towards eleven o'clock there was a lull in the fighting allowing the front to stabilise. The French were tired and this brief pause enabled them to get their breath back. On the other 1 500 prisoners with 7 Cannon and some flags. After this attack, the Russian cavalry arrived. Nansouty's Cuirassiers also came up in support. Grouchy pretended to withdraw, drawing towards him the Russian squadrons who were then charged on their flank by the French Cuirassiers and pushed back into the town, where the French followed them. Millet's brigade set itself up in Heinrichsdorf. The French cavalry had to charge fifteen times before the Russians could be reduced.

With the left wing secured, Lannes regrouped Oudinot's division which he placed in support of Dupas' division, defending Posthenen against Bagration's attacks. The arrival of Verdier's division enabled them to stop this attack.

With Mortier arriving on the battlefield and threatening the Russian centre, Benningsen launched a column against him made up of Engelhard's troops, reinforced by regiments from the 7th and the 8th Divisions. The French were driven back to the woods at Domau and an Eagle from the 15th of the Line was taken. In this action Mortier had his horse killed under him. In spite of this retreat, the 8th was able to deploy.

Dombrowski and his Poles were in front of Domau Wood; the 4th Light were sent into Heinrichsdorf and a powerful battery of 32 cannon was placed on the left of Dupas, under

Above.
Napoleon arriving at Posthenen at about midday. Lannes had indeed already engaged battle; he was going to change it into a great victory. *(RR)*

Bottom. **Grouchy's Dragoons discovering the battlefield an aide de camp brings them the order to charge.** *(RR)*

side the Russians, thinking only an isolated corps was facing them, were quite distraught by the fierce and unexpected resistance which Lannes had put up. Benningsen however did not for a moment doubt his own ability to reduce the French to silence.

Napoleon arrives

It was midday when Napoleon appeared at Posthenen followed by Ney and Victor whose corps soon arrived. To Lannes, who greeted him, the Emperor declared: *"I've brought you the army."* Then asking Oudinot where the Alle was, the latter replied: *"There, behind the enemy. I'd willingly push their bums into the water if I had some more men!"*

Napoleon, using his telescope to survey the lay out of the battlefield, at once saw the advantages he could get from it. Indeed, the Russians were deployed with their backs to the Alle which could only be crossed by means of the bad ford at Kloschenen and over four bridges, all of them in Friedland. The Emperor retorted to the generals who advised him to put the battle off till the following day because they were outnumbered: *"One doesn't surprise an enemy twice with the same mistake."* Benningsen had gone astray on the left bank of the Alle and this time Napoleon had every intention of making him pay this mistake dearly. At that time of year the sun set late so he had time to get his reinforcements up, to organise his manoeuvre and carry it out. Since Ney and Mortier had arrived he set his troops out as follows.

He put Mortier, supported on his own left by Grouchy's and Beaumont's cavalry, and the 9th Hussars on the left around Heinrichsdorf.

In the centre supported by the Windmill stream on their right was Lannes' corps. Verdier was in front supported by Oudinot. Nansouty flanked them, covered by a powerful artillery battery.

In the centre, in front of Posthenen, Napoleon placed Victor and his 1st Corps together with la Houssaye's Dragoons. The Imperial Guard, due to arrive at about 4 p.m., would take its place behind the village.

On the right, supported by Latour-Maubourg's Dragoons, the Cuirassiers and the Saxon Chevau-Légers, was Ney's corps whose Bisson Division was on the edge of Sortlack Wood; it had formed into two columns with the Marchand Division on the inside, forming the right of the disposition. The 3rd Hussars with the 10th and 15th Chasseurs à Cheval under Colbert, were up in support of the 6th Corps infantry.

The Order of Battle

Napoleon handed out his orders to his marshals and generals then sent them back to their respective units. However, he took Ney's arm and held him back a moment, explaining to him and pointing to Friedland and its bridges: *"There's your objective; just march there without worrying about what's going on around you. Break through into that thick mass no matter what the cost, enter Friedland, get hold of the bridges, and don't worry about what's going on to the left, to the right or behind you. The army and I will be there to keep an eye on things."*

It was the best mission a man like Ney could be given; by doing so, the Emperor knew that nothing would not stop Ney or distract him from his objective: he would enter the battle like the lion he was and would only stop once the mission was accomplished. Proud and full of enthusiasm, Ney left to join his troops who were waiting for the attack to start, lying on their bags in Sortlack Wood. They were resting before the attack, because they were the ones who were going to charge.

At two o'clock, Napoleon had Berthier write the order of battle and send it to all his corps commanders. *"Maréchal Ney will take the right, backing onto General Oudinot's present position. Maréchal Lannes will be at the centre which starts to the right of Maréchal Ney, i.e. almost on a level with the village of Posthenen. The part of the right formed by General Oudinot at the moment will support slightly to the left to reinforce the left; and Maréchal Lannes will keep his divisions together as much as possible. With this deployment, he will be able place himself along two axes. The left will comprise Maréchal Mortier who will not advance at all; any movement to be made will be made by our right, pivoting on the left. General Grouchy, with the cavalry on the left wing, will manoeuvre in order to make as much mischief for the enemy as possible who, under vigorous attack from our right, will feel the need to beat a retreat. General Victor will make up the reserve. He will be placed in front of the village of Posthenen together with the Guard, both infantry and cavalry. Latour-Maubourg's division will be under Maréchal's Ney's orders. La Houssaye's division will be under General Victor's orders. The Emperor has the reserve in the centre. We must only advance on the right and the initiative for the move must be left to Maréchal Ney, who must wait for the Emperor's orders before starting. At the moment when Maréchal Ney gets started, all the cannon must open fire at double the rate, firing in the direction that covers his attack."*

Napoleon thought that it would take the various corps two hours to reach their kick-off points and he wanted the troops to have an hour's rest before the battle; so he decided that the signal for the attack would be given at 5 o'clock, by the batteries of the Artillery of the Guard. As the sun did not set before 10 p.m., the Emperor knew that this gave him enough time to throw the Russians into the Alle. As a precaution, he called both Murat and Davout back; they had been marching on Königsberg and he knew they could not be back before nightfall; but they would help to tighten the noose which was drawing around the Russians.

Ney, the Lion of Friedland

17.00. The artillery of the Guard fired three salvoes as the signal to start. The attack began. Ney was immediately unleashed. He launched his divisions forward out of Sortlack Wood preceded by a swarm of Tirailleurs, driving back the Russian Tirailleurs. The Marchand Division advanced on Sortlack Village whereas Bisson, on the left, covered his flank and launched an attack on Gortchakov's corps which rapidly gave way to the fury of the French led by this lion. A counter-attack by the Russian cavalry was repulsed by Bisson's division and the corps artillery.

Top, right.
The Emperor and Maréchal Ney: "March without looking about you…" *(RR)*

Above, from left to right and top to bottom.
The Russian General Benningsen and the French Dragoon General Latour-Maubourg. General Bagration and Grand Duke Constantine, commanding the Russian Imperial Guard. *(RR)*

Opposite. **General Dupont, hero of Friedland.** *(RR)*

Below. **Sénarmont's "charge".** *(RR)*

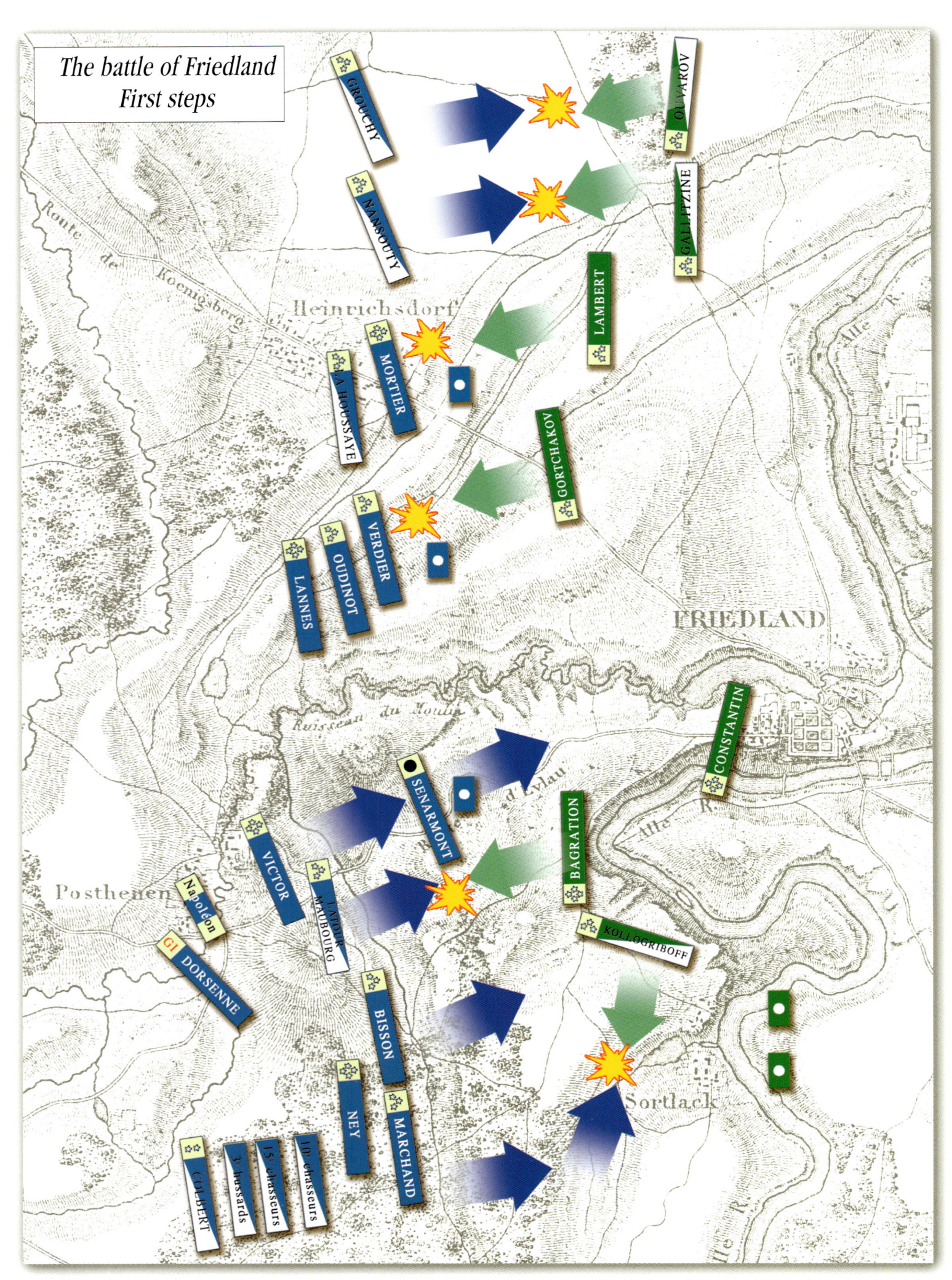

The battle of Friedland
First steps

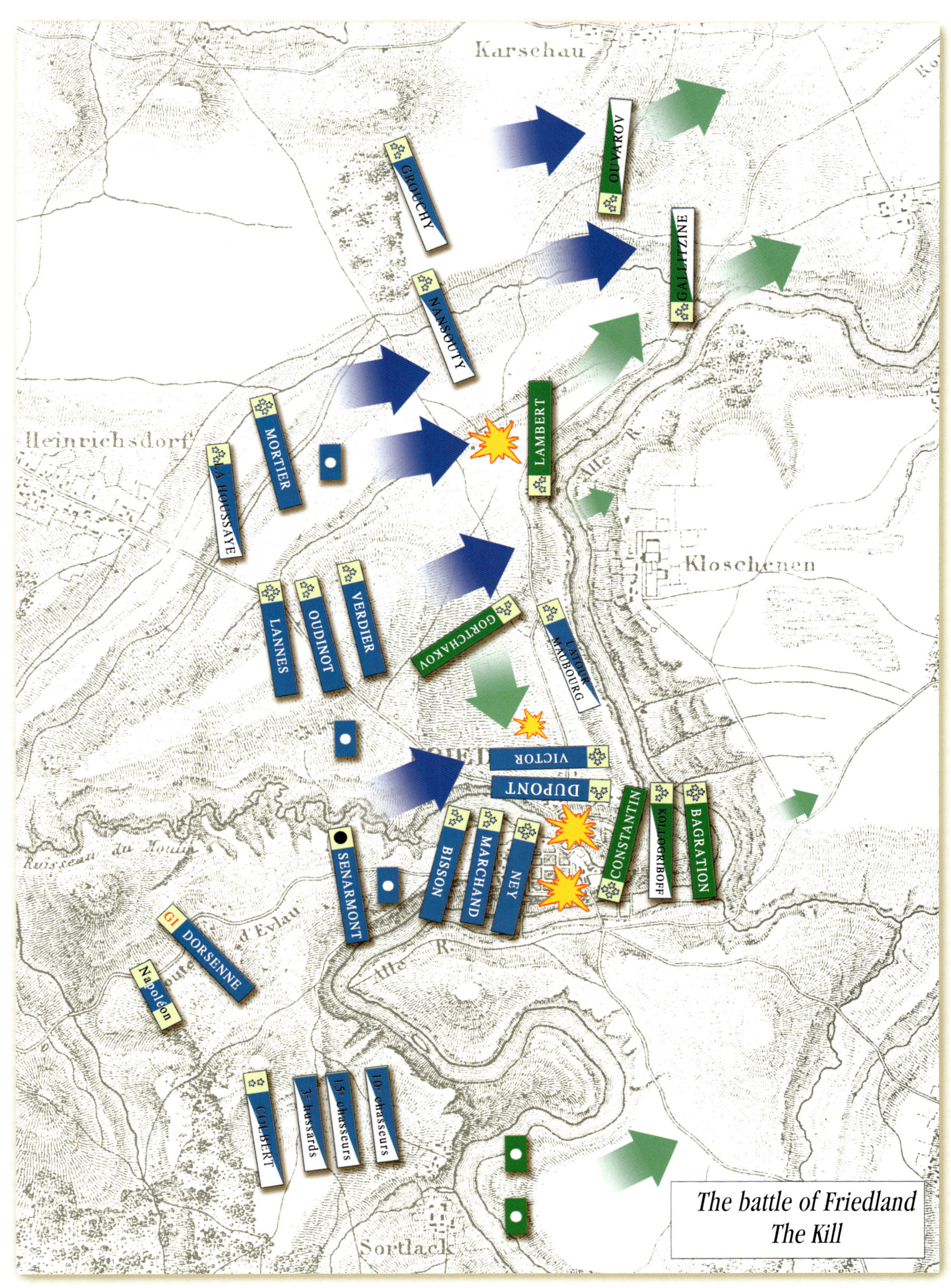

*The battle of Friedland
The Kill*

Above.
The Marchand, Bisson and Dupont divisions join up in the streets of Friedland and the Russian army is caught in the trap. *(RR)*

After chasing the Russians from the village, Marchand's division advanced but found itself caught in the crossfire from the artillery of the Russian Guard and the batteries that Benningsen had had placed on the right bank of the Alle. These cannon fired flat out and the cannonballs removed entire ranks, cutting great swathes among the French ranks which were caught broadside on. The Colonel of the 69th of the Line in Maucune's brigade was killed and the battalion commanders were soon out of action. Ney's artillerymen tried to muzzle their opponents, but they were outnumbered. Caissons exploded, shells rained down and the grapeshot burst making a *"horrible clicking sound among the raised bayonets"* as Levavasseur, one of Ney's aide de camps, noted.

All the division wavered and stopped. It was at this moment that Bagration chose to launch a counter-attack with the Cavalry of the Guard under Kollogriboff. This elite cavalry bore down on Bisson's division which was bowled over by the shock and had to pull back. Some of the battalions started off in disorder in spite of the energy their officers spent trying to rally them. The situation was critical at that moment. It was during this engagement that the Eagle of the 69th was thought to have been lost.

Fortunately, Dupont, one of the best Major-Generals in the Grande Armée, saw the danger and at once launched his division to help the wavering 6th Corps. In collusion with Latour-Maubourg and his Dragoons together with Ricci's artillery from Victor's corps, he bore down on the flanks of the Russians who, disunited by the fighting, were forced back. The Russians lost 80 men and several officers.

Once they had rallied, the Bisson and Marchand divisions started marching forwards again, encouraged by Ney, at the top of his form.

Meanwhile on the left wing, Mortier was energetically defending Heinrichsdorf against the attacks by Gortchakov's infantry which were repelled several times. Grouchy, on the far left of the line, blocked Uvarov who was trying to complete a turning movement.

Sénarmont's Charge

In order to reduce the batteries to silence - those that were slowing Ney down - Napoleon ordered Sénarmont to gather all the 1st Corps artillery together and silence the Russian guns. The general immediately formed two fifteen-gun batteries and kept ten in reserve. Moving up in front of the infantry line, he moved his cannon to within 400 yards from the Russians and opened fire with devastating effect. The right-hand battery went to Ney's help and fired back at the batteries which were on the right bank of the Alle. The left-hand battery was pushed up to within 200 yards of the Russian infantry and started firing grapeshot. Napoleon, who was a bit worried by his own boldness, sent Mouton off to find out what was going on. Sénarmont retorted: *"Leave me and my gunners alone, I'll answer for everything."* To prove it, he had the shooting stopped, the 30 guns loaded with grapeshot and moved up to 150 yards from the immobile Russian infantry. Rent apart by the firing, the Russian infantry could not hold the line and started to break up and fall back. In order to get the situation under the control, Bagration got the Guards to intervene but the salvoes of grapeshot got the better of them too and they also started to retreat. It was now that the whole of Bagration's left started to waver; all the more so as Lannes' artillery was also bombarding them.

Helped in this way by the artillery, the Marchand, Bisson and Dupont Divisions resumed the attack and pushed the Russians into the bend made by the Alle and into Friedland. Bagration launched the Infantry of the Guard into another charge but Dupont's 9th Light stopped them and in turn charged. After a brief fray, the Russian Guard started to fall back again, pursued by the French under Dupont who in the rush crossed the Windmill Stream.

Dupont's division found itself both on the rear of Gortchakov's wing and blocking the Russian infantry in Friedland and on the bridges, which suddenly got very quickly congested. The French attacked the town, moving along the Königsberg road. On the Eylau road Ney did the same, with the 59th of the Line leading. The three divisions entered the town and the enemy fled in full rout, abandoning artillery and caissons. Because Sénarmont's artillery still carried on shooting at the bridges, escape on the right bank was dangerous, but the pressure from the French was terrible although the Russians defended themselves fiercely.

When the bridges were destroyed, a number of soldiers jumped into the river and tried to swim across the Alle, which was only fifty or so yards wide at that spot. Many drowned. Dupont and Ney joined up in the town centre, congratulated each other and went off to continue fighting. The last Russians were either killed or captured.

The kill

With Friedland under control, Napoleon had his left wing move forward. Lannes, Mortier and Grouchy went over to the attack. Gortchakov saw the danger and decided to attack, sending a column at Friedland and another at Heinrichsberg. Victor drove off the former and Lannes' and Mortier's combined artillery got the better of the latter. The rout was complete. Some Russians managed to cross the Alle at the Kloschenen ford, but many of them got drowned. Part of the cavalry and a column of infantry managed to get away by moving along the left bank. All the other Russians were killed or captured.

At nightfall, the remnants of the Russian army withdrew towards the Pregel via Allenburg and Welhau. The Dragons of the Guard under Arrighi and the Saxon Cuirassiers started the chase. Kamanski and Lestocq abandoned Königsberg the following day meaning that the army had to retreat to the Niemen. Murat and Davout tried to intercept them, but Benningsen managed to get his troops across the river, then had the bridges burnt down.

Above. **The Dragoons of the Imperial Guard also took part in pursuing the defeated Russian army.** *(RR)*

Below. **The town of Friedland.** *(RMN)*

Above.
Napoleon at Friedland. At the end of the day of the battle, the Russian army no longer existed. When Königsberg fell, the two Emperors met at Tilsitt.
(© RMN)

The Losses at Friedland

In his report, Benningsen played down the results and claimed not to have wanted to give battle seriously and that no set battle had taken place at Friedland. He gave very low figures as far as casualties were concerned. In Dentzel's report however which was drawn up for Berthier, the following can be found:

For the Russians

6 438 Russians were buried on the battlefield, 4 566 in Friedland or 11 004 found on the battlefield.

For Both, the Russian losses were 10 000 killed, 6 000 wounded, five generals wounded and two killed, 80 cannon taken. Flags and several prisoners were captured during the chase.

For the French

— Victor's 1st Corps
— Dupont's division lost 56 killed among which 3 officers, 503 wounded among whom 24 officers. The artillery losses were 56 men.
— The Lapisse and Villatte Divisions which had been kept in reserve and only suffered only 28 killed including 4 officers.
— La Houssaye's 4th Division, under Victor had 42 killed including 3 officers and 58 wounded including 7 officers.
— Ney's 6th Corps, mentioned by Derode including Latour-Maubourg's Dragoons, lost 132 officers killed and 102 wounded, as well as 258 killed and 2 280 wounded among the men.
— Mortier's 8th Corps mentioned losing 425 men killed including 14 officers, 2 195 wounded including 91 officers.
— Lannes corps lost 18 officers killed, 158 wounded and 15 missing, as well as 455 killed, 3 090 wounded and 392 missing among the men.
— Grouchy's Dragoons lost 166 killed.
— Nansouty's Cuirassiers lost 128 killed, 230 wounded and 30 missing.
— Major-Generals Drouet d'Erlon, Latour-Maubourg and Dombrowski were wounded as were Generals Carré, Coëhorn, Harispe, Lebrun, Mouton, Vedel and Conroux.

The total losses for the French army were 11 062 men out of action.

The capture of the 15th of the Line's flag is debatable and has not been verified.

NAPOLEON'S GENERAL STAFF

The Emperor's aides-de-camp

Bertrand. He was with the Army of Italy, then in Egypt where he was wounded. He was made Gd Aigle of the OLH in 1809, Grand Maréchal du Palais in 1813 and Aide-Major-Général in 1814. He was mentioned in dispatches at Montmirail with Lefebvre, for the attack on Marchais. He accompanied the Emperor to Elba, Waterloo and then to St. Helena where he witnessed his death. Elected a Deputy in 1831, he organised the return of Napoleon's ashes in 1840. He was buried in the Invalides next to the Emperor.

His own aide-de-camp was Favereau. In Belgium in 1833, he was appointed Maréchal de Camp in 1839. CrLH in 1845.

Duroc. A veteran of Italy and Egypt, he was Napoleon's aide-de-camp from 1799. Marengo. He was promoted to General in 1801 and Major-General in 1803. He was made Grand Maréchal du Palais and Gd Aigle of the LH in 1804. He signed the armistice at Posen. Made Duke of Frioul in 1808, he was decorated with the Order of the Couronne de Fer in 1809. Senator, he was killed with Kirgener on 23 May 1813 at Görlitz.

De Savoie Carignan. Prince, Gendarme d'Ordonnance in 1807. He was a Captain in the 3rd Cuirassiers then Napoleon's Ordnance Officer in 1808 and Baron in 1809. He was appointed Colonel to the 6th Hussars in 1812 and served in Belgium in 1815. He was appointed Maréchal de Camp in 1821, then served in Spain and was made GdOLH in 1823. He died in 1825 and was buried in Turin.

Bongars de Roquigny. He was an Ordnance Officer from 3 January 1807 and was made a Baron in 1809. He became an aide-de-camp to Berthier and was made a Colonel in 1812. A General in 1813, he was retired in 1815. He was made CrLH in 1821 and retired in 1832.

Bacler d'Albe. A veteran of Italy and Egypt, he was the head of Napoleon's Topographical Unit and was made OLH and General in 1813.

Athalin. Ordnance Officer to Napoleon in 1811, he was the assistant chief of the Emperor's Topographical Unit. Colonel and aide-de-camp to Louis-Philippe in 1830, he was made GdOLH in 1831 and Lieutenant-General in 1840. He was retired in 1848.

Bonne. Geographical Engineer. Appointed Colonel in 1808, he was

THE FRENCH ARMY

Mouton. He was made a General and an aide-de-camp to Napoleon in 1805 then was present at Austerlitz. Present also at Eylau, wounded at Friedland, he was made Cr of the Couronne de Fer and Major-General in 1807. He recaptured the village of Essling at the head of the Fusiliers of the Guard and was made a Count. He went to Russia in 1812, and left with the Emperor at Smorgoni. He was made GdCx of the Réunion in 1813 but was taken at Dresden. In 1815 he was at Ligny and at Plancenoit where he was captured. Outlawed, he returned to France in 1818, was elected a deputy in 1828 and was returned several times. He was made GdCxLH in 1830, Maréchal de France in 1831 and Peer in 1833. He died in 1838.

Lefebvre-Desnouettes. Aide-de-camp to Napoleon in 1800 he was an Equerry in 1804. He was made CtLH in 1805 and a General in 1806. He was aide-de-camp to Jérôme in 1806 and 1807. He was appointed Colonel Major of the Chasseurs à Cheval of the Guard and was made a Count and a Major-General in 1808. He commanded the Chasseurs à Cheval of the Guard in Russia. He was made GdCx of the Reunion in 1813. He fought with Nansouty at Brienne. When the Emperor returned, he tried to take la Fère with Lallemand; he hid with Rigau then returned to his post. He fought at Quatre-Bras and at Waterloo; then he was outlawed and condemned to death. He was struck off all the lists and went into exile in the US. He tried to return in 1822 but died at sea when his ship was wrecked.

Bacler d'Albe. The head of Napoleon's Topographical Unit, he was made a Baron in 1809, then OLH and General in 1813. He died in 1821.

Savary. Napoleon's aide-de-camp in 1805, he was also appointed Major-General in the same year. He commanded the 5th Corps from 31 January 1807 to 3 March 1807 when he was replaced by Masséna. He won at Ostrolenka and was made GdCxLH on 25 February 1807. He served at Heilsberg and at Friedland where he commanded the Fusiliers of the Guard. He was made Duke of Rovigo in 1808. As one of Malet's victims, he was put in prison for several hours. A Peer in 1815, he was then outlawed and condemned to death. He sought refuge in Smyrna, then Graz, then London. Acquitted in 1819, he was in Rome in 1823 then was in command in Africa in 1831. He died in 1833.

Napoleon's Ordnance officers

Marbœuf. Wounded five times and captured at Wittenberg, he was freed after Tilsitt. He was awarded the LH in 1807 and made a Baron in 1809. He was a Squadron Commander in the Chasseurs à Cheval of the Guard in 1810, then Colonel of the 6th Lancers in 1811. He died in Russia.

De Ponthon. Officer of Engineers, he was a veteran of Egypt where he fought at Abukir. He was promoted to Colonel and joined the Emperor's cabinet in 1810. The following year he was made a Baron. He was made a General and CSL in 1814. Lieutenant-General in 1838, he was retired in 1848.

From left to right and top to bottom.
Generals Bertrand, Duroc, Mouton and Lefebvre-Desnouettes. *(RR)*

made Chevalier in 1809, then Baron in 1813, OLH the following year. He served in Belgium during the Hundred Days and was retired in 1833.

Branger. He was seconded to the General Staff after 22 January 1807 and was OLH the same

From left to right and top to bottom:
Bacler d'Albe, Generals Savary and Songis and Maréchal Berthier. *(RR)*

year then Chevalier in 1810. He was Colonel of the 32nd of the Line in Spain and took part in the fighting at Orthez. He served on the Rhine in 1815.

The Engineers were under the command of **Chasseloup-Laubat.** Battalion Commander in the Engineers in 1793, he took over command of the Engineers in the Army of Italy in 1796. He was in command on several other occasions. He was promoted to Major-General in 1799 and Inspector-General of Fortifications the following year. He was made Cr of the Croix de Fer in 1805. He took over command of the Engineers in the Grande Armée on 19 October 1806 and conducted the siege of Danzig under Lefebvre in 1807. He was a Senator and was made GdCx of the Reunion in 1813. After voting for the Emperor to be deposed, he was made a Peer and GdCxLH in 1814. He was made a Marquis in 1817.

Léry. Appointed General in 1796, he was made a Baron in 1811 and Gd Cordon of the LH. He served at Lyon in 1815 and was made a Viscount in 1818.

The Artillery was headed by **Songis des Courbons.** He was appointed Major-General in Egypt in 1800. Commander-in-Chief of the Artillery, he was made Gd Aigle of the LH in 1805, Couronne de Fer in 1806 and a Count in 1809. He was replaced by Lariboisière on 15 June 1809 and died the following year.

Maréchal Berthier was Major-General. He liked young émigrés and young nobles with titles; it was his snobbish side.

BERTHIER'S AIDE-DE-CAMPS.

Girardin d'Ermenonville. He was with Berthier from 30 June 1803. Colonel in the 8th Dragoons in 1806 with Milhaud, he was wounded near Willenberg. He was at Friedland. Promoted to General in 1812 he went back to Berthier. He was made a Major-General for his conduct at Champaubert in 1814, then Grouchy's Chief-of-Staff in 1815. He was made CrSL and GdOLH in 1825. He was retired in 1848.

Lejeune: Officer of Engineers, he was Berthier's aide-de-camp after 1800. Wounded at the siege of Saragossa where he distinguished himself several times. He was captured and wounded and his escort massacred by the guerrillas in April 1811. He was imprisoned in England, returning the following 30 July. He replaced Romœuf on Davout's staff. He was made a General in 1812 and was retired in 1813. He served with Harispe in 1833 and was made GdOLH in 1841. He died in 1848. Lejeune was a famous painter and left a number of works depicting battles and uniforms.

Talleyrand-Périgord. Aide-de-camp to Pino in Italy, he went over to Berthier in March 1807. He fought in Russia and was captured in 1813. As a General he was fired by Napoleon during the Hundred Days. As the Duke of Dino, he was married to the Princess of Courland who followed Talleyrand after living ten years with him. He was made a Lieutenant-General in 1828.

Lagrange (Lelièvre, Comte de). An aide-de-camp since 1805, he was an Equerry in 1810, General in 1812 and Lieutenant-General in 1814. GdOLH in 1836, he was elected to the Senate in 1859.

Le Camus, Baron de Montignon. Made CtLH on 1805 and General in 1806, he was Victor's Chief-of-Staff in 1814. Wounded at Craonne, he then retired. He was retired in 1825.

Montholon. Aide-de-camp to Klein at Austerlitz, he was made a Colonel in 1809, General and Chamberlain to the Empress in 1811. Aide-de-camp to the Emperor at Waterloo, he followed him to St. Helena. Napoleon's executor. His wife was Napoleon's last love. Elected Deputy in 1849, he died in 1853.

Canouville. His father, an émigré, had served the Princes. He returned in 1802, was elected Deputy in 1810, was made a Baron and Maréchal de Camp in 1817. He became a Counsellor of State. He was Pauline Bonaparte's lover.

Bosset. He was Capitaine-adjoint on the Staff of Oudinot's Mixed Grenadier Division. He was sent to Berthier's staff on 24 May 1807. Awarded the LH on 6 July 1807, he commanded the Neuchâtel battalion. He died at Smolensk on 29 October 1812.

THE IMPERIAL GUARD

The Guard was commanded by Maréchal Bessières.

Bessières. He commanded the Guides in 1796 and was present at Rivoli and in Egypt. He was made a General in 1800 and then Major-General in 1802. He commanded the Cavalry of the Guard and was made a Maréchal in 1804, among the first group. He was Gd Aigle of the LH in 1805. He commanded the Guard in 1807 and charged at Eylau, then at Friedland. He was made Duke of Istria in 1809. He commanded the Army of the North of Spain in 1811. He left to fight in Saxony and was killed at Rippach on 1 April 1813.

NEW UNITS

Several new units appeared during the Polish Campaign. One of them did not last long – the *"Gendarmes d'Ordonnance"* – the others entered History: the Fusilier-Grenadiers, the Fusilier-Chasseurs and the Polish Chevau-Légers.

The *Gendarmes d'Ordonnance*

This corps was created following on a circular from the Emperor dated 24 September 1806. The idea was to let former aristocrats have another opportunity to serve France. *"…Any man aged between 18 and 40, rich enough to equip himself, to buy a horse and to cover his own expenses, can come to Mainz and get in touch with Maréchal Kellermann… Those who enter the cavalry must have a guaranteed income of at least 600 francs per annum from their family or themselves…"*

De Ségur was responsible for setting up the unit; their Colonel-General was Maréchal Kellermann. They had to pay for their equipment but they were assimilated to the Chasseurs of the Guard.

Viscount Laval de Montmorency, the son of the Marquis and Louis XVI's Maréchal, commanded the 1st Company. Made a Maréchal de Camp in 1788, he was made a Captain in the Company on 4 November 1806. A Count in 1808, he was at Essling and was given leave in 1809. The company had a strength of 135 men.

The Count of Arberg, a Belgian, commanded the 2nd Company. In this company de Norvins, de la Bédoyère and d'Espichal should be mentioned, as they were all future writers.

The 3rd Company under M. de Sourdis only consisted of 72 horsemen; it joined up later.

A fourth company was under the command of the Prince de Savoie-Carignan; it was being formed up at Mainz.

The setting up of Captain d'Astorg's fifth company had just been started.

The Gendarmes d'Ordonnance were laid off on 12 July 1807 but remained within the army, the officers being incorporated in the Line with the higher rank. The arrival of these privileged men, among whom there were many émigrés, did cause some jealousy. They were offered the choice posts in their favourite unit, the Light Cavalry. They had famous names, many were courtesans. As of 1812, these men joined the headquarter staffs who were all too happy to rub shoulders with all these great names, sheltering beside Napoleon and Berthier, who was flattered to have them next to him.

In 1812, Berthézène voiced his disapproval since the old Grognards who had got their promotion the hard way, were very shocked to see all these former aristocrats getting all their privileges back again and quickly obtaining the choice jobs for themselves. Lachouque

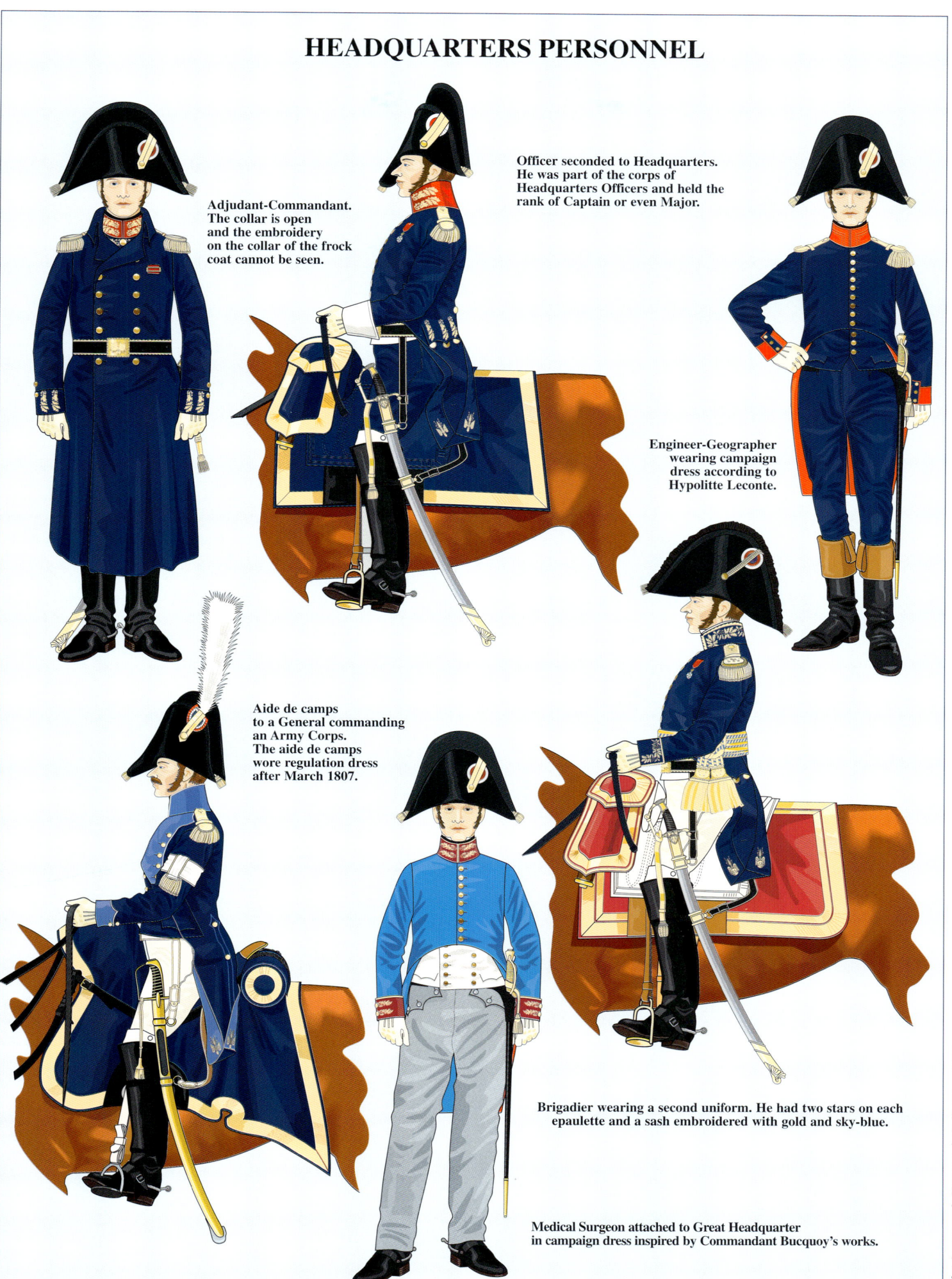

HEADQUARTERS PERSONNEL

Adjudant-Commandant. The collar is open and the embroidery on the collar of the frock coat cannot be seen.

Officer seconded to Headquarters. He was part of the corps of Headquarters Officers and held the rank of Captain or even Major.

Engineer-Geographer wearing campaign dress according to Hypolitte Leconte.

Aide de camps to a General commanding an Army Corps. The aide de camps wore regulation dress after March 1807.

Brigadier wearing a second uniform. He had two stars on each epaulette and a sash embroidered with gold and sky-blue.

Medical Surgeon attached to Great Headquarter in campaign dress inspired by Commandant Bucquoy's works.

Left, top to bottom.
Gendarmes d'Ordonnance and Fusilier-Chasseurs.
(Compositions by Jack Girbal. Author's Collection and RR)

Below.
The gendarme d'ordonnance de la Garde, see by a contemporary artist. *(RR)*

mentioned that Napoleon said on 24 September: *"… I want to open up the (military) career to those who were separated from the motherland by the circumstances of the Revolution and who want to follow this career, which is natural for the French. I don't know what'll come of it…"* France's nobility had the place of honour.

The Fusilier of the Guard

It was decided to form them on 18 September 1806 and the Fusilier-Chasseurs were created by Imperial Decree dated 19 October 1806. The Fusilier-Grenadiers were created the following 15 December. Each regiment comprised two four-company battalions with a strength of 120 men each. They were formed up with difficulty by 21 December 1806, when they left hurriedly for Mainz – they had not even been issued with greatcoats. They reached Osterode on 21 February and took part at Heilsberg and at Friedland. They were commanded by their Colonel Major, Friederichs, and Savary.

The destinies of the Fusilier-Grenadiers and Fusilier-Chasseurs were united and they served with glory all over the Empire's battlefields, often used as the first reserve, in order to spare the blood of the Old Guard, which was much too precious to shed.

The Fusilier-Grenadiers

Colonel Friederichs. Battalion Commander in the Foot Grenadiers of the Guard, he was appointed Colonel Major of the Fusilier Grenadiers on 1 January 1807. He brought back the flags from Eylau to Paris on 8 March 1807. He went to fight in Spain in 1808. He was promoted to General in 1809, and then made a Baron and CtLH. He took part in the Russian Campaign during which he was promoted to Major-General. Wounded at Leipzig, he died following an amputation.

Harlet. Coming from the Foot Grenadiers of the Guard, he was appointed Battalion Commander in the Fusilier-Grenadiers on 16 February 1807. He was made a Baron in 1810 and a General in 1813. Taken prisoner at Leipzig, he only returned to France in July 1814. He was then made CSL. He served during the Hundred Days and was wounded at Waterloo. He was made GdOLH in 1833 and was retired the following year.

There were 1300 Fusilier-Grenadiers when they left Paris.

The Fusilier-Chasseurs

Colonel Boyer de Rebeval. A veteran of the Italian campaign, he was battalion Commander in the Chasseurs à pied of the Guard before being appointed Colonel Major of the Fusilier-Chasseurs on 28 March 1807. He was made a Baron in 1808 and then CtLH in 1809. He was in command of the Chasseurs à Pied of the Guard in Russia and was wounded at the Moskova. Made Major-General in 1813, he was brilliant in 1814 and wounded at Craonne. He was available in January 1815; he was on the non-active list in 1818.

The Polish *Chevau-Légers*

Napoleon decided to create them on 2 March. Dombrowski was in charge of organising them and Krasisnki was their Colonel, helped by two French Majors:

Delaitre, from the Mamelukes where he was replaced by Denne; and, in particular, Dautancourt from the Gendarmerie d'Elite who was soon to be considered as the father of the Polish Chevau-Légers.

According to Napoleon's wishes, these Poles had to be rich in order to be able to pay for their equipment and they had to be educated. They were assimilated to the Guard. They were not equipped with lances, although they did ask to be issued with them. It was only after the Austrian campaign that the lance was finally adopted.

Napoleon was overzealous and the regiment was not yet ready for battle at Friedland;

THE IMPERIAL GUARD—INFANTRY

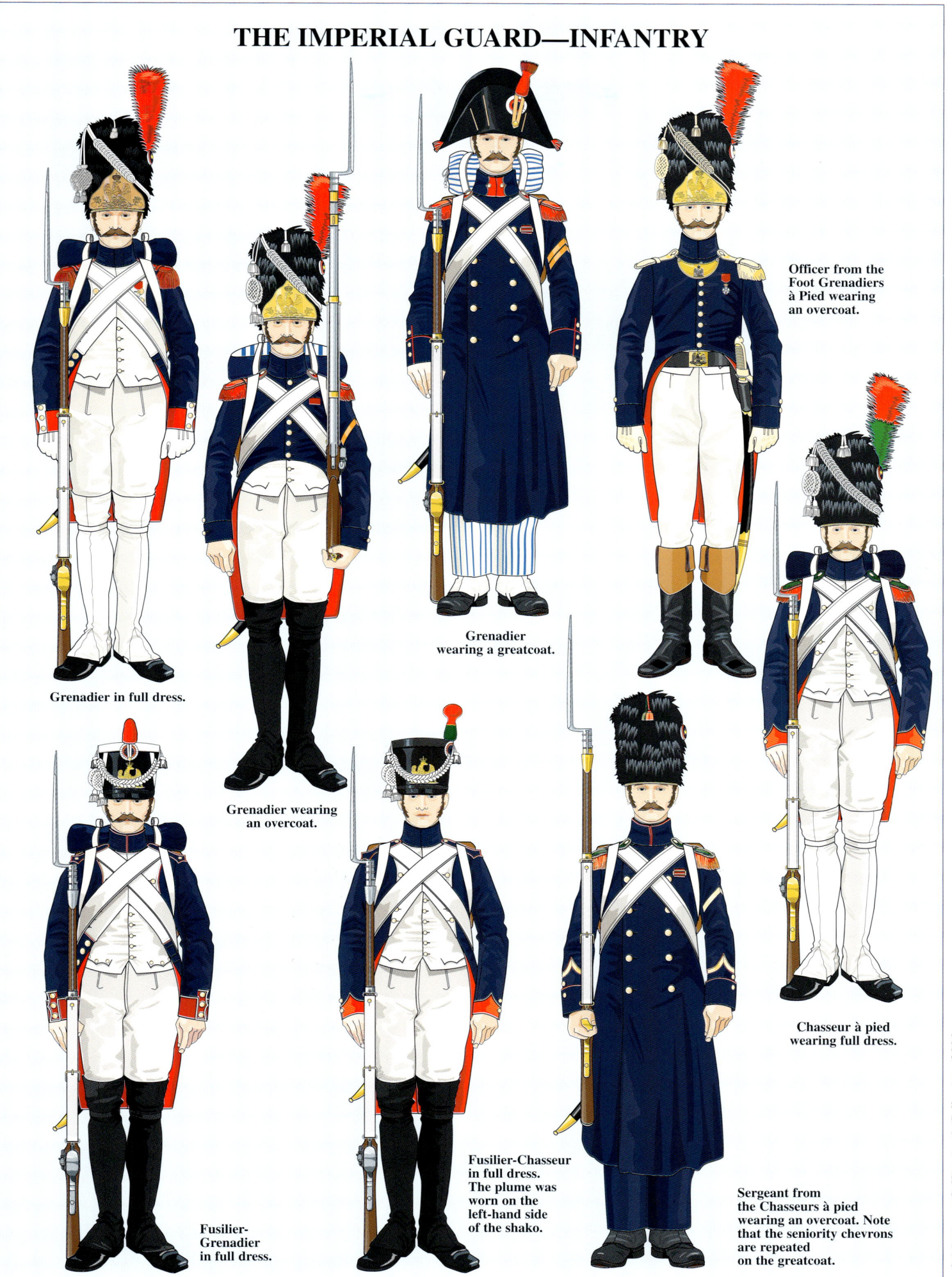

Grenadier in full dress.

Grenadier wearing an overcoat.

Grenadier wearing a greatcoat.

Officer from the Foot Grenadiers à Pied wearing an overcoat.

Chasseur à pied wearing full dress.

Fusilier-Grenadier in full dress.

Fusilier-Chasseur in full dress. The plume was worn on the left-hand side of the shako.

Sergeant from the Chasseurs à pied wearing an overcoat. Note that the seniority chevrons are repeated on the greatcoat.

IMPERIAL GUARD—CAVALRY

Grenadier à Cheval wearing a coat.

Grenadier à Cheval wearing an overcoat. No doubt the regiment charged during the Battle of Eylau wearing this uniform.

Dragoon Trumpeter of the Guard wearing an overcoat.

Chasseur à Cheval from the Guard wearing a tailcoat. This coat replaced the Hussar-style dress, which was too delicate to be worn when campaigning.

Dragoon Guards wearing overcoats. At this period, the overcoat was the item most often worn on campaign.

Chasseur à Cheval of the Guard wearing a tailcoat with a rotunda cape to protect him from the weather.

IMPERIAL GUARD—CAVALRY

Trooper form the Gendarmerie d'Elite wearing an overcoat. He is carrying an *An-XI* model cavalry sabre and an *An-IX* model carbine with its bayonet.

Trumpeter from the Gendarmes d'Elite wearing an overcoat.

In 1806, the Guard only had one Horse Artillery regiment.

Dragons à Pied attached to the Guard and already present at Jena.

Battalion of the Marins de la Garde (Sailors of the Guard). He is wearing the *caracot* as campaigning uniform.

Gunner from the Horse Artillery.

only a few volunteer Polish officers took part. The regiment entered the realms of glory immediately at Somosierra and thereafter the Poles of the Guard shone on all the battlefields from Madrid to Moscow until the final maelstrom at of Waterloo.

The Dragoons

The Dragoon Guards Regiment was created by Imperial Decree on 15 April 1806. This regiment was permitted to join the elite unit because of the way the it had behaved during the previous campaign. The men that made up the regiment came from the Dragoon regiments of the Line and in September 1806, the first two squadrons were up to full strength. The regiment was commanded by Arrighi de Casanova. With him were Fiteau and Letort.

Arrighi de Casanova. A veteran of the Italian and Egyptian campaigns, he was an aide-de-camp to Berthier in 1799 and fought at Marengo. CtLH in 1804, he was promoted to Colonel of the Dragoons on 19 May 1806. He was present at Friedland and was made a General the same year, then Major-General in 1809, replacing Espagne. He served under

From left to right and top to bottom.
An officer of the new cavalry regiment of the Guard: Polish Chevau-légers.
It was only after the Austrian campaign that the lance was finally adopted.

Majors Dautancourt and Letort, general Hulin and general Michel. *(RR)*

Above.
***Grenadiers and chasseurs à pied
are the infantry regiments of the "Old Guard".*** *(RR)*

Davout at Wagram and under MacDonald in 1814. He was retired in 1821, then in 1833. With him were:

Fiteau. He served in Italy and in Egypt and was made CtLH in 1805. He was made Colonel Major of the Dragoons of the Guard on 13 September 1806. He was awarded the Couronne de Fer in 1808, was appointed General in 1809 and was made a Count in 1810. He committed suicide a short while later in a moment of madness.

From left to right and top to bottom:
General Soulès, Major Curial, General Walther and Colonel-Major Lepic. *(RR)*

Colonel-Major Guyot from the Chasseurs à Cheval of the Guard. He was made a Baron in 1808 and fought until Waterloo where he was wounded. *(RR)*

Letort. A veteran of the Italian campaign, he was appointed Major of the Dragoon Guards on 8 October 1806. He was made a Baron in 1810 and a General in 1813. He commanded a brigade of the 1st Cuirassier Division the same year. He commanded the Dragoon Guards at the end of 1813, 1814 and 1815. He had been made a Count and CtLH in 1814, and aide-de-camp to Napoleon in 1815, during the Hundred Days. He was killed at Charleroi on 15 June 1815.

Joséphine was the regiment's Godmother and the regiment was often called the Empress' Dragoons.

Alongside these new units, the older regiments of the Guard were still there unchanged. They were still:

The (foot) Grenadiers

They were commanded by General Hutin and were made up of two regiments.

Hutin. He commanded the Grenadiers since 1802. He was made a Major-General in 1807. He was made a Count in 1808, Cr of the Couronne de Fer and GdOLH in 1811. He was wounded by Malet in 1812. GdCx of the Reunion in 1813. He was Governor of Paris in 1815 and outlawed, withdrew and retired.

Major Dorsenne commanded the 1st Regiment.

Dorsenne. Mentioned in Italy, he was wounded in Egypt. He was a Major in the Foot Grenadiers on 3 May 1805 then was promoted to Colonel in the Guard and then General after Austerlitz. He distinguished himself at Eylau and was appointed Grenadier Colonel of the Grenadiers in 1808, then Major-General after Essling where he was wounded in the head. He was made GdOLH in 1811. He died the following year after being trepanned following on his wound at Austerlitz. Friant replaced him.

Major Michel commanded the 2nd Regiment.

Michel. He served at Austerlitz and transferred to the Grenadiers with the rank of Major on 1 May 1806. He served at Jena and Eylau and was appointed Colonel Major of the 1st Grenadiers on 16 February 1807. He was made a Baron in 1808, General in 1811 and Major-General in 1813. His right arm was shattered at Montmirail and he was cared for in Paris. He was made a Count on 23 March and was wounded again at Pantin. He was Colonel of the 1st Chasseurs at Waterloo where he was seriously wounded. He was, it seems, the author of Cambronne's famous "saying".

The Velites were commanded by Friederichs, the Colonel of Fusiliers.

The Chasseurs à pied

They were under the command of General Soulès.

Soulès. Wounded at Castiglione and at Arcola, he distinguished himself at Marengo and was awarded a Sabre of Honour in 1801. He was made a General and CtLH in 1804. He was present at Jena, Eylau and Friedland. He was a Senator in August 1807. Retired in 1808, Peer in 1804, he did not serve in 1815 but voted for the death of Ney.

The 1st Chasseurs were commanded by Major Gros. **Gros.** Wounded three times, he was made CtLH in 1804, a Major in the 1st Chasseurs of the Guard in 1808, then a General and Couronne de Fer in 1807. Under the command of Dorsenne in 1809, he was appointed Regimental Colonel in 1810. Wounded at Dresden and at Leipzig. He was with Christiani in 1814, he was retired the same year and then again in 1815.

The 2nd Chasseurs were under the command of Major Curial. **Curial.** A veteran of Egypt and Italy, he was appointed Major in the Chasseurs in 1806. After Eylau, he was promoted to Colonel of the Guard. He was wounded at Heilsberg, promoted to General on 25 June 1807; he was Colonel of the 2nd Chasseurs at the end of 1807 and was made Chevalier of the Order of the Couronne de Fer and a Baron in 1808. Gd Cx of the Reunion in 1813, Count in 1814, then GdCxLH and Peer in 1815, the year in which he was put on the non-active list. He voted for Ney to be deported and served in Spain in 1823.

THE CAVALRY OF THE GUARD

Regrouped in a division, the cavalry was under the command of General Walther.

Walther. Major-General in 1803, he was made Gd Aigle of the LH and Chamberlain in 1806. Cr of the Couronne de Fer, he charged at Eylau with the Grenadiers à Cheval of whom he was the Colonel. He was made a Count in 1808. After the Russian campaign, he served under Nansouty in Saxony in 1813 and was killed on 24 November 1813. He was then replaced by Guyot.

General Dahlmann was in command of the Chasseurs à Cheval whose Colonel-in-Chief was Prince Eugène. He was mortally wounded at Eylau. (RMN)

The Chasseurs à Cheval

The nominal Colonel was Prince Eugène but the real Colonel was Dahlmann.

Dahlmann. A veteran of Italy and Egypt he served in the Guides à Cheval. He was made OLH in 1804 and replaced Morland who was killed at Austerlitz. He was made a General in 1806. He was mortally wounded at Eylau during the big charge.

Guyot. He was Colonel Major in 1805 then, at Eylau he was with the Chasseurs of the Guard. He became their Colonel on 16 February 1807. He was made a Baron in 1808, General in 1809, Chamberlain and CtLH in 1811. He replaced Walther in the Grenadiers à Cheval in 1813 and served under Nansouty in 1814. Wounded at Waterloo, he was retired in 1816 and then 1833. Not to be confused with his cousin, the General in the Light Cavalry.

Among the officers the following should be mentioned:

Clerc. He entered the Grenadiers à Cheval in 1800 then went over to the Chasseurs the following year as Adjudant-Major. He was made a Squadron Commander in 1805. He was made OLH in 1806 and became Colonel of the 1st Cuirassiers after Wagram to replace Berkheim who had been promoted to General. He was made a Baron. He took part in the big campaigns and was Chevalier of the Couronne de Fer in 1813 then Maréchal de Camp in 1814. He did not serve during the Hundred Days. He was made GdOLH in 1814 and died two years later.

Bohn. A veteran of Italy, he joined the Chasseurs à Cheval on 5 September 1803 with the rank of Captain and was awarded the LH. He was made Squadron Commander in 1805 and OLH the following year in 1808. He was made Colonel of the 7th Chasseurs in 1809 but was mortally wounded at the Battle of Raab.

Thiry. Distinguished himself in Italy, he was made Squadron Commander in the Chasseurs on 15 September 1805. He was wounded at Eylau and was made a Major. He was made CtLH and a General in 1809. In Russia, he was wounded three times at the Moskova. He served during the Hundred Days and was retired in 1815.

Franc. He entered the Chasseurs à Cheval of the Consular Guard in 1800 and his conduct at Austerlitz earned him the rank of Squadron Commander on 18 December 1805. He was made OLH the following year. Wounded at Wagram, he was made a Baron and the Colonel of the 10th Cuirassiers. He retired in 1812.

Daumesnil. Guide in Italy and Egypt, he was made OLH in 1806. Wounded in the leg at Wagram, he had to be amputated. He was made a Baron in 1810, a General in 1812, Governor of Vincennes. His refusal to surrender to Blucher was celebrated. He was made CSL in 1815 and Lieutenant-General in 1831.

Cavrois. He was made Squadron Commander of the regiment on 18 December 1805 for his good conduct during the campaign. He was made OLH in 1806, Chevalier in 1808 and Colonel in 1809. He was wounded at Brienne then put on the non-active list.

The Grenadiers à Cheval

They were under the command of General Walther who was also in command of the Cavalry of the Guard. Effective command was in the hands of the Regimental Major who was Colonel Lepic.

Lepic. In the Army of the West then in that of Italy, he was present at Marengo. He was appointed Colonel Major of the Grenadiers à Cheval on 18 December 1805. He was wounded four times at Eylau after his famous apostrophe to his men: *"… Grapeshot is nuts…!"* He was made a Colonel a few days later. He was made a Baron and CtLH in 1809 and then

Polish Chevau-Légers and Dragoon of the Guard. (RR)

Chasseurs à Cheval of the Guard. (RR)

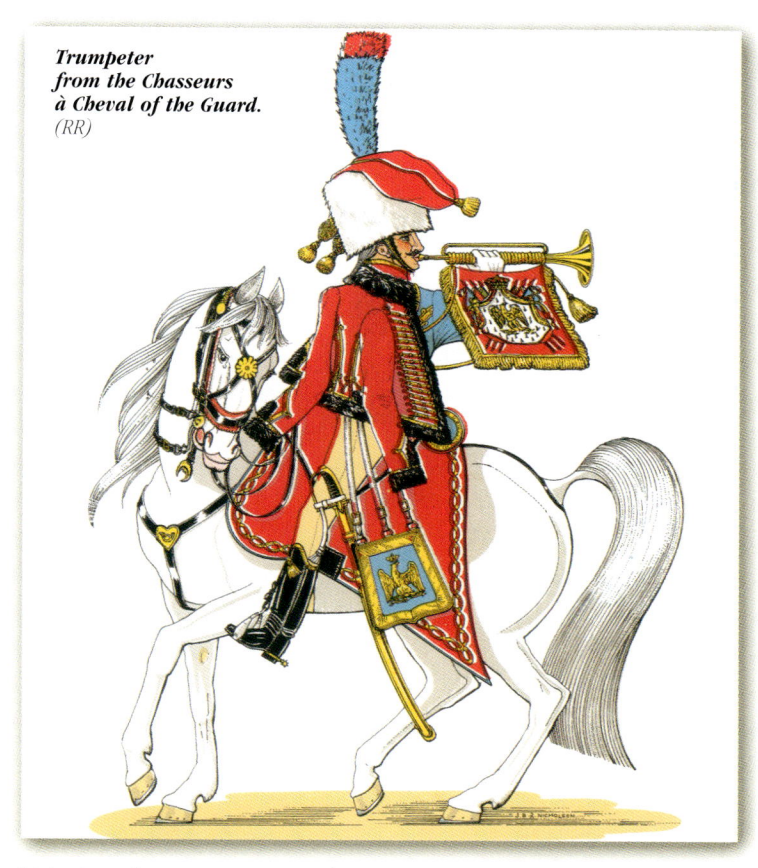

Trumpeter from the Chasseurs à Cheval of the Guard. (RR)

Gendarme d'Elite. (RR)

Major-General in 1813. He was retired in 1815.

Colonel Chastel was the second Regimental Major. **Chastel.** He served in Italy, at Toulon and in Egypt. He was made second Colonel Major on 18 December 1805 and then Colonel on 16 February 1807. He was made a Baron in 1808, General in 1811 and Major-General the following year. After serving in Russia and in Saxony where he was made CtLH and in France, he was put on the non-active list on 1 September 1814. During the Hundred Days, he commanded a division of dragoons in Exelmans' Corps. Put on the reserve list, he was retired in 1825.

The Gendarme d'élite

The Gendarmes d'Elite were under the command of Savary; they were not strictly speaking a fighting unit although on numerous occasions the Gendarmes took up their swords and charged alongside their other brothers-in-arms in the Guard.

Henry. With the Army of Helvetia, he was wounded at Zurich. He was allowed to join the Gendarmerie in 1801 and became Squadron Commander in 1805. He served in Prussia in 1806, in Poland in 1807 and in Spain in 1808. He was promoted to Major Colonel on 30 May 1808 and was made a Baron in 1809. He was General of the Gendarmerie and CtLH in 1812. He was retired in 1815.

Deschamps. Wounded at Valmy, he entered the Gendarmerie in 1798 then into the Gendarmerie d'Elite in 1802. He was Palace Fourrier for the Emperor from 1806 to 1814 and as a result followed him throughout all his campaigns. He was made CtLH in 1814 and joined him on Elba. A Colonel during the Hundred Days, he retired in 1818.

Grenadier à Cheval of the Guard. (RR)

Gendarme d'Elite and Sapper. (RR)

From left to right and top to bottom.
Maréchal Murat, Generals Belliard, Nansouty and Defrance. *(RR)*

Flahaut de la Billarderie. Son of Talleyrand and Mme de Souza, he was aide-de-camp to Murat from 1802. He was made Squadron Commander of the 13th Chasseurs on 25 January 1807. In 1813, he was aide-de-camp to Napoleon and was made a Count. Peer in 1815, he was at Quatre-Bras with Napoleon. Outlawed he went to England. GdCxLH in 1838, he was Grand Chancelier of the LH in 1864 and was then awarded the Military Medal in 1866. He died September 1870.

Déry. Wounded at Marengo. He was an aide-de-camp since 1805. He was made OLH in May 1807. He was at Heilsberg. General at Naples in 1809, he was made a Baron in 1810, then a French General in 1811. He was killed in Russia at Winkovo.

Detrès. A veteran of the Italian and Egyptian Campaigns, he received a Sabre of Honour in 1801. He was with the 7th bis Hussars which became the 28th Dragoons in 1803. Promoted to General in 1807, he was at Capri then Naples in 1810. He resigned when Murat defected.

Picquet. Aide-de-camp, he was appointed Colonel of the 6th Dragoons on 13th February 1807. He was made a General in 1813. He commanded the 1st Gardes d'Honneur in 1814. Made GdOLH in 1815, he was wounded at Waterloo. Lieutenant-General in 1831.

D'Avranges d'Haugeranville. He was at Eylau and at Friedland. Promoted to General, he was captured in 1813.

● NANSOUTY'S 1st DIVISION

Nansouty. A contemporary of Napoleon at Brienne, he was promoted to General in 1799 and then Major-General in 1803. He took command of a division of heavy cavalry on 3 August 1805 and led it over all the battle fields until 1807. He was made GdOLH in the same year. He was made a Count and First Equerry to the Emperor in 1808. He commanded a reserve cavalry corps in 1812 and was wounded at the Moskova. He commanded the Cavalry of the Line in 1813, then that of the Guard in 1814. He was then made CSL. He died in 1815.

Nansouty's aide-de-camp was his nephew, Lieutenant Beuverand.

Beuverand. After serving as a junior officer with the 12th and 6th Cuirassiers, he became his uncle's aide-de-camp on 24 January 1807. He was Chief-of-Staff of the Cavalry of the Guard during the French Campaign. He was promoted to Maréchal de camp in 1815. Made CtOLH in 1821, he was in Spain in 1823, and then retired in 1827.

— Defrance's Brigade

Defrance. Took part at the Battle of Valmy; with the Army of Italy he was at Marengo. He became Ecuyer Cavalcadour to the Emperor in 1804 and General in 1805. He took command of the Carabinier Brigade on 21 September 1806. He was made a Chevalier of the Croix de Fer in 1807, Count in 1808 and then promoted to Major-General in 1811. In Russia, he charged at

MURAT'S CAVALRY RESERVE

Murat led the Imperial cavalry in numerous charges during this campaign; from the glory of Eylau to the absurdity of Heilsberg, this *"buffoon of a brother-in-law"* - as Lannes liked to say – nonetheless showed that the French cavalry was the best in Europe.

The Chief-of-Staff was General **Belliard**. He was a veteran of the Italian campaign and was promoted to General after Arcola. He took part in the Egyptian campaign where he was made a Major-General. He was Murat's Chief-of-Staff from 30 August 1805 to 1808 when he became Governor of Madrid. Meanwhile he took part in all the big campaigns and battles. He was made a Count in 1810 and Colonel-General of the Cuirassiers. He left to fight in Russia where he was Murat's Chief-of-Staff again. His left arm was broken at Leipzig. He commanded the cavalry in Champagne instead of Grouchy in 1814, before being made CSL and a Peer. He was sent to Murat on a mission on 22 April 1815. He was made Ambassador of France to Belgium in 1832 where he died of apoplexy the following year.

On Murat's staff there were also the following:

Biarnois de Baine. Promoted to Squadron Commander in 1806, he was on the staff of the cavalry reserve until 1808 and his departure for Spain. Chief-of-Staff to Roussel d'Urbal in 1814, he was made OLH the same year. He retired in 1822.

Buchet. Served in the Navy and in Guadeloupe from 1797 to 1803. He was seconded to Murat's staff. He was Colonel of the 6th of the Line in 1813, and of the 35th in 1815. Promoted to Maréchal de camp in 1823, he was made GdOLH in 1854.

Brunet or Brunet-Denon. Murat's aide-de-camp from 1800. Wounded at Austerlitz. He remained attached to the staff in spite of his promotion to Squadron Commander. He was promoted to Colonel of the 24th Chasseurs on 25 June 1807. Wounded in the arm at Essling and had to be amputated. He was made a Baron and OLH then taken off the active list in 1809. Made Maréchal de camp in May 1815, he retired in 1848 and was made GdOLH in 1860.

Murat's Aide-de-camps

Beaumont. A veteran of Egypt, he was made Squadron Commander and aide-de-camp to Murat in 1799. He distinguished himself at Marengo and was made a General after Austerlitz. He became Murat's first aide-de-camp on 9 March 1806. On 14 May 1807, he took command of the 1st Corps' Light Cavalry and served under Victor at Friedland and was subsequently made CtOLH. He went to Spain and was made a Baron in 1808. He was made a Major-General in 1812 but died at Metz on 16 December 1813.

Manhès. He was one of Milhaud's nephews. He was an aide-de-camp until 1815, *"one of the bravest"* according to Murat. Promoted to the Neapolitan rank of General then to a French one, and made a Count, he remained with Murat in 1814 and 1815. He was made Lieutenant-General in 1816 and CrLH in 1825. Retired in 1848, he died of cholera in Naples in 1854.

French cuirassiers charging.
(Composition by Jack Girbal, Author's Collection)

THE CARABINIERS AND THE CUIRASSIERS

Like the Cuirassiers, the Carabiniers were considered as elite troops and as a result wore a red fringed epaulette. There were two Carabinier regiments wearing the same uniforms distinguished by the facings and the numbers on the pewter buttons.

Carabinier.

Carabinier Trumpeter.

Carabinier Officer.

Cuirassier wearing a coat.

Brigadier from the 1st Cuirassier Regiment.

Generals d'Hautpoul and Berkheim. (RR)

the Moskova. He commanded the Division of the Gardes d'Honneur in 1814 and was non-active in 1815. He was made a Commandeur of SL in 1820 and GdCxLH in 1829.

The 1st Carabiniers
Colonel Laroche. OLH in 1806, he was Regimental Major at Eylau. Replacing Prince Borghese who had been promoted to General, he was promoted himself to Colonel on 14 May and was at Friedland where he was wounded several times. Wounded also at the Moskova, he was promoted to General in 1813. He was in charge of the remounts in 1814. Elected in 1815, he was available in 1820.

The regiment was at Hoff, Ostrolenka, Guttstadt and Friedland where five officers were killed and seven wounded.

The 2nd Carabiniers
Colonel Morin. Joined the cavalry as a simple horseman in 1782, and rising through all the ranks, he was promoted to Colonel in 1803. He was made CtLH in 1805; he was promoted to General on 25 January 1807 and replaced by Blancard. Made a Baron in 1812, he was retired in 1813.

Colonel Blancard. Sabre of Honour in 1802, he was made OLH in 1807 and Baron in 1810. He was promoted to General in 1813 and replaced by Desève. He was wounded at Waterloo during the charges for the Mont Saint-Jean Plateau. Made CtLH in 1832, he was retired in 1848.

The regiment took part in the same battles as the 1st. At Friedland four officers were wounded.

— Lahoussaye's then Doumerc's Brigade

Lahoussaye. He was appointed General and made CtLH in 1804. Promoted to Major-General, he left his brigade to take command of a Dragoon division in place of Sahuc on 14 May 1807 with which he fought at Friedland. He left for Spain and was made a Baron in 1808. He was in Russia and was seriously wounded at the Moskova before being captured at Vilna. Returned to France in June 1814, he was made CSL then put on the non-active list. He was retired in 1833.

Doumerc. He was aide-de-camp to Pichegru from 1793. Appointed General on 31 December 1806, he replaced Lahoussaye and fought at Friedland. He was made a Baron in 1808 and was promoted to Major-General in 1811. In Russia he was at Polotsk and distinguished himself at the Berezina. Made CSL in 1814, he was retired in 1825 and made GdCxLH in 1832.

The 2nd Cuirassiers
Colonel Chouard: Squadron Commander in the 1st Carabiniers, he was wounded at Austerlitz then made a Colonel with the 2nd Cuirassiers. He was made a Baron in 1808 and a General in 1811. He was in Russia and was wounded at the Moskova. Major in the Dragoons of the Guard in 1813, he was CSL and CrLH in 1814. He served during the Hundred Days then retired.

The regiment was present at Eylau and at Friedland.

The 9th Cuirassiers
Colonel Paultre de la Motte. Squadron Commander in 1800. He was appointed Colonel of the 9th Cuirassiers on 31 December 1806. He had three horses killed under him at Friedland. He was promoted to General in 1811 and fought in Russia. Authorised to return to France for health reasons, he was made CSL in 1814, GdOLH in 1815 and CrSL in 1825. He was allowed to retire in 1830.

The regiment was at Guttstadt and at Friedland.

— Saint-Germain's Brigade

Saint-Germain. Appointed General in 1805, he was made a Baron and a Major-General in 1809. He commanded the 2nd Cavalry Corps in 1814 and was made GdOLH. He served in the Alps in 1815 then was put on the non-active list. He retired in 1826 and then again in 1832.

The 3rd Cuirassiers
Colonel Richter. After serving in Italy where he was wounded at Lodi, he took part in the Egyptian Expedition. He was at Pultusk and was made Colonel of the 3rd Cuirassiers on 31 December 1806. He fought at Eylau and Friedland before being made Chevalier of the Couronne de Fer at the end of 1807, then Baron in 1808. He was wounded at Essling. Promoted to General in 1811, he was at the Moskova in 1812. He was made a Lieutenant of the King in 1817 then CrLH in 1825. He retired in 1827, then 1832.

The regiment was at Eylau and Friedland.

The 12th Cuirassiers
Colonel Dornès. He was appointed Colonel of the regiment on 27 December 1806. He was made an OLH on 14 May 1807. He distinguished himself at Friedland. He became a Baron in 1808. He took part in the Austrian Campaign and was promoted to General in 1809. In Russia he charged at the Moskova but was killed at Vilna.

The regiment was mentioned in despatches at Eylau and Friedland.

● D'HAUTPOUL'S 2nd DIVISION

D'Hautpoul. Promoted to General in 1794, he became a Major-General in 1796. On 24 August 1805, he took command of the 2nd Heavy Cavalry Division which he led brilliantly at Austerlitz. Senator in 1806, he was also made Grand Aigle of the LH. He distinguished himself at Hoff on 6th February 1807 and at Eylau, two days later, where he charged several times and was wounded. He died in great pain.

Saint-Sulpice. A General since 1806, he became Ecuyer Cavalcadour of the Empress in 1804. In charge of the 2nd Brigade in the Division, he charged at Eylau where he was wounded. He therefore replaced d'Hautpoul. He was made a Count in 1808. He commanded the Dragoons of the Guard in Russia. He was made CSL and GdOLH in 1814 and a Peer in 1831.

— Clément's Brigade

Clément de la Roncière. A veteran of the Sambre and the Meuse, and Italian campaigns, he joined to the 3rd Division of Dragoons where he commanded the 16th Regiment. He was made a General on 31 December 1806 and took command of the brigade. Wounded eleven times at Eckmühl, he was promoted to Major-General and left to run the military school at Saumur. He was made CSL in 1814 and GdOLH in 1835, when he retired.

The 1st Cuirassiers
Colonel Berkheim. Squadron Commander and Equerry to the Emperor since 1805, he was appointed Colonel of the 1st Cuirassiers replacing Guiton, who left to take over command of the division's second brigade. He himself was promoted to General in 1809, then Baron the following year. He was in Russia then Saxony, where he was at the head of the Guards of Honour after being made CtLH and Major-General. He served in 1815, and then was put on the non-active list.

Certain authors put Berkheim with Latour-Maubourg at Friedland.

The regiment was at Hoff, Eylau, Heilsberg and Königsberg.

The 5th Cuirassiers
Colonel Noirot. A veteran of Toulon, he was appointed Colonel of the regiment in 1802. He was brilliant at Austerlitz and made CtLH. He was promoted to General on 31 December 1806 and was in Klein's division. Wounded at Hoff, he returned to France to convalesce. He served in Spain in 1809. He was made a Baron in 1813 and CSL in 1814. He was retired in 1824.

Colonel Quinette de Cernay. He was appointed Colonel of the regiment on 31 December 1806, replacing Noirot. Promoted to General in 1811, he was put on the non-active list, accused of embezzlement in the regiment. Reinstated in 1813, he served in Saxony then in Champagne. He was retired in 1824.

The regiment was at Hoff and among the heroes of the Moskova, in the Great Redoubt with Caulaincourt.

— Guiton's Brigade

Guiton. Grenadier à Cheval in the Consular Guard in 1800, he was Colonel of the 1st Cuirassiers in 1803. After Austerlitz, he was made CtLH. He was appointed to the second brigade on 1 April 1807, replacing Saint-Sulpice. He was made a Baron in 1808. He was retired in 1814. He served during the Hundred Days, fought at Quatre-Bras and at Waterloo where he was wounded. He was retired the same year.

The 10th Cuirassiers
Colonel Lhéritier. Baron, he was wounded at Essling then promoted to General in 1809. He was at Polotsk in 1812 and was made Major-General in 1813. He commanded the 6th Division of Milhaud's 5th Corps in 1814. Made CtLH, he was wounded at Waterloo.

The 11th Cuirassiers
Colonel Fouler. Appointed Colonel of the regiment in 1801, he distinguished himself at Austerlitz and was made a General on 31 December 1806. Wounded at Heilsberg, made a Count

THE CUIRASSIERS

Brigadier from the 2nd Cuirassiers.

Officer from the 2nd Cuirassiers.

Trooper wearing a coat and forage cap.

Trooper from the 6th Regiment.

Officer from the 10th Cuirassiers.

Trumpeter from the 11th Cuirassier Regiment.

Officer from the 8th Cuirassiers wearing social dress.

The coat with lapels appeared during the first quarter of 1806. As the changeover was carried out as and when the clothes wore out it is therefore quite probable that 9-button coats were worn alongside coats with lapels.

According to the plate by L. Rousselot it dates from 1809. As there are no other documents for the 1807 period, one can presume that he wore the coat with lapels at that date.

André Jouineau © Histoire & Collections 2006

105

in 1808, he was wounded and captured at Essling then freed after the armistice. He was promoted to Major-General in March 1814. He was made GdOLH in 1815, took up service once again as Equerry to the Emperor during the Hundred Days, and then was retired at the end of the year.

Colonel Brancas. He distinguished himself at Jemmapes and then at Neerwinden. He was promoted to Colonel of the 11th Cuirassiers to replace Fouler. Made OLH in 1807 then a Baron in 1809, he was mortally wounded at the battle of Essling.

The regiment was mentioned in despatches at Friedland.

● ESPAGNE'S 3rd DIVISION

Espagne. A General in 1799, he was present at Hohenlinden the following year. Promoted to Major-General he transferred to the Army of Italy then that of Naples. He served under Lefebvre at Danzig then returned to the cavalry reserve on 28 March 1807. Wounded at Heilsberg, he was made GdOLH in July and a Count in 1808. He was mortally wounded during a charge at Essling.

— Fouler's Brigade

Fouler (see the 11th Cuirassiers)

The 7th Cuirassiers

Colonel Offenstein. He was in command of the regiment from 1800. He was made OLH in 1804. Seriously wounded at Heilsberg, he was promoted to General and made a Baron the following year. He served in 1815, at Waterloo, and then was retired in 1816.

The regiment was at Heilsberg.

The 8th Cuirassiers

Colonel Merlin. Succeeded Espagne at the head of the regiment in 1803. He was made CtLH in 1804, then Baron in 1808. He was wounded at Essling and was promoted to General. On the non-active list in 1815, he was retired in 1832.

The regiment was at Heilsberg. It embrigaded with the 5th Cuirassiers at the Moskova in order to capture the Great Redoubt.

— Reynaud's Brigade

Reynaud. A veteran of Egypt, he was made CtLH in 1805. He was promoted to General after Golymin where he commanded the 20th Dragoons, on 31 December 1806. A Baron in 1809, he was wounded at Wagram. On the non-active list in 1814, he was retired in 1821.

The 4th Cuirassiers

Colonel Herbault. Squadron Commander in the Grenadiers à Cheval of the Consular Guard, he distinguished himself at Marengo. He was appointed the Regimental Colonel in 1803, and was made OLH the following year. He was seriously wounded at Heilsberg. He was made a Baron in 1808, the year of his death.

The regiment was at Heilsberg and Friedland.

The 6th Cuirassiers

Colonel Rioult-Davenay. He was in command of the regiment since February 1805. He was made CtLH in 1806. He was brilliant at Heilsberg and made a General on 25 June 1807, then OLH in 1808. A Baron in 1809, he joined the Army of Italy and was mortally wounded at the Battle of the Piave, on 8 May 1809.

In the regiment there was a certain Gonneville, who wrote his memoirs.

The regiment was at Heilsberg and Friedland.

GROUCHY'S DRAGOONS

● KLEIN'S 1st DIVISION

Klein. He was involved in all the great battles of the Revolution: Valmy, Jemmapes and Fleurus, then with the Army of the Sambre and the Meuse. He was made a General in 1794, and then in 1799 he was promoted to Major-General in the Army of Helvetia whose cavalry he commanded. He was appointed to the 1st Division of Dragoons of the Grande Armée and took part in all the fighting until Eylau. He was made a Senator in 1807 then was made a Count the following year. Peer and CSL in 1814, he was promoted to GdCxLH in 1834.

Latour-Maubourg. Emigrated with La Fayette, he returned to France in 1799. Made a General after Austerlitz. Commanding the 1st Brigade of the 3rd Division of Dragoons, he distinguished himself during the fighting at Czarnovo on 23 December 1806, taking command of Lasalle's brigade (5th and 7th Hussars) and was wounded at Deppen. He was promoted to Major-General on 14 May and replaced Klein. He fought at Heilsberg and Friedland where he was wounded. He was made a Baron and served in Spain in 1808. He returned in 1812, he was in Russia and wounded at the Moskova. He was made a Count in 1813, CSL and GdOLH in 1814. He did not serve in 1815; he retired and voted for Ney's execution. He became Minister of War in 1819.

The division's Chief-of-Staff was **Bertrand.** A former aide-de-camp to Moreau, he was appointed to this job on 13 July 1805. He was wounded at Eylau and at Friedland. He was promoted

From left to right and top to bottom.
Generals Grouchy, Klein and Digeon.
(RR)

to General in 1808 and made a Baron and CtLH 1809. He was on the non-active list in 1814 and served during the Hundred Days. He was wounded at Belfort. He retired in 1815 and was placed in the reserve in 1832.

General Klein's aide-de-camp was Matharel after 17 January 1807.

Matharel. Made OLH in 1813, he was Maréchal de camp in 1821. He retired in 1832.

— Fenerol's Brigade

Fornier, called **Fenerol.** Appointed General in 1803, he was made CtLH the following year. He was killed at Golymin by a shell burst. He was replaced by Perreimond.

Perreimond. A General in 1794, he was discharged in 1796. His return to active service was confirmed by Imperial decree in February 1807. He was made a Baron and OLH in 1808. He then served in Spain and Italy until 1814 when he was put on the non-active list. He retired as Maréchal de camp in 1816. CSL in 1827.

The 1st Dragoons

Colonel Oullembourg. Aide-de-camp to Bessières in 1805, he was promoted to Colonel of the 1st Dragoons on 19 June 1806 and then was appointed General on 4 April 1807, commanding the 2nd Brigade (4th and 14th Dragoons) of the division. He charged at Friedland. He was made a Baron in 1808 and left for Spain. He was made CSL and CtLH in 1814. Retired 1832.

Colonel Dermoncourt. Took part in the taking of the Bastille, he also served in Italy, at Rivoli and in Egypt. He was appointed Colonel to the regiment to replace Oullembourg on 5 April 1807. During the Polish Campaign, he fought at Golymin, Hoff, Eylau, Heilsberg and distinguished himself at Friedland. He was made a General in 1813 and was made CtLH. He served with Piré in 1814, and then defended Neuf-Brissach until peace was restored. He retired in 1821. He married the Duchess of Berry in 1832 and was again retired the following year.

The regiment was at Golymin, Heilsberg and Friedland. In 1811, it was changed into the 1st Regiment of Chevau-Légers Lancers.

The 2nd Dragoons

Colonel Pryvé. He was in command of the regiment since 1803. He was made CtLH after Austerlitz. He captured three cannon at Golymin and was wounded at Eylau. He was then promoted to General on 14 May 1807 and replaced by Ismert. He served under Dupont in Spain and was captured at Baylen. He only returned to France in 1814 and retired in 1818.

Colonel Ismert. A veteran of Marengo and Austerlitz, he was appointed Colonel on 8 May 1807. Made OLH in 1808, he served in Spain until 1813 and was then promoted to General and made Chevalier of the Couronne de Fer. He returned to fight in Champagne in 1814. He retired in 1815.

The regiment was at Golymin, Eylau, Heilsberg and Friedland.

— Fauconnet's Brigade

Fauconnet. A General in 1796, he was at Hohenlinden and was made CtLH in 1804. He took

THE DRAGOONS

For each regiment, we have used the full dress coat in order to show the pocket and the facings.

Sapper from the 1st Dragoon Regiment wearing full dress.

Subaltern from the 2nd Dragoons Regiment.

Subaltern from the 3rd Dragoons Regiment. Note the cloth shabrack, not usually found in the Dragoon's equipment.

Officer from the 4th Dragoon Regiment wearing social dress.

Trumpeter from the 12th Dragoon Regiment.

Trooper from the Elite Company of the 12th Regiment wearing an overcoat over his full dress coat.

over command of the brigade on 13 December 1805, replacing Lasalle. He made Major-General on 7 January 1807. He was on half pay on 1 June 1814 and was retired in 1815.

Oullembourg. Took over command of the brigade on 4 April 1807. See 1st Dragoons.

The 4th Dragoons

Colonel Lamotte. A veteran of Italy, he was appointed Regimental Colonel on 13 January 1806. He was wounded at Deppen, at Eylau and at Friedland. He was made a Baron in 1808, promoted to General the following year and retired in 1812. He returned to active service for the Saxon campaign. He distinguished himself in Champagne and was made CtLH in 1814.

Squadron Commander Birgy (called **Perquit**). LH in 1804, he was in the regiment on 7 January 1807 and was wounded at Friedland. OLH in 1808, he was appointed Colonel to the 6th Chevau-Légers Lancer Regiment in March 1813. On the non-active list in 1814, he served during the Hundred Days. He was promoted to Maréchal de camp in 1831 and retired the following year. CtLH in 1850.

The regiment was at Golymin, Deppen, Hoff, Eylau, Heilsberg and Friedland.

The 14th Dragoons

Colonel Bouvier des Eclaz. He was present at Austerlitz. He was promoted to Colonel of the regiment on 22 September 1806. He was wounded both at Eylau and Heilsberg. He was made a Baron in 1808, a General in 1810 then CtLH and Chevalier de la Couronne de Fer in 1811. He served in 1815, when he retired.

The regiment was present at Golymin, Watersdorf, Eylau, Heilsberg and Friedland.

— Picard's Brigade

Picard. A veteran of Italy, promoted to General in 1803, and then made CtLH in 1804. He took command of the brigade on 13 December. He was wounded at Eylau by a Biscayen shot which went right through him; he was replaced by Digeon. He was made a Baron in 1808; he was discharged the following year and retired the next.

Digeon. Captured two standards and was wounded at Austerlitz, then wounded before Straslund in January 1807, he was promoted to General and replaced Picard on 31 March 1807. After fighting at Heilsberg and Friedland, he left for Spain where he was made a Baron and Chevalier of the Croix de Fer in 1813. He commanded the cavalry in the Army of Lyon in 1814, and then was made CSL. Viscount in 1816, he became an aide-de-camp to the Comte d'Artois and a Peer in 1819. GdCxLH in 1821, he was Minister of War in 1823 and aide-de-camp to the King in 1824.

The 20th Dragoons
Colonel Reynaud. See Espagne's division
The regiment was at Eylau and Friedland.

The 26th Dragoons
Colonel Delorme. He distinguished himself at Rivoli where he captured 200 men. In 1800, he was made brigade commander (Colonel) for the 17th Cavalry regiment, the future 26th Dragoons. He was retired on 16 February 1807. He was replaced by Chamorin.

Colonel Chamorin. After Arcola, Marengo and St Domingo, he was appointed Squadron Commander in 1,804 in the 3rd Cuirassiers before joining the Grenadiers à Cheval of the Guard in September 1805. On 16th February 1807, he was promoted to Colonel of the 26th Dragoons. Wounded at Heilsberg, he nevertheless played an important role at Friedland. He went to Spain and was made CtLH in 1808 then a Baron the following year. Promoted to General on 5 March 1811, he was killed at Campo-Mayor at the head of his men.

The regiment was at Watersdorf, Hoff, Eylau, Heilsberg and Friedland.

● GROUCHY'S 2nd DIVISION

Angot-Darsonval. LH, was the Chief-of-Staff after 1806. He was made OLH in 1811. He served in Belgium in 1815, and was retired with the rank of Maréchal de camp.

Roget's Brigade

Roget. A General since 1799, he was CtLH in 1804 and was present at Austerlitz and Zedenhick. He was promoted to Major-General on 30 December 1806, he was replaced by Bron. Retired in 1815.

Bron de Bailly. An Italian and Egyptian campaigns veteran where he was made a General in 1800. CtLH in 1804. After Poland where he was in command of the depot at Danzig for a time he was sent to Spain with Junot's corps. Baron in 1813, he was retired in 1815.

The 3rd Dragoons
Colonel Grézard. LH in 1804, he was made the Regimental Colonel on 24 September 1806; OLH in 1807. Promoted to Colonel in the Gendarmerie in 1810, he was replaced by Berruyer. Retired in 1824.

The regiment was at Eylau and Friedland.

The 6th Dragoons
Colonel LeBaron. A former sailor, he served under Grasse. He was promoted to Brigade Commander (Colonel) of the regiment in January 1796. He was awarded the LH in 1806 and was made OLH the following year. He was killed on 6 February 1806 in the fighting at Hoff and was replaced by Piquet, Murat's aide-de-camp.

The regiment was at Hoff, Eylau and Friedland.

— Milet's Brigade

Milet. He was at Marengo and was made a General in 1800. CtLH in 1804. He took part in Austerlitz and in the business at Zedenhick. He was present at Friedland and then the following year he went to Spain. He was retired in 1812.

Carrié de Boissy. Colonel in the 22nd Dragoons in 1800. He took part in the Duke of Enghien's arrest. He was made CtLH in 1805. Promoted to General on 4 April 1807, he replaced Milet and was wounded at Friedland. He was made a Chevalier and went to Spain where he was captured in 1812, returning to France only in June 1814. A Deputy in 1815, he was retired the same year.

The 10th Dragoons
Colonel Dommanget. Wounded at Friedland he was replaced by Squadron Commander Pillay for the whole of the battle. He was promoted to General in 1811 and CtLH in 1813. He was in the 2nd Brigade with Roussel d'Urbal with the 11th and 12th Chasseurs and the 2nd Lancers in 1814. He was present at Ligny and Waterloo. He was arrested in 1817 on charges of conspiracy, and was put into the Cartier mental home but was freed in 1818. He was retired in 1825.

The 11th Dragoons
Colonel Bourbier. He was at the head of the regiment since 1805, after Austerlitz. He was wounded at Eylau and died at Landsberg on 9 February 1807. He was replaced by Dejean.

Dejean. The son of the General, one of the Emperor's ministers. He was appointed Regimental Colonel on 13 February 1807. He was promoted to Brigadier in 1811 and served in Montbrun's regiment in Spain. He served in Champagne and was promoted to Major-General in 1814. He was sent to Napoleon's brother, Joseph, by Napoleon himself, to try and prevent Paris from capitulating on 30 March, but he arrived too late. He served as aide-de-camp to the Emperor during the Hundred Days and was then exiled. He returned in 1818. GdCxLH in 1844.

The regiment was at Eylau and Friedland.

● BEAUMONT'S 3rd DIVISION

Beaumont. In 1794, he was arrested and condemned to death as a suspect. Led to the scaffold, he was rescued in the nick of time by his Dragoons. He was promoted to General in 1795, served in Italy. He was made a Major-General in 1802, and took command of the 3rd Dragoon Division of the cavalry reserve. After brilliant campaigning in Austria and Prussia, he was replaced by Milhaud on 30 December 1806. He was a Senator and he was made Couronne de Fer in 1807, a Count in 1808, Peer and CSL in 1814. After serving in 1815, he voted for Ney's death during the later's trial. He was made GdCxLH in 1824.

Milhaud. A Montagnard deputy, he voted for the death of the King. He was promoted to General in 1800, he was present at Austerlitz then was in temporary command of Soult's 4th Corps' cavalry before taking command of a light brigade in Murat's reserve. He was at Golymin, and then was promoted to Major-General at the same time as Lasalle, on 1 January 1807. He was present at Eylau then at Königsberg. A Count in 1808, he served brilliantly in Spain, was made GdOLH in 1810. He commanded the 5th Cavalry Corps in 1814. He served at Ligny and at Waterloo, and then was outlawed as a regicide. Pardoned in 1817, he was discharged in 1832.

— Latour-Maubourg's Brigade

Latour-Maubourg. See the 1st Dragoon division. He was replaced on 30 December 1806 by Maupetit

Maupetit. A veteran of the Italian Campaign. He was wounded twice at Marengo. CtLH in 1805, he was made a General on 30 December 1806. He was at Eylau and Friedland and was made a Chevalier of the Couronne de Fer in 1807. A Baron in 1808, he served in Spain but was sent back because he was deaf. He died in 1811.

The 5th Dragoons
Colonel Lacour. The Regimental Colonel since 10 April 1804, he was wounded at Austerlitz. Retired in 1815, he was made an Honorary Maréchal de camp in 1818.

The regiment was at Eylau and Friedland.

The 12th Dragoons
Colonel Girault de Martigny. A Colonel since 13 January 1806. Wounded at Eylau, he was made OLH in 1807, then a Baron in 1808. He was mortally wounded at Ocaña in 1809.

The regiment was at Eylau, Heilsberg and Friedland.

— Marizy's Brigade

Marizy (called **Vagnair**). A General in 1803, he was made CtLH in 1804. He was wounded at Austerlitz. He took over command of the brigade in October 1806. In 1808, he was made a Baron and left for Spain where he was murdered in 1811.

THE DRAGOONS

Trooper from the Elite Company of the 14th Regiment of Dragoons.

Trooper from the 16th Dragoon Regiment.

Subaltern in second uniform, also worn while campaigning, with the helmet.

Trooper from the 26th Dragoon Regiment.

Trooper from the 20th Regiment wearing cantonment dress.

Trooper from the 21st Dragoon Regiment wearing campaign dress.

The overcoat was most often used when campaigning during the early years of the Empire.

109

André Jouineau © Histoire & Collections 2006

The 8th Dragoons
Colonel Girardin d'Ermenonville. Wounded at St. Domingo, he was aide-de-camp to Berthier in 1803. He was made the Colonel of the 8th Dragoons on 27 December 1806. He was wounded at Friedland and was made a Baron and Lieutenant of the Emperor's Hunt in 1808, then a Count in 1810. He served in Champagne in 1814 and was promoted to Major-General. Grouchy's Chief-of – Staff in 1815. Made CSL in 1821, GdOLH in 1825 and was retired in 1848.

The regiment was at Eylau, Heilsberg and Friedland.

The 16th Dragoons
Colonel Clément de la Roncière. See d'Hautpoul's division. He was replaced by Colonel Vial on 31 December 1806.

Vial. He was in Italy then in Egypt where he was made Squadron Commander. He was a Major in the 4th Dragoons; he was promoted to Colonel in the 16th Regiment on 31 December 1806. OLH in 1807, he left for Spain in 1809 where he was killed at the Battle of Ocaña.

The regiment was at Eylau and Königsberg.

— Boyé's Brigade

Boyé. Born a German, he was made a General in 1794, then CtLH in 1804. He left to command of the Cavalry depot at Breslau on 13 March 1807 before replacing Montbrun at the head of the Wurtemburg cavalry on 17 June. He retired in 1812 and was naturalised in 1817.

The 9th Dragoons
Colonel Maupetit. See Latour-Maubourg's Brigade.

Queunot. He was made Colonel of the 9th Dragoons to replace Maupetit. He was made a Baron and left for Spain where he served until 1811 and his promotion to the rank of General. He served in Russia and was wounded at the Moskova. He retired in 1813.

The regiment was at Jonkovo, Hoff, Friedland, Willemsdorf and Königsberg.

The 21st Dragoons
Colonel Mas de Polart. He was appointed the Regimental Colonel in 1801 and was wounded at Eylau. He was made a Baron in 1808. He was in Westphalia with Jérôme who made him a General. He was made a French General on 26 February 1814, and then followed the King. Lieutenant-General in 1815, he was made a hereditary Count and GdOLH in 1815. On the reserve list in 1839, he was Mayor of la Ferté-Milon until 1842.

The regiment served at Allenstein, Hoff, Eylau and Königsberg.

● SAHUC'S 4th DIVISION *(replaced by Lahoussaye on 14 May 1807)*

Sahuc. He served under Kellermann at Valmy. Promoted to General in 1799, he was made CtLH in 1804, then Major-General in January 1806. He succeeded General Bourcier. He was replaced on 14 May 1807 by Lahoussaye. He was made a Baron in 1808, and died of typhus in 1813.

In 1806 and 1807 his aide-de-camp was Charmont, who was awarded the LH. Adjudant-Commandant in 1813, he served in 1815, and then was put on the non-active list. He was retired in 1823.

Lahoussaye. See Nansouty's heavy cavalry division.

— Laplanche's Brigade

Laplanche. Made A General in 1803, he was made CtLH the following year. After serving under Bourcier, he joined Sahuc in September 1806, was made a Baron in 1808, and served with Lasalle. He was retired in 1810.

The Brigade was made up of the 17th and 27th Dragoons.

The 17th Dragoons
Colonel Beurmann. He was in the Chasseurs of the Consular Guard in 1800. After being wounded twice at Austerlitz, he was made Colonel of the 17th on 27 February 1806. He went to Spain in 1808, where he was made a Baron and was wounded at La Corunna. Promoted to General in 1811, he was made CtLH the following year. He was on the non-active list in 1814.

The regiment was at Eylau, Königsberg and Friedland.

The 27th Dragoons
Colonel Lallemand. A Baron, he was made a General in 1811; he took part in the putsch which brought Napoleon back from Elba, and was made a Peer. He fought at Ligny and was wounded at Waterloo. Exiled, imprisoned on Malta, he founded the sanctuary in Texas. He returned to France and was a Peer in 1832.

The regiment was at Friedland.

— Margaron's Brigade

Margaron. He was made a General in 1803, then CtLH in 1804. He was wounded at Austerlitz. He was made a Baron in 1809 and Major-General in 1813. He was CSL in 1814. Available in 1815, he was then on the non-active list. GdOLH in 1835. The brigade was made up of the 18th and 19th Dragoons.

The 18th Dragoons
Colonel Lafitte. He was wounded and captured at the Battle of Rivoli and took part in the Egyptian expedition. He was made Regimental Colonel on 20 September 1806. He was made a Baron in 1808, then General and CtLH in 1813. He served in 1815, against the Duke of Angoulême. Retired in 1823.

The regiment was at Mohrungen and Friedland.

The 19th Dragoons
Colonel Saint-Geniès. In Egypt he was in command of the Dromedary Camel Corps. He was Colonel of the 19th from 1806; he was made a Baron in 1808. He left for Spain where he was promoted to General before fighting in Russia. Wounded and captured, he only returned to France in July 1814. He served in 1815, before being made a Viscount in 1822 and GdOLH in 1831. He was available in 1834.

● LORGE'S 5th DIVISION

Lorge. See with Masséna. At first part of the cavalry reserve, the division was subsequently attached to the 5th Corps.

LASALLE'S LIGHT CAVALRY

At the end of 1806, **Lasalle** was in command of his legendary *"infernal brigade"* comprising the 5th and 7th Hussars. He was promoted to Major-General on 30 December and on 1st January 1807 and took command of the Light Cavalry Division of the Reserve.

His aide-de-camp was **Wathiez**. He was present at Austerlitz. Wounded at Heilsberg, he went to Spain. Promoted to General and made a Baron in 1813, wounded twice at Hanau, he served in Exelmans' division in 1814 before being suspended. He served during the Hundred Days and was wounded at Waterloo. He was promoted to Lieutenant-General in 1837 and was made GdOLH in 1843.

— Pajol's Brigade

Pajol. Colonel in the 6th Chasseurs in 1799, he was awarded a Sword of Honour the following year. He was made a General in 1807 and replaced Latour-Maubourg. He was made a Baron in 1808. He was with Montbrun in 1809. He was made a Major-General in 1812 and served with Davout but was seriously wounded at Mojaisk. He replaced Sebastiani in 1813, in command of the 2nd Corps and was made a Count. He commanded the 2nd Reserve Corps at Melun in 1814 and after Montereau, where he was wounded, he was sent back to Paris for care. With Grouchy at Ligny and at Wavre in 1815, he was made Gd Aigle of the LH in 1815. Hostile to the Bourbons, he founded societies and took part in the 1830 Revolution. GdCxLH in 1830 and Peer in 1831. He was married to César Berthier's daughter and was related to Oudinot.

General Lasalle. (Composition by Jack Girbal, Author's Collection)

THE CHASSEURS À CHEVAL

Subaltern from the 1st Chasseur à Cheval Regiment. Normally the officers in the Chasseurs wore a rank epaulette on the left-hand side; however this was not necessarily systematic.

Trumpeter from the 3rd Chasseurs à Cheval. He is still wearing the Hussar-style dress which at the time could have been worn alongside the Chasseur coat if one assumes the regulation - that all uniforms were only changed as and when they wore out - was always obeyed.

Trooper from the 7th Chasseurs à Cheval. He is armed with a Chasseur sabre as others were armed with the Light Cavalry sabre An XIII Replacements were used when the old weapons were no longer serviceable.

Trooper from the 11th Chasseurs à Cheval. Trooper from the 20th Chasseurs à Cheval.

THE HUSSARS

Trooper from the 2nd Hussars wearing campaign dress, according to Colonel Barbier.

Trooper from the Elite Company of the 3rd Hussars wearing campaign dress, according to a drawing by P. Benigni. The plume is protected by a twill sheath.

Trooper from the 3rd Hussar Regiment, according to Martinet.

Officer wearing town dress, and Trooper from the 4th Hussars.

Trumpeter from the 4th Hussars wearing campaign dress.

André Jouineau © Histoire & Collections 2006

The Brigade was made up of the 5th and the 7th Hussars.

The 5th Hussars

Colonel Déry. A former aide-de-camp to Murat, he replaced Colonel Schwarz at the end of 1806. He was made OLH, wounded at Heilsberg, promoted to General in 1809, served at Naples and was made a Baron in 1810. Made a General in 1811, but was killed the following year.

The regiment was at Golymin, Liebstadt, Heilsberg and Königsberg.

The 7th Hussars

Colonel Colbert de Chabanais (called **Edouard de**). He took part in the Egyptian Campaign where he was wounded. Wounded at Austerlitz, he was appointed Regimental Colonel on 30 November 1806 to replace Marx. Promoted to General in 1809, he was in command of the cavalry of Lannes' 2nd Corps in Austria; he was wounded at Wagram and was made a Baron. He was promoted to Colonel of the 2nd Lancer Regiment of the Guard in 1811 and to Major-General in 1813. He took part brilliantly in the French Campaign where he led his Red Lancers at Quatre-Bras and Waterloo; he was put in prison. Released, he was placed on the non-active list then in the reserve in 1833. He was wounded by Fieschi's bomb in 1835. Raised to the rank of GdCxLH in 1837, he was retired in 1848 and died in 1853.

The regiment was at Deppen, Guttstadt, Heilsberg and Friedland.

— Watier de Saint-Alphonse's Brigade

Watier de Saint-Alphonse. In 1804, he was Ecuyer Cavalcadour to the Emperor. Promoted to General on 24 December 1805, after Friedland he went to Spain with Moncey. Made Count de Saint-Alphonse in 1809 and Major-General in 1811, he took part in the Russian campaign and took an active part in capturing the Great Redoubt at the Moskova. He was present at Waterloo and then was put on the non-active list. He was made GdOLH in 1821.

The brigade was made up of the 11th Chasseurs à Cheval and the Bavarian and Wurtemburg Chevau-Légers.

The 11th Chasseurs

Colonel Jacquinot. Aide-de-camp to Duroc at Austerlitz, he was appointed Colonel in 1806 and took command of the regiment. He was made a Baron in 1808 and General in 1809. He commanded the cavalry in Davout's corps brilliantly in Austria. After the Russian campaign, he fought in Saxony and was seriously wounded at Dennewitz. He was promoted to Major-General on 26 October 1813. He fought with Subervie at Waterloo. On the non-active list in 1816, he was made CrSL in 1826 and GdCxLH in 1826.

The regiment was at Eylau, Danzig, Guttstadt, Heilsberg and Friedland.

— Bruyère's Brigade

Bruyère. A former aide-de-camp to Joubert and Berthier, he brought Desaix back to the battlefield at Marengo. Promoted to General on 30 December 1806, he took command of the 3rd Brigade the following day. He distinguished himself at Eylau in a charge against a column of Russian grenadiers during which he was wounded. He was made a Baron in 1808, promoted to Major-General in 1812; he was in Nansouty's 1st Corps. He was mortally wounded in 1813.

The brigade comprised the 1st Hussars, the 13th Voltigeurs and the Royal Italian Chasseurs. Later, the 24th Chasseurs were attached to the brigade.

1st Hussars

Colonel Bégougne de Juniac. A Marengo veteran, he was a Major in the regiment when he distinguished himself at Golymin capturing a standard from the enemy. He was promoted to Regimental Colonel and OLH on 6 January 1807. He was wounded in action at Hoff. He was made a Baron and Couronne de Fer in 1808. He was retired because of his wounds in 1810.

Squadron Commander Nicolas. A veteran of the Sambre and Meuse, and Italian campaigns, he was promoted to this rank in September 1806. He was wounded at Eylau and was made OLH for his good conduct. He took part in the Russian campaign during which he was made Colonel of the 11th Chasseurs. Made CtLH in 1814, he served during the Hundred Days. He was promoted to Maréchal de camp in 1823 and was retired in 1835.

The regiment was at Golymin, Allenstein, Eylau, Heilsberg and Friedland.

The 13th Chasseurs

Colonel Demengeot. A former aide-de-camp to Oudinot, he was made Regimental Colonel in September 1806. He was wounded at Golymin then at Eylau and was made OLH. He was made a Baron in 1808 and retired the following year. CtLH in 1849.

The regiment was at Golymin, Ostrolenka, Liebstadt, Eylau and Friedland. It had a strength of 29 officers and 693 men on 1 January 1807.

The 13th Chasseurs was one of the rare French cavalry regiments in which none of its Colonels was ever promoted to General, either during the Revolutionary or the Imperial periods.

From left to right and top to bottom.
Generals Pajol, Edouard de Colbert and Bruyère.
Maréchal Bessières. *(RR)*

The 24th Chasseurs

Colonel Maurin. He was promoted to Regimental Colonel in 1802 and then General on 25 June 1807. He left for Spain and was captured by the English in 1808, returning only in 1812. He was made CtLH in 1813 and CSL the following year. He served during the Hundred Days and was wounded at Ligny. Retired in 1825, he committed suicide in 1830.

— Durosnel's Brigade

Durosnel. See 7th Corps.

The brigade was initially composed of the **7th** and **20th Chasseurs** and was reinforced by the 22nd Chasseurs coming from Soult's 4th Corps. It was attached to Lasalle's division after the 7th Corps was disbanded.

At the beginning of the campaign, the French cavalry was split into two reserve corps. The first was under Murat, the second under the command of Maréchal Bessières. The latter corps was disbanded in January and its units shared out among the others.

BESSIERES' CAVALRY CORPS

— Tilly's Brigade

The 2nd and 4th Hussars

● GROUCHY'S DIVISION

Boguet and Millet Brigades
The 3rd, 6th, 10th and 11th Dragoons

● SAHUC'S DIVISION

— Margaron and Laplanche Brigades

The 17th, 18th, 19th and 27th Dragoons

● D'HAUTPOUL'S DIVISION

— Saint-Sulpice and Guiton Brigades

The 1st, 10th, 5th and 11th Cuirassiers

THE HUSSARS

Officer from the 5th Hussar Regiment.

Trooper from the 5th Hussar Regiment.

Trooper from the 7th Regiment of Hussars wearing town dress.

Standard-Bearer from the 5th Hussar Regiment. This job was assigned to a Maréchal des Logis-chef appointed by the Colonel.

Trumpeter from the 8th Hussar Regiment.

Trooper from the 8th Hussar Regiment wearing full dress.

Senior officer from the 7th Hussar Regiment wearing campaign dress.

BERNADOTTE'S 1st CORPS

Maréchal Bernadotte was wounded and was replaced by Victor on 6 June.

Victor. He received a Sword of Honour for Marengo and was made a Gd Aigle of the LH in 1805. Chief-of-Staff to Lannes during the Prussian Campaign, he was given command of the Polish Dombrowski Division on 4 January 1807, then the 10th Corps on 5 January. He was captured by a party of 25 Schill's Prussian Chasseurs when travelling to Stettin on 20 January. He was exchanged on 8 March, he took command of the corps which was besieging Graudentz. On 6 June he replaced Bernadotte who was wounded in command of the 1st Corps which he led brilliantly at Friedland earning him his Maréchal's baton the following 13 July. He served in Spain after 1808 and in Russia in 1812 where he commanded the French rearguard at the crossing of the Berezina. After fighting at Leipzig, he took part in the Campaign for France but he had his command withdrawn from him because he dallied on the march to Montereau. He rallied Louis XVIII whom he followed when he fled to Ghent in 1815. As a Peer he was Minister of War in 1821.

The Chief-of-Staff was **General Maison.**

Maison. Aide-de-camp to Bernadotte in 1797 then again in 1804, he was made a General in 1806 and took command of the 2nd Brigade of Rivaud's division. He became Chief-of-Staff of the 1st Corps on 30 November of the same year. Made a Baron in 1808, he was a Major-General in 1812, a Count in 1813. In 1814, he was in command of the Army of the North in Belgium. He was made GdCxLH the same year. He was made Maréchal de France in 1829.

Bernadotte's Aide-de-camps

Jan de la Hamelinaye. He was made a General and a Baron in 1809. He was put in command of the 2nd Division of the Paris reserve on 11 January 1814. He gave up his command because he was ill. He was at Tours in 1815. He was made GdOLH in 1820 then a Count in 1822. He was retired in 1832.

Gentil de Saint-Alphonse. Appointed aide-de-camp on 14 February 1807, he served in Russia in 1812 and with the 2nd Corps in 1813.

Gérard. Assigned to Bernadotte in 1795, he became his aide-de-camp in 1799. He was made a General in 1806. At Friedland he was in command of the 2nd Brigade of Villate's division. He was Chief-of-Staff of the 1st Corps in 1809. He served in Spain and under Davout in Russia where he replaced Gudin who was killed. He was GdCX of the Reunion in 1813 and GdCxLH in 1814. He was made a Maréchal de France in 1830; he died in 1852.

The artillery was commanded by **Sénarmont** replacing **Faultrier** who was captured at Marienwerder. After fighting at Austerlitz, he was made a General in 1806. He was one of the heroes of Friedland and as such was made a Baron, awarded the Couronne de Fer and made a Major-General in 1808; he was killed at Cadiz in 1810.

● DUPONT'S DIVISION

Aide-de-camps were **De Warenghein** was Dupont's aide-de-camp from July 1806. He was captured at Baylen but returned to France with his General. He was awarded the LH and made Chevalier in 1809 after the Austrian Campaign. Maréchal de Camp in 1815, but this appointment was cancelled. He was OLH in 1822 then retired in 1837.

Barbarin de la Martinie. Aide-de-camp to Dupont after 1799 and to Maison in the Army of the North in 1815. He served in Spain in 1823 and was made CtLH. He was allowed to retire in 1830.

— La Bruyère's Brigade

La Bruyère. On 21 February 1807 he replaced Rouyer who had joined Soult's staff. He had been made a General in 1803 and made CtLH in 1804. He distinguished himself at Friedland and was made GdOLH in 1807, then a Baron in 1808. He was killed in Madrid the same year.

The brigade was made up of the three battalions of the 9th Light only.

— Legendise's Brigade (replaced by Barois)

Legendre. a veteran of the Italian campaign, distinguished at Marengo. His conduct at Austerlitz earned him the rank of General on the following 24 December. He was Chief-of-Staff to Dupont and signed the capitulation at Baylen on 22 July 1808. He was nevertheless made a Baron the same year. Retired in 1809, he was recalled to service in 1811. CtLH in 1814, he was retired in 1824.

Barois. A veteran of Marengo, in the Grande Armée, he was Colonel of the 99th of the Line, Marchand's brigade, Dupont's division. He was made General of the same brigade on 14 February 1807. He served in Spain and was made a Baron in 1809. He was made Major-General in 1811. He commanded the 1st Division of the Young Guard in 1813 then served under Maison in Belgium in 1814. During the Hundred Days, he fought at Ligny and at Waterloo where he was wounded. CSL in 1819, he was retired in 1848.

The brigade comprised the 32nd and the 96th of the Line.

The 32nd of the Line

Colonel Darricau. See Rivaud's division.

The 96th of the Line

From left to right and top to bottom: Maréchal Bernadotte and General Victor who succeeded him at the head of the 1st Corps on 6 June. Generals Maison, Sénarmont, Gérard, Dupont and Drouet.

Colonel Barois. After being put in command of the brigade he was replaced by Colonel Cales.

Colonel Cales. A veteran of the Siege of Toulon, he was promoted to Colonel on 14 February 1807. Wounded at Somosierra and at Talavera, he was retired in 1810.

● RIVAUD'S and LAPISSE'S DIVISION

Rivaud. A veteran of Italy, he was Chief-of-Staff to Berthier in the Army of Rome.

He was made a General in 1798, wounded at Marengo, made Major-General in 1802. He fought at Austerlitz. He broke his arm when he fell from his horse on 30 January 1807 and had to be replaced by General Lapisse on 6 February. Chevalier of SL in 1814, he was made GdCxLH in 1825. He was retired in 1831.

Lapisse. A General in 1799, he was made CtLH in 1804. He was made a Major-General in 1806, awarded the Couronne de Fer and made a Baron in 1808; he was killed at the battle of Talavera on 28 July 1809.

— Dumoulin's Brigade

Dumoulin. Promoted to General in 1800, he was transferred to Italy on 31 December 1806. He was made GdOLH in 1825. Retired in 1830. He succeeded General Maison at the head of this brigade after the latter became Chief-of-Staff to the 1st Corps.

The brigade comprised the 16th Light and the 45th of the Line.

The 16th Light

Colonel Dellard. He replaced Harispe at the head of the regiment on 10 February 1807. He was made a Baron in 1809 and a General in 1813. CRLH in 1831.

The 45th of the Line

Colonel Barrié. He was made CtLH and a Baron in 1808, then a General in 1810. After serving in 1815, he was put on the non-active list then retired in 1825.

— Darricau's Brigade

Darricau. A veteran of Italy and Egypt, he commanded the 32nd of the Line before being made a General on 14 February 1807. He was awarded the Couronne de Fer in 1811 and was made GdOLH in 1815. He served during the Hundred Days then was put on the non-active list.

The 8th of the Line

Colonel Autié. He had been in command of the regiment since 5 October 1803. He became OLH in 1804. Mentioned in despatches at Austerlitz, he was made a Baron and CtLH in 1808. He was killed in action at Chiclana in Spain in 1811.

The 54th of the Line

Colonel Philippon. OLH in 1804, he was made a Baron and a General in 1808. Captured at Badajoz where he was the Governor after a heroic defence, he escaped from England the following year and returned to service in the Grande Armée. He retired in 1813.

— Sarrut's Brigade

Sarrut. A General since 1803, he was wounded at Eylau. His brigade was part of Augereau's 7th Corps and was assigned to the 1st Corps on 21 March. He was made a Baron in 1810, then Major-General in Portugal in 1811. He was wounded at Vittoria and captured but died of his wounds on 21 June 1813.

Levasseur was his aide-de-camp.

The 24th of the Line

Colonel Semellé: In the regiment since 1801, he was first wounded at Golymin, and then seriously wounded again at Eylau, then again at Friedland. He was appointed General on 1 July 1807, Baron in 1808 and became Victor's Chief-of-Staff in the same year. He was made a Major-General in 1811, retired in 1824 and made GdOLH in 1831.

The 63rd of the Line

Colonel Lacuée. Aide de camp to his uncle in 1793, he was a Colonel in the regiment from 1805. During the Battle of Eylau, he was wounded twice and against the surgeon's advice, he carried on fighting. He was then killed by a bullet in the lower abdomen.

Colonel Mouton-Duvernet. Wounded at Arcola, he replaced Lacuée on 10 February 1807. He was made a Baron in 1808, CtLH in 1812, and Major-General in 1813 and was captured at Dresden. He was Governor of Lyon during the Hundred Days and was shot on 27 July 1816.

● DROUET/VILATTE'S DIVISION

Drouet, Comte d'Erlon. Major-General in 1803, he was at Austerlitz then in the Tyrol. He was made a GdCx of Bavaria then GdCxLH in 1814. He commanded a corps at Waterloo. Outlawed, he was condemned to death the following year the pardoned in 1825. He was made a Maréchal de France in 1843. He left the command of his division to become Augereau's Chief-of-Staff on 24 January 1807. He was the replaced by Vilatte.

Vilatte d'Outremont. A General in 1803, he was mentioned at Echlingen; he was made a Major-General on 25 February 1807, then a Baron in 1808. He served with Soult and replaced Darricau under Clausel. He fought at Toulouse on 10 April 1814, then during the Hundred Days. GdCxLH in 1820, the CrSL in 1823, he was in the reserve in 1831.

— Frère's Brigade

Frère: A General in 1802, he was in command of the infantry of the Consular Guard. He was made CtLH in 1804, then Major-General in 1808, then a Count in 1809. He was at Lille in 1815, and retired in 1825.

The Brigade only consisted of the **27th Light.**

Colonel Charnolet. At the head of the regiment since 1803, he was made CtLH the following year. He was retired on 8 March 1807 with the rank of Brigadier. He was made a Baron in 1809 and CrSL in 1816.

Colonel Lacoste. A veteran of Egypt, he was wounded at St. Jean d'Acre. He was promoted to Colonel and replaced Charnotet on 30 March 1807; he served in Spain and was made a Baron in 1809, CtLH in 1809, and General in 1813. He was captured at Rheims on 12 March 1814 and died the following month.

— Werlé's Brigade

Werlé. A General in 1803, he was made CtLH in 1804 and a Baron in 1808. He was killed at the Battle of Albuhera in 1811. He was replaced by Gérard on 15 March 1807.

Gérard. He served Bernadotte after 1795. Wounded at Austerlitz he was appointed General in 1806. He commanded a brigade in the Desjardins Division in the 7th Corps. He replaced Werlé on 15 March then became Bernadotte's Chief-of-Staff on 23 August 1807. GdCx of the Reunion in 1813, he distinguished himself in 1814 and was made GdCxLH the same year. He served in the Hundred Days at Wavre and at Ligny where he was wounded. He was Maréchal de France in 1830.

The brigade was made up of the 94th and the 95th of the Line.

The 94th of the Line

Colonel Razout. Helped Bonaparte on 18 Brumaire. He was made a General on 14 February 1807, then a Major-General in 1811. He was wounded at Krasnoie and put on the reserve list; he was made GdOLH and Count in 1813. He was captured in 1813 and died in 1820.

Colonel Combelle. Succeeded Razout. Wounded at Toulon, he was a veteran of the Egyptian and Italian Campaigns. He was promoted to Colonel and took command on 14 February 1807. He was CtLH in 1808, Baron in 1810 and General in 1813. He was wounded at Dresden, made a Major-General on 7 September 1813 but died from his wounds on the 15th.

The 95th of the Line

Colonel Pecheux. He was at Austerlitz and fought in Spain. He was made a General in 1810 and Major-General in 1813. He was besieged in Hamburg with Davout. LH in 1814, he served at Waterloo under Gérard. He was made GdOLH and retired in 1825.

— Tilly's Cavalry Brigade

Tilly. He was appointed a General on 21 April 1793 and Major-General on 2 December the same year. At the head of the 1st Cavalry Corps he was at Mohrungen. He left for Spain in 1808, was made a Chevalier in 1809, a Baron in 1809, and Count and GdOLH in 1814. He was elected deputy in 1815 and retired at the end of the same year.

2nd Hussars

The 2nd Hussars was commanded by **Colonel Gérard.** Baron in 1808, he was promoted to General the following year. He fought in Russia in 1812 and was made Major-General in 1813. He was captured at Dresden. Chevalier SL in 1814, he was on the non-active list in 1815. GdOLH in 1830.

4th Hussars

Colonel Burthe. Aide de camp to Masséna in Switzerland; he was at Austerlitz. He fought in Spain. He was made a Baron in 1808 and a General in 1810. He was wounded at the Moskova and was captured but returned in July 1814. Retired in 1825.

5th Chasseurs

Colonel Bonnemain. Appointed to command the regiment, he was made a Baron in 1808 and a General in 1811; he served under Exelmans in 1815. He joined the Gendarmerie. GdOLH in 1829, he was made a Peer in 1815 and was retired in 1845.

DAVOUT'S 3rd CORPS

His Chief-of-Staff was **Fournier de Loysonville,** Marquis of Aultane. He was an officer under the *Ancien Régime*, appointed General in 1799, then Major-General on 31 December 1808 for his conduct at the head of Gudin's division at Pultusk. He was made a Baron in 1808. He was also GdOLH, GdCxSL and GdCx of Baden.

The assistant Chief-of-Staff was **Adjudant-Commandant Hervo.** He was promoted to General and made CtLH in March 1807. He was killed in 1809 near Eckmühl.

Musquinet de Beaupré was an officer on the Staff and was the Maréchal's father-in-law and also Friant's uncle. He was made a General on 4 March 1807, then a Baron in 1809, but died from exhaustion during the retreat from Moscow.

The Corps' Engineers were commanded by **Battalion Commander Bonnay de Breuille**. He was made a Major on 4 March 1807, then OLH and Chevalier in 1810. Retired in 1822.

● MORAND'S DIVISION

Morand. A veteran of the Italian and Egyptian Campaigns, he was made a General in 1800 and Major-General in 1805. He distinguished himself at Auerstadt, Golymin, Eylau, Eckmühl and Wagram. He took part in the Russian Campaign. He was made GdCx of the Reunion in 1813. He held Mainz until April 1814. He was Napoleon's aide-de-camp in 1815 and took part at Plancenoit and at Waterloo. He was sentenced to death and then acquitted in 1819. Retired in 1825 and made GdCxLH in 1830.

THE INFANTRY OF THE LINE

Fusiliers. In 1807, certain companies still had a hat whilst others already wore a shako.

Fusiliers and a Corporal from the same company. The Corporal had the right to carry a *sabre-briquet*.

Grenadiers from the 24th Regiment wearing a bearskin hat.

Grenadier from the 63rd Regiment of the Line wearing a shako

Chasseurs from the 1st Battalion of the Garde de Paris. This unit was considered as "out of the Line" infantry.

Voltigeur from the 21st Regiment of the Line and Voltigeur wearing a greatcoat.

117

From left to right and top to bottom.
Maréchal Davout commanding the 3rd Corps of the Grande Armée. Two of his divisionaires, Morand and Friant and General Gilly, one of Friant's Brigadiers.

— Bonnet d'Hornière's Brigade

Bonnet d'Hornière. An officer under the Ancien Régime, he joined up again in 1791; He was made OLH in 1804 and made a General on 24 December 1805. He took command of the second brigade in Morand's division the following March. He was mortally wounded at Eylau.

Divisional vanguard, the Brigade was only made up of the two battalions of the 13th Light, a total of 1 535 men.

The 13th Light

Colonel Guyardet. Wounded at Auerstadt, he distinguished himself at Golymin. He was made OLH in 1807, Baron in 1810 and General in 1811.

Battalion Commander Brice was mentioned in despatches. He was made a Colonel in 1811. He was in Hamburg in 1813, served in 1815 and was made CtLH.

Battalion Commander Thévenet. He was wounded at Marengo, Auerstadt and Eylau. He served in Spain where he was wounded twice. Made a General in 1813, he was wounded in 1814. Served in 1815 and then put on the reserve list. Retired in 1825 then taken back in 1831.

Hanetin. A veteran of Rivoli, retired in 1814.

— Guiot's brigade

Guiot de Lacour. A General in 1800. He was made CtLH in 1804; he took command of the brigade on 1 April 1807. He was made a Baron in 1808 but was mortally wounded at Wagram.

The brigade was made up of the 51st and 61st of the Line.

The 51st of the Line

Colonel Baille. A veteran of the Egyptian Campaign, he was wounded at Golymin. He was made a Baron in 1808 then became the first aide-de-camp to Morand and OLH in 1809. He was promoted to General in 1811 and made a Baron in 1814. After serving in 1815, the year he was made CtLH, he was put on the non-active list then retired in 1832.

Bony. A veteran of Castiglione, Arcola and Hohenlinden, wounded at Auerstadt, he was brilliant in Spain. General in 1813, Réunion, Chevalier and also OLH. Captured at Leipzig, he returned and served at Waterloo. Retired then CrLH in 1820, retired in 1825, then again in 1835.

Aulard. Colonel at Wagram, OLH, Baron and General in 1814, killed at Waterloo.

Bosse. A hero of Arcola, OLH in 1813, and retired in 1816.

Ladrières. Rifle of Honour, he was killed in Spain in 1811.

The 61st of the Line

Colonel Nicolas. Captain then Battalion Commander with the Foot Grenadiers of the Consular Guard. He had commanded the regiment since August 1805. Wounded at Auerstadt, he was promoted to General and CtLH on 23 October 1806; He served in Spain. He served in 1815 and retired in 1825. He was replaced by **Colonel Faure** on 20 October 1806, OLH in 1804, but mortally wounded at Friedland.

— Brouard's Brigade

Brouard. A veteran of the Egyptian Campaign, he was made OLH in 1804 and General in 1805. He was wounded at Czarnovo before Golymin. He was made a Baron in 1808, elected deputy and appointed Lieutenant-General in 1815. This appointment was cancelled but he was reinstated in 1831. He was retired in 1832.

The 17th of the Line

Colonel Lanusse. Murat's aide-de-camp, he was promoted to Colonel on 30 April 1806, he distinguished himself at Golymin, Eylau and Heilsberg. He was promoted to General in 1808. He was in Naples with Murat where he became the Maréchal du Palais. Made Baron in 1810, he married Pérignon's daughter. He was made CtLH and Major-General in 1813, served in 1815, he was then on the non-active list, then retired in 1833.

The 30th of the Line

Colonel Valterre. Battalion Commander in 1795. He served in the regiment from 1797, was put in command of it in 1800 and led it into battle at Marengo. He was made CtLH in 1805, wounded at Eylau, promoted to General in January 1808, but kept his command until October. Baron in 1809, he was retired in 1819.

● FRIANT'S DIVISION

Friant. General from 1794, he took part in the Italian and Egyptian Campaigns. He was promoted to Major-General in 1799. A hero of Austerlitz, he was made Gd Aigle of the LH in 1805, then Count in 1808. He distinguished himself at Auerstadt, Golymin, Eylau, Eckmühl and Wagram. In Russia, where he was wounded, he commanded the Grenadiers of the Guard. He was Chamberlain in 1813 and then served with Mortier in 1814. He was made a Peer in 1815 then fought at Waterloo where he was wounded again. He was retired in the following September.

— Lochet's brigade

Lochet. He was a soldier in the Queen's Regiment. He was made a General on 29 August 1803 and CtLH the following year. He was brilliant at Austerlitz, was killed by a bullet in the forehead at Eylau, and was then replaced at the head of the brigade by General Gilly.

Gilly. A General in 1799. He took command of the brigade in March 1807. He was made Major-General in 1809, GdOLH in 1811. After serving with Maison in 1814, he was made a Count in 1815 and elected as a deputy. Outlawed, he was pardoned in 1820. He was allowed to retire in 1825.

Thoulouse. Italy, mentioned in Egypt. He took command of the regiment at Eylau. Baron in 1808, he was made a Colonel on the battlefield at Wagram and OLH. Died at Valoutina in 1812.

The brigade was made up of the 33rd and the 48th of the Line.

The 33rd of the Line

Colonel Pouchelon. A veteran of Italy, he succeeded Colonel Saint-Raymond who had died of illness on 11 December 1806. He was appointed Colonel on 7 January 1807 at the head of the 33rd. He was raised to OLH the same year, made a Baron in 1808 and General in 1812. He was wounded at Leipzig in 1813. He served with Augereau in 1814 with the Army of Lyon. He was allowed to retire in 1816.

The regiment distinguished itself at the Battle of Eylau during the capture and the defence of Kuschitten, confronting the Prussians under Lestocq.

The 48th of the Line

Colonel Barbanègre. He was in the Consular Guard in 1800; he was appointed Colonel of the 48th in August 1805 and led his regiment into battle at Austerlitz, Auerstadt and Eylau. He was made CtLH in December 1805, a Baron in 1808, and a General the following year. In Russia, he was wounded twice at Krasnoie and was captured in 1813 at Stettin, returning to France the following year. He covered himself with glory at the siege of Hunninge in 1815. Put on the on-active list in 1820.

— Grandeau's Brigade

Grandeau. Lieutenant in the National Guard in 1789, he was made a General in 1799 and a Baron in 1808. On 17 August 1812, in Russia he was made a Major-General. He was captured at Stettin where he was ill. GdOLH in 1814, he served at Besançon in 1815. He died in 1832.

The brigade comprised the 108th and 111th of the Line, but the latter regiment, which stayed behind, did not take part in the Battle of Eylau.

The 108th of the Line

Colonel Rottembourg. Made a Colonel in 1808, he succeeded Colonel Higonet, killed at Auerstadt. He was made a Baron in 1809 and a General in 1811. He took part in the reorganisation of the Young Guard in 1813 and was made Major-General. He served under Oudinot during the Campaign for France. He was made CrSL in 1825 and GdCxLH in 1828. He was retired in 1834.

THE INFANTRY OF THE LINE

Drummer from the Grenadier Company of the 18th of the Line and

Drummer from the Fusiliers of the same regiment.

Sapper from the 25th Infantry Regiment.

Drum-Major from the 2nd Regiment of the Garde de Paris.

Officer from a company of Fusiliers.

VALEUR ET DISCIPLINE I.ᴇʀ BATAILLON

L'EMPEREUR DES FRANCAIS AU 32.ᴍᴇ RÉGIMENT D'INFANTERIE DE LIGNE.

When campaigning, as the officers wore very sober dress there was little to distinguish one regiment from another except for the number on the buttons. In the Elite Companies, the Grenadier officers worn a bearskin hat and the Voltigeur officer could be made out by his chamois collar.

1804-type flag of the 32nd Infantry Regiment of the Line according to the book by P. Charrié on the flags and standards of the First Empire. The 32nd was given three Eagles, but unfortunately none of them has come down to us.

Commandant Schmitz, the future General, was mentioned as having replaced Colonel Rottembourg for the Battle of Eylau.

Captain Higonet, the brother of the Colonel at Auerstadt, was hit in his left leg by a bullet and sustained severe bruising in the lower abdomen at the Battle of Eylau. Wounded at Eckmühl he transferred to the Foot Grenadiers of the Guard as a Captain in June 1809. Had one of his feet frozen during the retreat from Russia. Returned to the 108th as a Major and served at Hamburg under Davout. A Colonel in 1814, he served the following year during the Hundred Days and was wounded twice at Ligny and twice at Waterloo. Maréchal de Camp in 1823, he served in Morea in 1828 and was retired in 1848.

The 111th of the Line

Colonel Husson. He succeeded Colonel Gay on 28 October 1806. He was a veteran of Italy and Egypt, he was made a Baron in 1809 and General in 1811. CtLH in 1813, he was taken prisoner when Danzig capitulated in January 1814. He commanded a brigade of Bachelu's division at Waterloo. Retired in 1825.

The 111th of the Line and the 2nd Chasseurs were left under the command of General Grandeau to guard Myszienic in February 1807 and therefore did not take part in the Battle of Eylau.

The 15th Light under Colonel Desailly had been assigned elsewhere and was not included in the strength of the division for the duration of this campaign. It was however present at Königsberg in June.

● GUDIN'S DIVISION

Gudin de la Sablonnière. Was made a General in 1799 then Major-General the following year. In the 3rd Corps since 1804, he distinguished himself at Auerstadt, Pultusk and Eylau. Count in 1808, he became Grand Aigle of the LH in 1809, but was killed at Valoutina on 19 August 1812. Maréchal Davout considered him as his spiritual son.

His Chief-of-Staff was All-ain, made OLH in 1804 then CtLH in 1805. Took part in Austerlitz, retired in 1817.

Gudin des Bardelières, his brother, was his aide de camp. Made a General in 1812, he served in the Army of Aragon and at Limonest with Musnier in 1814 and with Rapp in 1815. He was made CrSL in 1820, Lieutenant-General in 1821, Viscount in 1822 and CrSL in 1826. He was retired in 1848.

Creutzer. Gudin's aide de camp. Russian campaign; he was made a General in 1813. OLH. He served in 1815 then was put on the non-active list. He married Maréchal Lefebvre's niece.

— Petit's Brigade

Petit. A former soldier in the Auvergne infantry. He was made a General in 1803 and CtLH in 1804. Wounded at Auerstadt and killed on 3 June 1809 at Pressburg.

The 12th of the Line

Colonel Muller. Succeeded from Colonel Vergez, wounded at Auerstadt and made a General. He was himself wounded on 26 December 1806 at Pultusk. He was made OLH in 1807 and a Baron in 1808. He was retired in 1809. He was Clarke's aide de camp in 1813. He was finally retired in 1819. It would seem that after he was wounded he did not retain command of his regiment.

Teulet. Sabre of Honour at Castiglione. OLH in 1804. He served in Spain where he was made a Colonel in 1813. Maréchal de Camp during the Hundred Days, but later revoked. Retired as a Colonel in 1821.

The 21st of the Line

Colonel Decouz. A former veteran of Toulon and Egypt, he fought at Austerlitz. He was made a Baron in 1808 then a General and CtLH the following year. Made Major-General in 1813, he commanded a brigade of the Young Guard in 1814 which he led in the battle of Brienne where he was mortally wounded.

De Vaugineuse. He was made a Colonel in the 1st Regiment of the Paris Guard.

Rome. Wounded and mentioned in despatches in Russia. Made a General in 1813 and CtLH. He served at Ligny then was put on the non-active list.

— Gautier's Brigade

Gautier. A veteran of Zürich and Italy, he was made OLH in 1804, then a Major-General the following year; wounded at Auerstadt, he was made a Baron in 1808. He died in 1809 as result of the wounds he received at Wagram.

The 25th of the Line

Colonel Cassagne. A veteran of Italy, he was wounded at Auerstadt. He was made a General in 1807 and a Baron the following year. He was with Vedel at Baylen, was made CtLH in 1811; Couronne de Fer and CR de la Reunion in 1813. He served in 1815, was retired in 1825 and was put in the reserve in 1831.

The Lieutenant Adjudant-Major Lavallée, a veteran of Egypt and LH, was killed at the Battle of Eylau.

The 85th of the Line

Colonel Duppelin. A former Battalion Commander with the Grenadiers of the Guard, he was made a Colonel on 20 October 1806 and took command of the 85th. He was made a General, CtLH and a Baron of the Empire in 1809. He died in 1813.

Fournier. He was the first to enter Regensburg and was mentioned in despatches for this action. Wounded several times at Wagram, he was made a General and CtLH in 1813. On half-pay and retired as Honorary Lieutenant-General in 1826.

— Marulaz's Cavalry Brigade

Marulaz. Born in the Palatinate, he fought at Zürich, received a Sabre of Honour in 1801 and was thus made CtLH in 1804. He was made a General in 1805 and served with Davout. Wounded at Golymin, he took Ostrolenka then charged at Eylau. He was made a Baron in 1808 and Major-General in 1809. He distinguished himself at Wagram by taking command of the 8th Hussars, his former regiment. He served then was retired in 1815. He was naturalised in 1817, retired in 1834.

The brigade was made up of the 1st, 2nd and 12th Chasseurs. However, the 2nd Chasseurs were left behind with the 111th of the Line and therefore did not take part in the Battle of Eylau.

1st Chasseurs

Colonel Exelmans. A former aide de camp to Murat, he was appointed to the regiment after Austerlitz. He was made a General on 24 May 1807 and a Baron in 1808. A Major in the Grenadiers à Cheval in 1812, he was also made a Major-General. He distinguished himself in 1813 and 1814. He played an important part in Napoleon's return from Elba and was made a Peer. He was at Ligny, Wavre and Rocquencourt. He defended Ney during his trial and was exiled in 1815. He returned in 1819, was made GdCxLH in 1830. Peer and Grand Chancellor of the LH. Made a Maréchal de France in 1851, he died the following year.

Meda. Took part in the arrest of Robespierre in 1794, distinguished himself at Marengo, was Squadron Commander in the 7th Hussars and took part in the 1805-07 Campaigns. On 24 May 1807, he was made a Colonel in the 1st Chasseurs. He died in Russia as a result of a wound received during vanguard fighting.

Simoneau (see Chasseurs). Aide de camp to Exelmans in 1812. Colonel of the 1st Chasseurs in 1815, wounded at Waterloo. Maréchal de camp in 1815, revoked, he was reinstated in 1830. CrLH. He was in Spain in 1823 and in Belgium in 1832.

Hubert. Colonel of the regiment in Russia in 1812, he was made a General in 1814 and served in 1815 then put on the non-active list. He was reinstated and was in Spain where he was made GdOLH and Lieutenant-General in 1823, retired in 1832.

Apart from Exelmans and Meda, the 1st Chasseurs included some outstanding horseman among its colonels such as Sahuc and Montbrun.

2nd Chasseurs

Colonel Mathis. A former Guide in St Dominica, he took over from Colonel Bousson who was seriously wounded at Auerstadt. He was made OLH the same year, a Baron in 1809 and Maréchal de Camp in 1815. This appointment was cancelled but restored in 1831; he retired the following year and died in 1841.

Delacroix. Commanded the 1st Squadron in 1807, he was Colonel of the 3rd then the 2nd Cuirassiers. Killed at Waterloo.

The 12th Chasseurs

Colonel Guyon. a veteran of Italy and Egypt, he was awarded a Sabre of Honour in 1799. Appointed Colonel of the regiment in March 1805, he was made a Baron in 1809, a General in 1811 and CSL in 1814. Put on the non-active list in 1820 he was made GdOLH in 1825.

In 1807, his brother, Dominique, a hero of Italy and Egypt was a Captain in the 3rd Dragoon Regiment was subsequently Squadron Commander in the 12th Chasseurs.

Aubry. Adjudant, a veteran of Marengo and Austerlitz, he was wounded at Auerstadt. Captain in 1810. Wounded and captured at the Moskova, returned in 1814. Wounded at Ligny. Retired in 1816 and the author of memoirs.

In the Artillery of the 3rd Corps there was also Colonel Charbonnel: a veteran of Italy and Egypt, Baron and General in 1809, he served in Russia and Spain. Major-General in 1813, Count the following year, GdCxLH in 1824 and Peer in 1841.

Each division had five 8-pounders, one 6-pound howitzer and two 4-pounders. In the pool there were six 12-pounders, three 8-pounders and three 6-pound howitzers.

SOULT'S 4th CORPS

The Maréchal's aides de camp were **Lameth** and **Saint-Joseph.** Lameth was the son of the Constituant and was awarded the LH, wounded at Heilsberg and appointed Squadron Commander. Killed in Spain in 1809.

Compans. Chief-of-Staff. General in 1799, he distinguished himself at Austerlitz and at Jena. Soult's Chief-of-Staff on 27 September 1806. He was made Major-General in November. He served with Davout in 1811, was wounded at the Moskova and again in 1813. He contributed to the

THE INFANTRY OF THE LINE WEARING WHITE COATS

Voltigeur from the 14th Infantry Regiment.

Fusilier from the 17th Infantry Regiment according to a drawing by the Burger of Hamburg.

Fusilier from the 28th Infantry Regiment.

Fusilier from the 33rd Infantry Regiment.

Voltigeur from the 3rd Infantry Regiment.

Sapper from the 14th Infantry Regiment. This regiment was wiped out at Eylau.

Grenadier from the 15th Infantry Regiment.

Drummer from the Voltigeur company of the 17th Infantry Regiment. The white coats were only worn by the parts of the companies to whom they had been issued.

Maréchal Soult commanding the 4th Corps of the Grande Armée, his Chief-of-Staff Compans and Legrand, one of his divisionaires. (RMN and RR)

defence of Paris and was made GdCxLH in 1814. Retired and Peer in 1815, he voted for Ney's execution.

His aide de camp was **Battalion Commander Bonnin**. Awarded the LH in 1809, he retired for health reasons in 1814.

Destabenrath. Assistant Chief-of-Staff. A veteran of Marengo, he had this post under Ney from 1805 to 1806 before joining Saint-Hilaire's staff then Soult's in 1 May 1807. He was made a General three months later, then Baron in 1808, CtLH in 1809 and CSL in 1814. He was retired in 1832.

Remond. Appointed Battalion Commander in the Engineers on 5 January 1807, he became Chief-of-Staff for the 4th Corps Engineers on the following 13 February. Wounded at Heilsberg, he nevertheless captured a Prussian battalion fleeing towards Königsberg. He went to Spain with Soult where he was made a General in 1811 and a Baron in 1813. Wounded, he was put on sick leave on 18 December of the same year. CSL in 1814, he retired in 1825. GdOLH in 1831.

Rouyer de Saint-Victor. Adjudant-Commandant, a former Marengo veteran, he was made a General in 1808 and retired in 1814.

The Corps' artillery was commanded by **General Lariboisière**. A General in 1803, he was made Major-General and Commander in Chief of the Artillery of the Guard on 3 January 1807. Dulauloy replaced him. GdOLH the same year, he was a Count in 1808. GdCx of the Couronne de Fer in 1809, he died of exhaustion in 1812.

Dulauloy. He was made a General in 1794 and Major-General in 1803, Chevalier in 1810, Count in 1811. GdCx of the Reunion in 1813, Couronne de Fer in 1814 and GdCxLH in 1815. He retired in 1815.

● **SAINT-HILAIRE'S DIVISION**

Saint-Hilaire. A veteran of Toulon and Italy, he was one of the great architects of the victory at Austerlitz for which he was awarded the Grand Aigle of the LH. A cannonball took his left foot off at Essling and he died from his wound. The Emperor had promised him a Maréchal's baton.

His aide de camp was **Captain Boudin de Roville**. Wounded at Eylau and Wagram, he was made CrSL in 1821 and GdOLH in 1825.

— **Candras' Brigade**

Candras. He was made a General and CtLH in 1804. He fought at Austerlitz, Eylau, Heilsberg and in front of Königsberg. He was killed at the Berezina.

The Brigade was made up of the 10th Light and the 36th of the Line.

The 10th Light
Colonel Pouzet. LH in 1804, wounded at Austerlitz, Jena and Eylau and Made a General on 10 February 1807. Made a Baron in 1808, he was killed by a bullet in the forehead at Essling.

Colonel Berthézène took over from Pouget, promoted to General. A Baron in 1808, he was appointed General in 1811 and Major-General in 1813.

The 36th of the Line
Colonel Berlier. He came from the Guard. Made a Colonel on 20 October 1806 and OLH. He was wounded at Eylau, made a Baron in 1810, then a General the following year. Wounded at Toulouse, he was made a Chevalier de Saint Louis in 1815.

— **Varé's Brigade**

Varé. Made a General in 1803, he was made CtLH in 1804, wounded at Eylau and killed at Thorn in 1807. He was replaced by Buget.

Buget. A Toulon veteran, he was awarded at Sabre of Honour and made a General in 1799, then CtLH on 1804. He was appointed on the 29 March. He was Heilsberg and wounded at Königsberg. Made a Baron in 1808, he served in 1815 and was retired in 1823.

The brigade consisted of the 43rd and 55th of the Line

The 43rd of the Line
Colonel Lemarois. He came from the 4th Corps staff. He was made OLH in 1804 and CtLH in the following year. He was made Regimental Colonel on 27 December 1805 and was killed at the Battle of Eylau. He was replaced by Baussain.

Colonel Baussain. Was awarded the LH in 1804. Wounded at Austerlitz, he refused to be taken care of and continued fighting. Made Colonel of the 43rd on the morrow of Eylau, he was wounded at Heilsberg. He was made a Baron and CtLH in 1808. Killed in Spain in 1811.

The 55th of the Line
Colonel Silbermann. At the head of the regiment since 1805, he was killed at Eylau. Perier replaced him.

Colonel Perier. LH in 1804, he was wounded at Austerlitz. Killed at Heilsberg and replaced by Colonel Schwiter.

● **LEVAL'S THEN CARRA-SAINT-CYR'S DIVISION**

Leval. General in 1795, he was made Major-General in 1799. He organised the Duke of Enghien's arrest. Wounded at Eylau, he was replaced by Carra-St-Cyr. He was taken prisoner in Spain in 1808 and led the escape from the hulk, Vieille Castille. He distinguished himself in the Iberian Peninsula and in France in 1814. Retired in 1832.

Carra-Saint-Cyr. Fought in America in 1782. General in 1795, he was in Turkey in 1797, took part in Marengo. He replaced Leval on 24 February 1807 and was made GdOLH in 1807 then a Baron in 1808, Count in 1814. Retired in 1815, he was Administrator of Guyana in 1817.

— **Schiner's Brigade**

Schiner. General in 1800, made CtLH in 1804, he distinguished himself at Eylau and was made a Baron the following year. He served in 1815 and was retired as Honorary Lieutenant-General in 1818, then again in 1832.

The 24th Light
Colonel Pourailly. Served in the Foot Grenadiers of the Consular Guard. Wounded twice at Eylau, made Baron in 1808, he lost his left arm at Wagram, was made a General in 1811 then CtLH in 1813. He was put on the non-active list for invalidity in August 1813 and finally retired in 1825.

Ferey's Brigade

Ferey, Baron de Rosengath. He served in the Vendée and at Marengo, appointed General in 1803 and CtLH in 1804. Wounded at Heilsberg, he was made a Baron and Major-General in 1813. Killed at Los Arapiles in 1812.

The brigade was made up of the 4th and the 28th of the Line.

The 4th of the Line
Colonel Boyledieu. Wounded at Heilsberg, he was made a Baron in 1808 and a General in 1811. He went over to the Young Guard in 1812 and died at Toulon in 1815.

The 28th of the Line
Colonel Toussaint. Replaced Colonel Edighoffen at the head of the 28th on 31 December 1806. He was a veteran of Italy, was made a Baron in 1809 and a General in 1813, fought at Ligny in 1815 then was put on the non-active list. Made Viscount in 1822, served in Spain in 1823, made GdOLH and CrSL in 1825. Available in 1826.

— **Viviès' Brigade**

Viviès de la Prade. OLH in 1804, he was made a General in 1805 after distinguishing himself at Austerlitz at the head of the 43rd of the Line. He replaced Schiner on 13 March 1806. He captured the Eylau cemetery during the fighting for Ziegelhof and distinguished himself the following day. He was wounded at Heilsberg and made a Baron in 1808. He was captured at Vilna in Russia and died of fever in February 1813.

The brigade comprised the 46th and 57th of the Line

The 46th of the Line
Colonel Latrille de Lorencez. Made a General in 1807 and a Baron in 1808, he went over to Gudin in 1809 and became Oudinot's son-in-law in 1811. He served with his father-in-law in 1812, was made Major-General in 1813 before being seriously wounded at Bautzen. Made GdOLH in 1814, he served in 1815, was awarded the CrSL in 1822 and was put in the reserve in 1839.

Colonel Richard. Appointed Colonel of the 46th on 12 February 1807, he replaced Latrille.

THE LIGHT INFANTRY

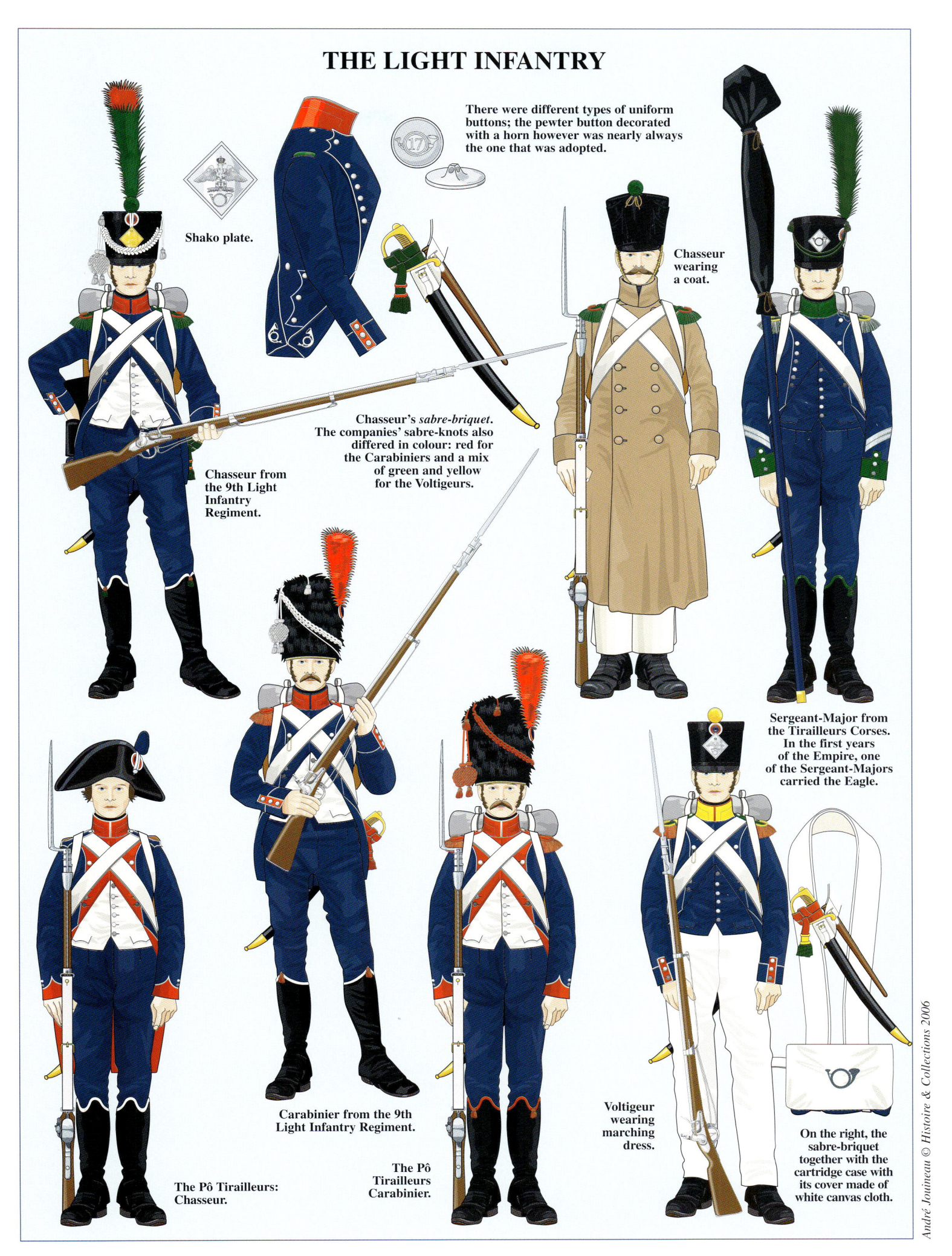

Shako plate.

There were different types of uniform buttons; the pewter button decorated with a horn however was nearly always the one that was adopted.

Chasseur's *sabre-briquet*. The companies' sabre-knots also differed in colour: red for the Carabiniers and a mix of green and yellow for the Voltigeurs.

Chasseur from the 9th Light Infantry Regiment.

Chasseur wearing a coat.

Sergeant-Major from the Tirailleurs Corses. In the first years of the Empire, one of the Sergeant-Majors carried the Eagle.

The Pô Tirailleurs: Chasseur.

Carabinier from the 9th Light Infantry Regiment.

The Pô Tirailleurs Carabinier.

Voltigeur wearing marching dress.

On the right, the sabre-briquet together with the cartridge case with its cover made of white canvas cloth.

From left to right and top to bottom:
Generals Barbanègre, Gudin de la Sablonnière, Claparède, Suchet and Marulaz. (RR)

Awarded the LH in 1804, he was made OLH in 1807. He died defending the village of Essling on 21 May 1809.

The 57th of the Line

Colonel Rey: He replaced Brun who had been promoted to General. He was made CtLH on 25 December 1805 and took part at Jena, Eylau and Heilsberg. He was made a General and a Chevalier of the Couronne de Fer in 1806. He fought in Spain and was at Toulouse in 1814; retired in 1832.

● LEGRAND'S DIVISION

Legrand. A General in 1793, he was promoted to Major-General in 1799. He drew attention to himself at Hohenlinden and was brilliant at Austerlitz. He was made Grand Aigle of the LH in 1806 and fought at Jena, Eylau and Heilsberg. He became a Count in 1808. He was seriously wounded at the Berezina and was made a Peer and CrSL in 1814. He died in 1815 as a result of his wounds.

Ledru des Essarts' Brigade

Ledru des Essarts. A former veteran of Italy, he was brilliant at Austerlitz and was promoted to General on 25 December 1805. He then replaced Merle at the head of his brigade. He was seriously wounded at Eylau and left for dead but nonetheless distinguished himself at Heilsberg and during the taking of Königsberg. He was made Baron des Essarts in 1809 and Major-General in 1811. In 1814 he protested against Marmont's Corps which defected. Chevalier of SL in 1814, he was GdCxLH in 1827 and retired in 1832.

The brigade comprised the 26th Light and the 18th of the Line.

The 26th Light

Colonel Pouget. Appointed to command the regiment on 1 February 1805. He was at Austerlitz, Hoff, Eylau and Heilsberg. He was made a Baron and a General in 1809. His left knee was shot off at Aspern. Wounded at Polotsk and Vitebsk where he was captured. He was at Toulon in 1815, retired in 1816. Made GdOLH in 1831 and retired again in 1832.

The 18th of the Line

Colonel Ravier. A veteran of Egypt, he became a Colonel in 1801. He was one of the members of the commission which judged the Duke of Enghien.

He was made CtLH in 1805 and a General in 1809. He served with Brune in 1815 and retired the same year.

— Levasseur's Brigade

Levasseur. Made a general in 1800, he was CtLH in 1804. Austerlitz then wounded at Eylau, he was replaced by Lamartinière. Baron in 1808, he died in 1811.

His aide de camp was **Canavas**, called **St-Amand**. Wounded at Eylau then at the Moskova. OLH, he served with the Dragoons of the Guard in 1813, with the 5th Dragoons in 1814 and served in 1814. Retired in 1821, he was made Maréchal de Camp in 1832 and made CrLH in 1835 and put in the reserve in 1839.

Lamartinière. Colonel in the 50th of the Line, he was made CtLH on 25 December 1805. His brilliant conduct at Eylau earned him the rank of General on the following 10 February. He was made a Baron in 1808. In Spain he was Marmont's Chief-of-Staff. Promoted to Major-General he was mortally wounded at la Bidassoa in 1813.

The brigade was made up of the 75th of the Line as well as the Battalion of Tirailleurs Corses and that of the Pô Tirailleurs.

The 75th of the Line

Colonel Lhuillier. A veteran of Rivoli and Egypt, he was wounded at Austerlitz. Wounded again at Hoff on 6 February 1807 he was made a General a few days later and replaced in the regiment by Colonel Buquet. He was made Chevalier of the Couronne de Fer in 1807 and a Baron the following year. Major-General in 1811, Chevalier of SL in 1814 and retired the same year.

Colonel Buquet. Aide de camp to Ney in 1799, he was wounded at Heilsberg. He was made a Baron in 1808, captured at Talavera but escaped from the hulk ships at Cadiz. Seriously wounded at the Moskova, he was made Major-General on the following 23 September. Made CtLH in 1813 and Chevalier of SL in 1819, he was retired in 1825.

The Tirailleurs Corses

They were commanded by **Battalion Commander d'Ornano**, a cousin of Bonaparte and a future Maréchal de France, up until 23 November 1806.

Battalion Commander Morandini took over from him. Wounded at Austerlitz, he was awarded the LH in 1806. Wounded twice at Eylau as well as at Heilsberg. In 1809 he was wounded at Ebersberg and captured by the Austrians but was freed once the peace treaty was signed. He was made Chevalier de SL in 1817 and died in 1831.

The Pô Tirailleurs

Battalion Commander Hulot was in command. Aide de camp to Soult in 1803, he was also in command of the battalion of the Tirailleurs du Pô. He was wounded at Austerlitz then at Eylau. He was made a Colonel in 1808 and *Chevalier de l'Empire* in 1810, General in 1812 and Baron in 1813. During the Hundred Days, he commanded Bourmont's division when the latter defected, and fought at Ligny and Wavre. He was retired in 1848.

— Guyot's Light Cavalry Brigade

Guyot. A cousin of the Guyot in the Guard, he came from the 9th Hussars and replaced Margaron from 7 November 1806. He was OLH in 1804 and a General in 1805. Took part at Guttstadt and Eylau but was killed on 8 June 1807 during the fighting at Kleinenfeld.

The brigade comprised the 8th Hussars as well as the 16th, 26th and 22nd Chasseurs.

The 8th Hussars

Colonel Laborde. Wounded at Jena and killed at Wagram.

The 16th Chasseurs

Colonel Maupoint. He was Regimental Colonel from 13 January 1806, was made a Baron in 1808, a General in 1811 and CtLH in 1814. He was allowed to retire in 1816.

The 22nd Chasseurs

Colonel Bordessoulle. He was awarded a Sabre of Honour in 1802, wounded on 9 June 1806 at Guttstadt, appointed General two weeks later, a Baron in 1810 but seriously wounded at the Moskova then made Major-General on 4 December 1812. He was made a Count in 1816, GdCxSL in 1821. He served in Spain and was made a Peer in 1823. He was retired in 1832.

During the campaign the regiment was attached to Durosnel's Brigade within the Light Cavalry Division of the Reserve.

The regiment was at Hoff, Eylau, Guttstadt, Heilsberg and Friedland.

LANNES' THEN MASSÉNA'S 5th CORPS

Masséna had been recalled from Naples where he had cleaned up Calabria thus reassuring Joseph. He joined the Emperor at Osterode and was given command of the 5th Corps in place of Savary who was already replacing Lannes who had been wounded. The latter was ill and depressed but was given back command for the march on Friedland where he regained his enthusiasm and Napoleon's friendship. Masséna stayed on the Omulev, in the direction of the Narev, and defended

LIGHT INFANTRY

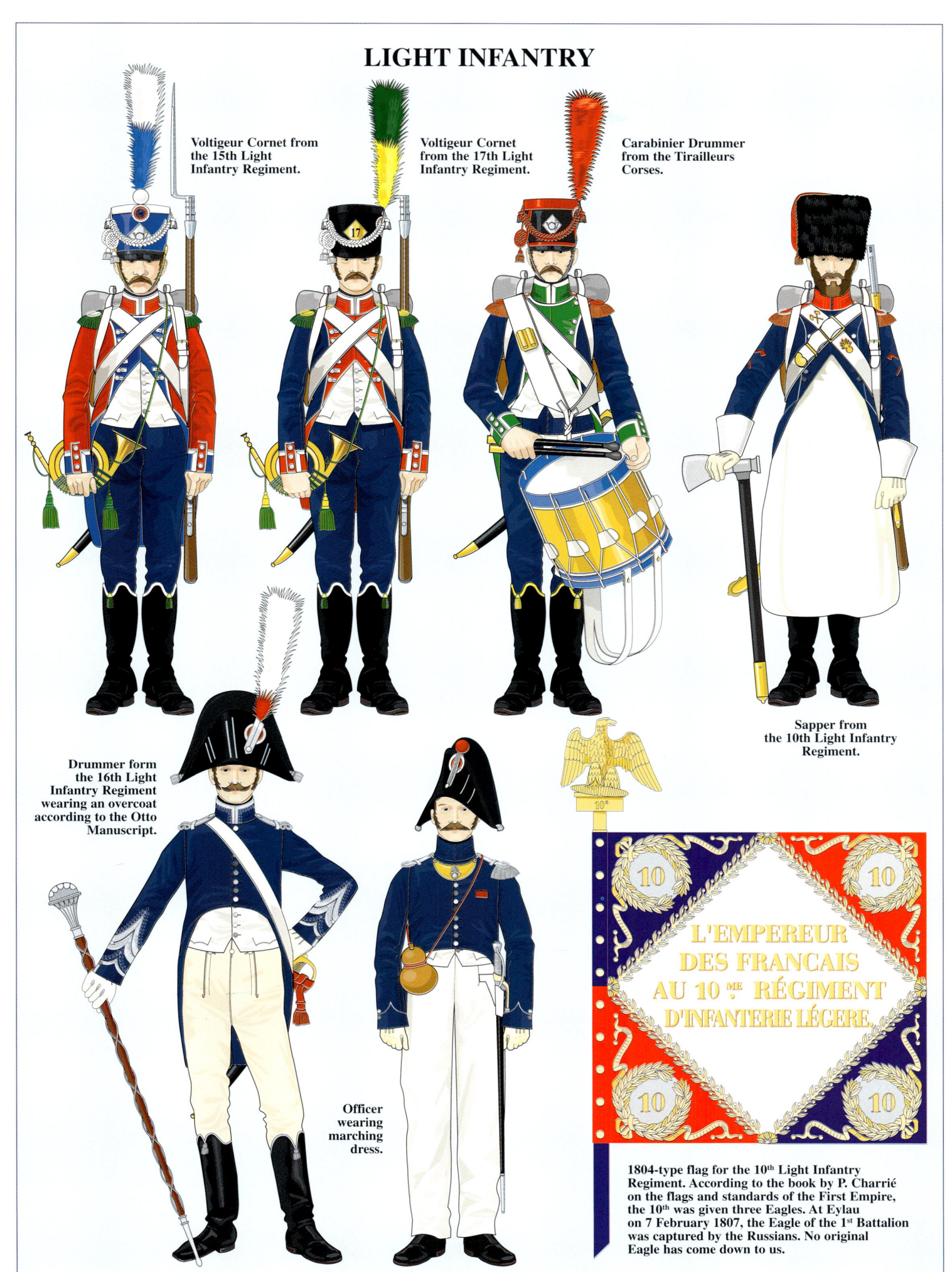

Voltigeur Cornet from the 15th Light Infantry Regiment.

Voltigeur Cornet from the 17th Light Infantry Regiment.

Carabinier Drummer from the Tirailleurs Corses.

Sapper from the 10th Light Infantry Regiment.

Drummer form the 16th Light Infantry Regiment wearing an overcoat according to the Otto Manuscript.

Officer wearing marching dress.

1804-type flag for the 10th Light Infantry Regiment. According to the book by P. Charrié on the flags and standards of the First Empire, the 10th was given three Eagles. At Eylau on 7 February 1807, the Eagle of the 1st Battalion was captured by the Russians. No original Eagle has come down to us.

himself at Ostrolenka at the far right of the French line. The corps included the two French divisions under Suchet and Gazan, and the Bavarians under de Wrède and Deroy together with Montbrun's cavalry and the Wurtemburg reinforcements. His task was to hold Pultusk, Sierock and Ostrolenka against Essen. He had to cover Warsaw and threaten the isolated Russians.

Savary commanded the 5th Corps from 31 January to 3 March 1807 when he was replaced by Masséna. The victor at Ostrolenka, he was made GdCxLH on 25 February 1807. He served at Heilsberg and at Friedland where he was in command of the Fusiliers of the Guard. He was made Duke of Rovigo in 1808. A victim of Malet in 1812, he was imprisoned for several hours. A Peer in 1815, he was then outlawed and sentenced to death. He fled to Smyrna, then Graz then finally London. Acquitted in 1819, he was in Rome in 1823 then was in command in Africa in 1831. He died in 1833.

● SUCHET'S DIVISION

Suchet. Grand Aigle of he LH in 1806, made a Maréchal in 1811, then Duke of Albuhera in 1812. He replaced Bessières in 1813 and commanded the Army of Aragon and of Catalonia. During the Hundred Days, he commanded the Army of the Alps and freed Savoy; he was then made a Peer in 1815, struck of the list of Peers and then reinstated in 1819.

The division's Chief-of-Staff was **Reille**, replacing Victor on 31 December 1806. He was Napoleon's aide de camp at Friedland. He was sent to keep an eye on Bernadotte in 1809, was made a Peer and GdCxLH in 1815; he fought at Quatre-Bras and at Waterloo. Maréchal de France and Senator in 1847, he was awarded the Military Medal in 1852. He married Masséna's daughter.

Saint-Cyr-Nugues was Suchet's aide de camp from 1802 and he became his Chief-of-Staff in 1808. He was made a Baron and a General in 1811. He served in the Alps in 1815. He was at Antwerp and was made a Peer in 1832 then GdCxLH in 1833. In the reserve in 1840.

Mesclop. Battalion Commander, he was on Suchet's staff from the time of the camp at St Omer. He was at Austerlitz, Saafeld, Jena and Pultusk. He was made OLH in 1811 and a General in 1813 in the Army of Aragon; retired in 1826, he was in the reserve in 1839.

— Claparède's Brigade

Claparède. A veteran of Italy, Saint Domingo and Dominica, he was made a General in 1802. He distinguished himself at Austerlitz where he directed the defence of the Santon. Wounded at Pultusk, he was at Ostrolenka; Count in 1808, he was appointed Major-General in the same year. He was in Spain with Oudinot then in Austria in 1809 where he distinguished himself again. He organised the Legion of the Vistula and commanded it and was made GdCxLH in 1815; he was one of Ney's judges. Peer in 1819.

This brigade formed the vanguard of the division and was only made up of the famous 17th Light.

The 17th Light

Colonel Cabanes de Puymisson. OLH in 1807, he was made a Baron in 1808 then General in 1810. He was retired in 1815.

— Dumoustier's Brigade

Dumoustier. A veteran of Marengo, he was Colonel of the 34th of the Line when he was made a General on 30 December 1806 for his conduct at Jena and Pultusk. He then replaced Reille in this post before serving under Mortier. Made a Baron in 1808, he was appointed Second Colonel under Curial with the Chasseurs à Pied of the Guard, then Major-General in 1811. Awarded the Order of the Couronne de Fer and made a Count, he was wounded at Dresden. GdOLH in 1831, he died following the amputation of his thigh after an accident.

The brigade comprised the 34th and 40th of the Line.

The 34th of the Line

Colonel Remond (called Remonda) replaced Dumoustier at the head of the regiment. He was made a Baron and CtLH in 1809 then a General in 1811. In 1814 he commanded a brigade of National Guards in Lyon. In 1815 he served in the Indre. Retired in 1825 then in 1832.

The 40th of the Line

Colonel Chassereaux. He was the Regimental Colonel since the beginning of 1806, he was made OLH in 1807, then Baron and CtLH in 1809. He was wounded several times in Spain and was made a general in 1811; in March 1814, he was responsible for organising mass conscription in the Loiret Department. Retired in 1825.

● GAZAN'S DIVISION

Gazan. Made a General in April 1799, he was then made a Major-General at Zürich on the battlefield by Masséna on the following 25 September. He was with Masséna at Genoa, then with Suchet and with Lannes. He distinguished himself at Pultusk and Ostrolenka on 16 February 1807. A Count in 1808, he was with Soult in Spain. GdCxLH in February 1815. He was opposed to Napoleon's return but served him in the 14th Military District. On the non-active list, retired in 1825, he was made a Peer in 1831 then retired again in 1832.

After fighting under Lannes, the division was placed in reserve occupying Sierock, Pultusk and Ostrolenka in order to protect Warsaw under Masséna. It remained covering Warsaw, and in reserve on the Narev and the Omulev during the last offensive towards Friedland.

— Campana's Brigade

Campana. Born in the Piedmont, he went into French service in 1794 and served in the Army of Italy. He was made a General and CtLH in 1805. Killed at the Battle of Ostrolenka. Taupin replaced him.

Taupin. Wounded at Marengo, he was awarded a Sabre of Honour in 1802 and was made CtLH in 1805. He distinguished himself at Ostrolenka and was promoted to General to replace Campana on 21 February 1807. He was made a Baron in 1808 and left for Spain. Made a Major-General in 1813, he was mortally wounded by eight shots during the Battle of Toulouse.

The brigade comprised the 21st Light and the 100th of the Line.

The 21st Light

Colonel Duhamel. A veteran of Italy and Egypt, he was wounded at St John of Acre. He was awarded the LH in 1804 and was raised to CtLH the following year. He died in Warsaw from a wound he got at Ostrolenka and was replaced by Lagarde.

Lagarde. A veteran of the Sambre and Meuse, and of Italy, he was wounded at Austerlitz. He was made a Baron and went to Spain in 1808 and distinguished himself during the whole of the campaign. He was made a General in 1813. On the non-active list, he received the CSL. He served during the Hundred Days and was wounded during the Namur affair. Put on the non-active list in 1818.

The 100th of the Line

Colonel Quiot du Passage. Wounded at Rivoli, he was Victor's aide de camp in 1798 and distinguished himself at Marengo. He left for Spain and was made a Baron in 1808. He was made a General in 1811, he fought in Germany where he was wounded and captured at Külm. He returned, was made CSL in 1814. He served during the Hundred Days and fought at Waterloo. He was made GdOLH in 1818 and retired in 1831.

— Graindorge's Brigade

Graindorge. A veteran of the Sambre and Meuse and in the Army of Helvetia, he was made a General in 1805. He was brilliant at Ostrolenka. He left to serve in Spain. He was made a Baron and CtLH in 1809 but was mortally wounded the following year at Busaco.

The brigade was made up of the 28th Light and the 103rd of the Line.

The 28th Light

Colonel Abbé. Holder of the Sabre and Pistols of Honour, he became aide de camp to Leclerc whom he followed to Saint Dominica. He was made a General on 1 March 1807 and was replaced in the regiment by Thierry. He went to serve in Naples, in Italy then in Spain in 1810 where he was made a Baron. He was promoted to Major-General in 1812. Under Lecourbe in 1815, he defeated the Austrians at Dannemarie on 27 June. He was retired in 1816.

Thierry. LH in 1804, he replaced Abbé when the latter became a General. He took part in the Austrian Campaign in 1809 with the Army of Italy and was killed at the Battle of Raab.

The 103rd of the Line

Colonel Taupin. He was in command of the regiment until he was promoted to head the 1st Brigade of Gazan's division. He was replaced by Rignoux.

Rignoux. He drew attention to himself at Eylau and was made a Baron in 1810, a General in 1811, CtLH in 1813, and CSL in 1814. He retired in 1819.

— Treillard's Light Cavalry Brigade

Treillard. Made a General in 1799, then CtLH in 1804, he was brilliant at Saafeld, wounded at Pultusk and made Major-General on 30 December 1806 and authorised to return to France. He was made a Baron in 1810, served in Portugal and in Spain. He returned in 1814 and served in Champagne at the head of a division of dragoons in Kellermann's 6th Corps. He was retired in 1815.

Debelle. A veteran of the Sambre and Meuse, made a General in 1805, replaced Treillard on 27 December 1806 then went over to the 3rd Division of Milhaud's Dragoons on 17 March 1807. He was made CtLH the same year and a Baron in 1809. After having suffered setbacks in Spain he was put on the non-active list then retired in 1812. In 1815, he was wounded fighting the Duke of Angoulême and was then outlawed. He was sentenced to death and then pardoned by Louis XVIII; he was reinstated with his rank and retired.

Montbrun. Distinguished himself at Austerlitz under Davout and was made a General on 24 December 1805. He was in command of the Wurtemburg cavalry in Vandamme's 5th Corps then was transferred to Jerome's 9th Corps in November 1806. He replaced Debelle on 17 March 1807 at the head of the cavalry brigade in Masséna's 5th Corps. He was made a baron in 1808 and charged with his Polish Chevau-Légers at Somosierra. He was made a Major-General in 1809, then a Count and a Chevalier of the Couronne de Fer. In 1810, he commanded the cavalry of the Army of Portugal. GdOLH in 1811. In Russia he commanded the 2nd reserve cavalry corps and was killed at the Moskova.

Montbrun was one of the Empire's best light cavalry commanders.

The brigade was made up of the 9th and 10th Hussars and the 21st Chasseurs à cheval.

The 9th Hussars

THE ARTILLERY

Trooper from the Horse Artillery.

Trooper from the Horse Artillery wearing campaign dress according to the Burger of Hamburg Manuscript.

Horse Artillery Trumpeter.

Artillery train driver.

Second-Lieutenant in the Artillery.

Gunner according to the Burger of Hamburg.

Drummer according to the Burger of Hamburg.

Driver of the *Train des équipages* at the time they were created in 1807.

Opposite, from left to right and top to bottom.
Maréchal Masséna, Generals Gazan, d'Ornano and de Wrède. (RR)

Right.
Maréchal Ney, commanding the 6th Corps of the Grande Armée. (RMN)

Colonel Gauthrin. A veteran of Toulon and Italy, he succeeded Colonel Barbanègre (no relation of the Barbanègre in the 48th of the Line) who was killed at Jena. He transferred to Oudinot's division on 5th May 1807. He was hit by a bullet in the forehead at Friedland, was made a Baron in 1808. He took part in the Russian Campaign during which he was captured. He only returned to France in August 1814. During the Hundred Days, he fought at Ligny then was put on the non-active list. He was retired in 1825.

The 10th Hussars

Colonel Briche. He served in the Army of Italy and fought at Marengo. He distinguished himself at Saafeld. He left for Spain in 1808 and was made a Baron and a General the following year. He was called back and distinguished himself in Germany in 1813 and was promoted to Major-General. He was brilliant during the Campaign for France and was made a Viscount in 1815, then GdOLH in 1821. Available in 1822.

Among its Colonels, the 10th Hussars included the future Generals Rigau and Beaumont and the legendary Lasalle.

The 21st Chasseurs

Colonel Berruyer. A veteran of Italy, he was wounded at la Trebia and at the crossing of the Mincio. Made OLH in 1808, he distinguished himself at Jena where the Emperor publicly congratulated him on the battlefield. He retired in 1808 and was made a Baron the same year.

● LORGE'S DRAGOON DIVISION

Lorge's (ex-Beker) 5th Dragoon Division was attached to Masséna's 5th Corps.

Lorge. General in 1797, he served in the Army of the Sambre and Meuse, in that of Helvetia then in that of Italy. He was made a Major-General in 1799. He replaced Beker, who had become Masséna's Chief-of-Staff on 25 May 1807. A Baron in 1811, he served in Spain and in Russia. He was available in February 1814 and was made CSL and GdOLH in the same year. He retired in 1825.

The division was made up of the 13th, 15th, 22nd and 25th Regiments of Dragoons.

The 13th Dragoons

Colonel Laroche. A former Guide in the Army of Italy, he served in Egypt where he distinguished himself at Heliopolis. He was awarded the LH in 1804. He took command of the regiment on 20 September 1806. He was made OLH in 1807 and a Baron in 1808. He left for Spain but died of illness at Talavera at the end of 1809.

The 15th Dragoons

Colonel Barthélémi. A former Squadron Commander in Bonaparte's Guides, he served in Egypt. He was made OLH in 1804. Took part at Austerlitz, was wounded at Pultusk, made a General in 1807 and a Baron in 1808. In 1814, he was awarded the CSL. He was retired in 1815.

Colonel Treuille de Beaulieu. LH in 1804, he was in the Grenadiers à cheval in 1805; OLH in 1806, he replaced Laroche who had been made a General. He was made Baron de Beaulieu in 1808 then was retired for invalidity in 1809. He was elected Mayor of Sélestat in 1811.

The 22nd Dragoons

Colonel Carrié de Boissy. Took part in the arrest of the Duke d'Enghien. He was CtLH in 1805, then a General on 4 April 1807. He was then replaced by Frossard. Wounded at Friedland, he went to fight in Portugal and Spain. He was made a Baron in 1810, then put on the non-active list then retired in 1815.

Colonel Frossard. He served in the Army of Italy, awarded the LH in 1805, he was made Regimental Colonel on 5 April 1807. He was made a Baron in 1808; he left for Spain and was retired in 1809.

The 25th Dragoons

Colonel Rigau. Wounded at Jemmapes in 1792, he refused the rank of General two years later. He served in Italy and was at Marengo, made CtLH in 1805, he was made a General in 1807, and then wounded at Ostrolenka. He was made a Baron in 1809; He was brilliant during the Campaign for France. He was awarded the CSL upon the King's return. He took part actively in the Eagle's return then was outlawed and sentenced to death and went into exile in the Champs d'Asile in Texas.

Colonel Ornano. A cousin of Bonaparte, he took part in the Saint Dominica expedition before becoming Berthier's aide de camp in 1804 and distinguishing himself at Austerlitz and at Jena. He was made Colonel of the 25th Dragoons to replace Rigau who had been made a General in 1807, then a Count in 1808 and a General in 1811. In Russia, he distinguished himself at the Moskova and was made Major-General. He transferred to the Dragoons of the Guard in 1813 and commanded them during the Hundred Days. He married Marie Walewska in 1816. He was Commandeur of SL in 1829, a Peer in 1832, GdCxLH in 1850, Gd Chancelier of the LH in 1852. He was awarded the Military Medal in 1853 and was made a Maréchal in 1861.

In order to reinforce the 5th Corps during its operations on the right flank of the French army, some of Jérôme's 9th Corps units were attached to it while he continued the occupation of Silesia with a series of sieges. **The reinforcements** were De Wrède's and Deroy's Bavarians, i.e.

Infantry: The 2nd, 3rd, 4th, 7th, 13th and 14th Regiments and four light battalions.

Cavalry: The 2nd Dragoon Regiment and the 3rd Chevau-Légers Regiment

A **Wurtemburg Division** with its horsemen.

The foreigners came either from Jérôme's 9th Corps or from Brune's Coastal Observation Corps with two French divisions, two Dutch divisions of which a part had been detached from the siege at Danzig, and one Spanish (la Romana).

MARÉCHAL NEY'S 6th CORPS

The Chief-of-Staff was **Du Bosc Dutaillis.** A former Italy and Egypt veteran, he was awarded Pistols of honour. He was a General after 1803 and a cannonball took off one of his arms on 9 June 1807 at Guttstadt. He was made a Major-General on 29 June. He was made a Count the following year and was awarded the Couronne de Fer. Retired in 1815, he was made a Peer in 1832, GdCxLH in 1845.

The Assistant Chief-of-Staff was **Mallerot** who was mortally wounded at Guttstadt.

The Maréchal's aides de camp were **Béchet de Léocour**. Squadron Commander, he had already been Ney's aide de camp in 1803 and was to be so again in Spain. He was made OLH and a Baron in 1808. He was made a General in 1814, retired in 1831.

La Boissière. He was in Ney's service from 1806 to 1812. He was made a General and OLH in 1813. He died of his wounds the same year.

Caillemer. Squadron Commander, he was sent to Spain with the 26th Chasseurs on 18 March 1807. Made OLH in 1808 and Chevalier in 1811, he was in Hamburg in 1813 and 1814. He served at Waterloo where he was wounded and captured.

Colonel Becqueley commanded the Corps' artillery.

● MARCHAND'S DIVISION

Marchand. Made a General in Italy in place of Joubert who was killed at Novi. He was made a Major-General on 24 December 1805. He transferred to the 6th Corps with Ney instead of Loison. On 6 June he fought at Deppen then at Friedland. Gd Aigle of the LH, followed Ney to Spain.

THE BAVARIANS

The Bavarian infantry formed two divisions within the 9th Army Corps and one division in the 5th Army Corps according to the 1 April 1807 report on the Grande Armée.

Corporal from Prince Karl's 3rd Infantry Regiment.

Drummer from the 2nd Infantry Regiment, Prince Royal.

1803-model flag. *Top:* blue on the reverse (identical on the obverse) of the battalion flag. *Bottom:* white obverse (identical on the reverse) for the "Colonel's" flag.

Von Preysing's 5th Infantry Regiment.

Saxe-Hilburghausen 4th Infantry Regiment.

Soldier and officer of Duke William's 6th Infantry Regiment.

129

André Jouineau © Histoire & Collections 2006

From left to right and top to bottom.
Generals Marchand, Auguste de Colbert, Bisson and Gardane. *(RR)*

— Vilatte's, Liger Belair's THEN Maucune's Brigade

Vilatte. Comte d'Outremont, made a General in 1803 and commanded the 1st Brigade of Bisson's division before transferring to Marchand's in February 1807. He was made a Major General on 25 February and went over to Bernadotte's 1st Corps.

Liger Belair. He replaced Villatte at the head of the 1st Brigade. He had been made a Brigadier-General in November 1806. He was replaced on 28 March 1807 by Maucune. He then left for Spain where he was captured at Baylen, but was made Major-General in 1811. He was made a Viscount in 1816, GdOLH in 1820 and GdCSL in 1826. He was retired in 1827 then again in 1832.

Maucune. A veteran of Arcola and Marengo, coming from the 39th of the Line whose Colonel he was. He was CtLH on 25 December 1805 and a General on 10 March 1807. He was made a Baron and Chevalier of the Croix de Fer in 1808, Major-General in 1811 and CSL in 1814. He was retired in 1818.

The brigade was made up of the 6th Light and the 39th of the Line.

The 6th Light

Colonel Laplane. A veteran of Italy, he distinguished himself in Egypt where his conduct at St John of Acre earned him a Sabre of Honour. He was made Brigadier-General in July 1807. He was made a Baron and a Major-General in 1810. He retired in August 1815 and was made GdOLH in 1835.

The regiment distinguished itself all during the campaign and thereafter bore the names Eylau and Friedland on its standard.

The 39th of the Line

Colonel Maucune was in command at first but he was replaced by Colonel Soyer when he was appointed to head the 1st Brigade of the 1st Division under General Marchand on 10 March 1807.

— Roguet's THEN Marcognet's Brigade

Roguet. A veteran of Italy he was made a General in 1803 in the second brigade of Marchand's division. He transferred to the 2nd Division under Bisson on 3 March 1807. He was wounded and captured at Guttstadt but freed after Tilsitt. He was made a Baron in 1808 and went over to the Imperial Guard in 1809. A Major-General in 1811 he served in Spain and in Russia. He commanded the infantry in the Old Guard at the beginning of 1813 and served under Maison in Belgium in 1814 and then was made a Chevalier. He fought at Waterloo as a Colonel in the Grenadiers. He was made GdCxLH and a Peer in 1831.

Marcognet. He had served in America from 1781 to 1783. Wounded at Hohenlinden, he was made a General in 1803. He commanded the 1st Brigade of Gardane's division then transferred to Marchand's 2nd Brigade. He was made a Baron in 1808 and then Major-General in 1811. CSL and GdOLH in 1814. He fought at Waterloo and was retired in 1832.

General Desenfans coming from the 8th Corps only stayed for a few days with the 6th Corps before being assigned to the siege of Danzig under Lefebvre. He died of illness at Mainz the following year.

The brigade comprised the 69th and 76th of the Line.

The 69th of the Line

Colonel Brun. Wounded at Toulon, he served in Italy and in Egypt. He was made CtLH in 1805, a General on 10 March 1807. He took command of the 3rd Brigade of the 1st Division which only comprised the 31st Light. Wounded at Friedland, he left to fight in Spain. He was made a Baron in 1810 and CSL in 1814. He was retired in 1815.

Colonel Fririon. He was made Regimental Colonel following Brun's promotion. Wounded by a Biscayen bullet at Friedland, he next left to fight in Portugal and Spain. He was made a Baron and OLH in 1808, General in 1811 and CSL in 1814. Retired in 1833.

76th of the Line

Colonel Faure (called Faure-Lanjonquière). A veteran of Italy, he became a Captain in the Grenadiers of the Consular Guard in 1800 then Battalion Commander the following year. He was made the Regimental Colonel in 1803, then OLH in 1804 and CtLH in 1805. Wounded at Friedland, he died the following day.

— Brun's Brigade

General Brun (see 69th of the Line)

This brigade was created on 1 April 1807 and only comprised the 31st Light.

The 31st Light

Colonel Mejan. A veteran of Italy, he was awarded the LH in 1803 then was made OLH the following year. He was wounded at Friedland, then left for Spain, was made a Baron in 1808 and was retired in 1809. He was taken back in 1810 and definitively retired in 1813.

● GARDANE'S THEN BISSON'S DIVISION

Gardane. Present at the siege of Toulon he was also a veteran of Italy and was wounded at Arcola. Made a General in 1797, he distinguished himself at Marengo and was awarded a Sword of Honour for his conduct and promoted to Major-General. He was made CtLH in 1804 and wounded on 4 February 1807. Ney who did not like him, had him replaced a month later by Bisson. He died of illness the following August.

Bisson. He replaced Gardane on 6 March. A veteran of Marengo, he was made a General in 1800 and then a Major-General, GdOLH and Couronne de Fer in 1805. He was brilliant at Friedland and was made a Count in 1808 before serving in Italy. He was obese, eating and drinking too much and died of apoplexy in 1811.

— Roguet's THEN Marcognet's Brigade (see under Marchand's division)

The brigade was made up of the 25th Light and the 27th of the Line.

The 25th Light

Colonel Morel. Awarded the LH in 1804, he had commanded the regiment since 1805 and was made CtLH at the end of the same year. He was wounded on 23rd February 1807 and was then retired and replaced by Anselme. He was made a Baron in 1808.

Colonel Anselme (called Baptiste). Awarded the LH in 1804, he came from the 50th of the Line where he was Battalion Commander. He was made OLH on 14 May 1807, then a Baron in 1808. He died in 1810 as a result of his wounds from the previous year.

The 27th of the Line

Colonel Bardet. He commanded the regiment from 1803. He was made CtLH in 1805 and was made a General on 12 March 1807 and was replaced by Menne. He was made a Baron in 1811. He was made a Major-General and served under Augereau in the Army of Lyon in 1814. He was made CSL in the same year. He was retired in 1815.

Colonel Menne. Appointed to the regiment on 12 March 1807, he was wounded at Friedland by a Biscayen bullet in the shoulder. He was made a Baron in 1808, CtLH in 1810 and General in 1811. He was wounded at Los Arapiles, made CSL in 1814 and was retired in 1815.

— Delabassée's Brigade

Delabasée. A veteran of Marengo where he was a Colonel in the 9th Light. He was made a General in 1803 and was made CtLH in 1804. He served in Spain, was made CSL in 1814 and retired the following year.

The 50th and the 59th of the Line made up the brigade.

The 50th of the Line

Colonel Lamartinière. He drew attention to himself at Ulm and was brilliant at Eylau, was made a General on 10 February 1807 and was replaced by Frappart. A Baron in 1808, he left to serve in Portugal and in Spain. He was Marmont's Chief-of staff in 1812 and Major-General

THE BAVARIANS

Loewenstein's 7th Infantry Regiment.

13th Infantry Regiment.

NCO from the 13th Infantry Regiment.

Drummer from the 13th Infantry Regiment.

6th Light Battalion.

Gunner.

Artillery train driver.

Trumpeter from the Prince Royal's 3rd Chevau-Légers.

From left to right and top to bottom:
Maréchal Augereau, commanding the 7th Corps, his aide de camp Marbot, the author of famous memoirs. Colonel Harispe, made a General in January 1807; Colonel Habert from the 105th of the Line, General Durosnel and Colonel Castex from the 20th Chasseurs (RMN and RR)

in the following year. He was wounded on the Bidassoa and died a few days afterwards.

Colonel Frappart. A child of the Picardy Regiment in 1778. LH in 1804, he was promoted to Colonel after Eylau and was made OLH. He was wounded at Deppen. He was made a Baron and CtLH in 1810, wounded in Spain in 1811 and was retired.

The 59th of the Line

Colonel Dalton-Shee. He was aide de camp to Hoche in 1795 and then to Berthier in 1800. He was made Regimental Colonel in 1805. He distinguished himself at Eylau and Friedland. He was made a General in 1809 and made a Baron in 1810. He was wounded at Smolensk and returned to France for treatment. He was made CSL in 1814 then was retired on half-pay. He was made Commandeur of SL in 1826 and GdOLH in 1833. He was retired in 1848.

— Auguste de Colbert's Cavalry Brigade

Colbert de Chabanais (Auguste). Aide de camp to Murat in Italy, he took part in the expedition to Egypt with his two brothers. He was made a General in 1805 and was killed in Spain by a bullet in the head on 9 November 1808. Ney said of him: *"I can only sleep well when I know that Colbert is in charge of my forward positions."*

The brigade was made up of the 3rd Hussars and the 10th and 15th Chasseurs à Cheval.

The 3rd Hussars

Colonel Lebrun. The son of the Empire's arch-treasurer, he was an aide de camp to Bonaparte at Marengo. He was appointed Regimental Colonel on 1 February 1804; he remained aide de camp to the Emperor and was at Austerlitz. He was made a General on 1 June 1807. He was wounded at Friedland. Made a Major-General in 1812. He was made CSL in 1814, a Peer and the Duke of Plaisance upon the death of his father in 1824. GdCxLH in 1833. He was retired in 1848. In 1853 he was awarded the Military Medal and was made Gd Chancelier of the LH.

Colonel Laferrière-Lévesque. A Major in the regiment, he replaced Lebrun on 8 March 1807. He was made a Baron in 1808. He was wounded three times in Spain, was made a General and awarded the Orders of the Couronne de Fer and of the Reunion in 1811. Made a Major-General in 1813, he commanded the cavalry of the Guard under Mortier in 1814. He had his leg torn off at Craonne. He was made Peer, GdCxLH and CSL in 1821.

The 10th Chasseurs

Colonel Subervie. Born at Lectoure like Lannes whose aide de camp he was in 1797. He was appointed Regimental Colonel in 1805 to replace Auguste de Colbert and served under Lasalle in Spain. He was made a Baron in 1809 and a General in 1811. He was wounded twice at the Moskova and was awarded the Couronne de Fer in 1813. He served in France in 1814 and in Belgium during the Hundred Days. He took part in the 1830 Revolution and was returned several times as the deputy for Lectoure. GdCxLH he was Gd Chancelier of he LH in 1848.

The 15th Chasseurs

Colonel Mourier. A veteran of Italy, he came from the Grenadiers à Cheval of the Guard.

He was the Regimental Colonel from 1805. He was captured at Guttstadt after being receiving five sabre blows, but he was freed after Tilsitt. He was made a Baron in 1810, a General in 1811 and CtLH in 1812. He was wounded at the Moskova and at the Berezina. He served with Berkheim in 1814, and then was put on the non-active list after the Hundred Days. He was retired in 1823.

The regiment returned from Italy and joined up with the 6th Corps on 1 April 1807.

The Royal Italian Chasseurs under **Colonel Zannetti** were attached to the Corps but left after Guttstadt.

AUGEREAU'S 7th CORPS

This corps was crushed at Eylau and the survivors spread throughout the other corps.

The Chief-of-Staff was **Pannetier, Comte de Valdotte.** Wounded at Rivoli, he was made a General in 1803 and CtLH the following year. After the 7th Corps was disbanded, he became Assistant Major-General to the Grande Armée. He was in Lyon in 1814 and was Lieutenant-General in 1815.

Among the Maréchal's aides-de-camp was **Captain Marbot** whose famous memoirs — although they were put into writing at a later date — do give us precious indications and information about the events during the campaign, and more particularly about the Battle of Eylau.

Marbot. Augereau's aide-de-camp in 1803, wounded twice at Eylau then became successively aide-de-camp to Lannes in 1807 and then to Masséna in 1809. He was awarded the LH in 1808 and made a Baron the following year. He took part in the Russian Campaign during which he was promoted to Colonel. He was made OLH in 1813 and Chevalier of SL in 1814. He served during the Hundred Days. He was made CtOLH in 1831 and GdOLH in 1836. He was retired in 1848.

● DESJARDIN'S DIVISION

Desjardin: A General in 1793, he was promoted to Major-General the following year. Made CtLH in 1804, he was mortally wounded at Eylau.

— Lapisse's Brigade

Lapisse. Transferred to Bernadotte's 1st Corps after the 7th Corps was disbanded.

The brigade was made up of the 16th Light and the 14th of the Line.

The 16th Light

Colonel Harispe. Commanded the regiment since 1802, wounded at Jena, he was promoted to General on 29 January 1807 and transferred to Verdier's division in the reserve corps on 10 April and in which he was wounded at Friedland. Major-General in 1810, he was made a count in 1813. He was wounded and captured at Toulouse. He was made GdCxLH and Peer in 1835 and Maréchal de France in 1851.

Colonel Dellard. He replaced Harispe after he was promoted. He went to Spain in 1808 where he was wounded several times. He was made a Baron in 1809 and a General 1813, put on the non-active list and made CSL in 1814; CtLH in 1831.

The 14th of the Line

Colonel Henriod. He was made Colonel of the regiment on 30 December 1806. He distinguished himself at Eylau where he was wounded, and again at Heilsberg. He went to serve in Spain until 1813. He was CtLH in 1808, a Baron in 1809. He retired and was awarded the CSL in 1815. He died in 1821. At Eylau, with Colonel Henriod wounded, command of the regiment passed to Squadron Commander Daussy. It was he who entrusted the regimental eagle to Mar-

132

WÜRTZBURG AND WURTEMBURG

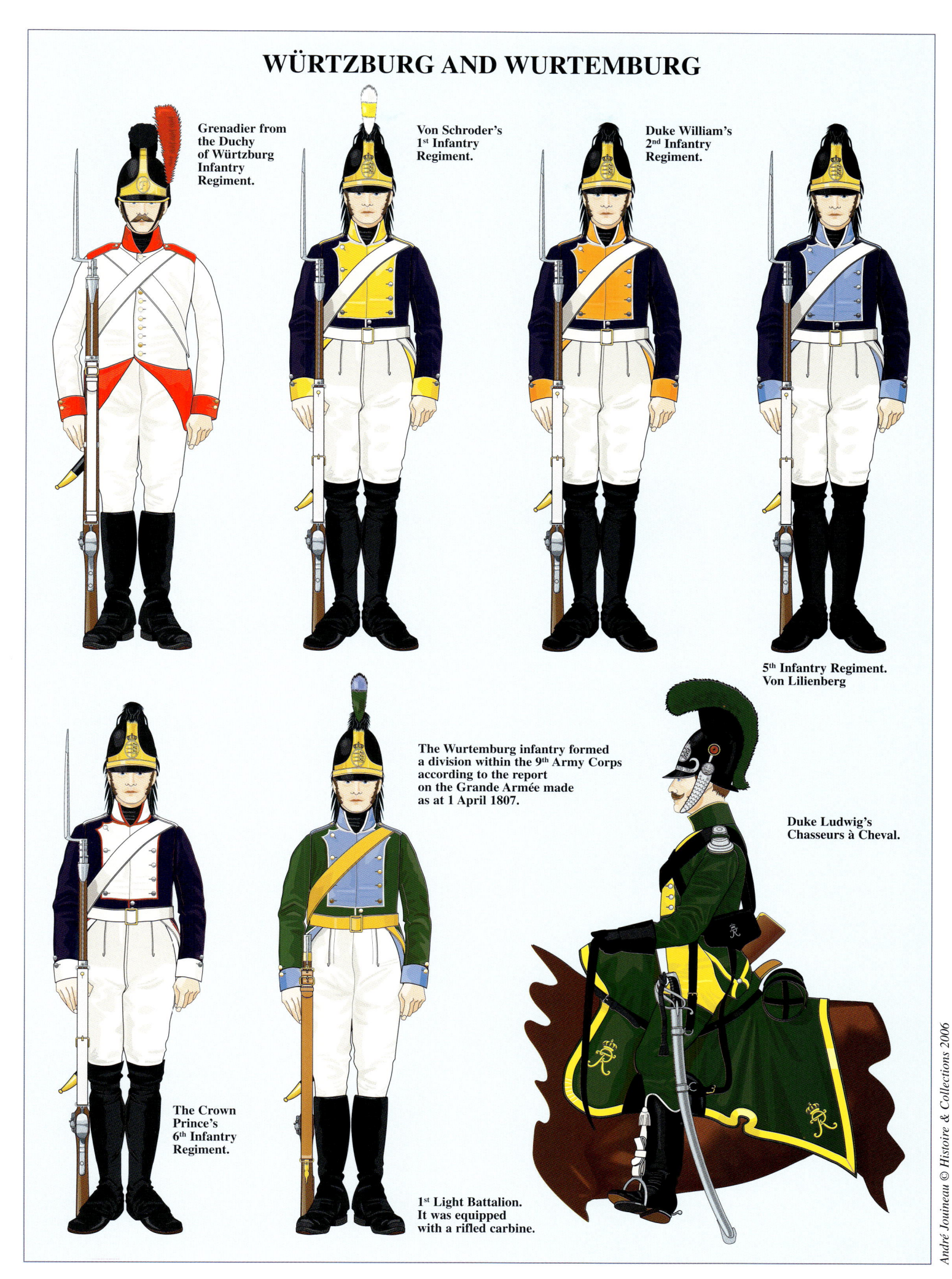

Grenadier from the Duchy of Würtzburg Infantry Regiment.

Von Schroder's 1st Infantry Regiment.

Duke William's 2nd Infantry Regiment.

5th Infantry Regiment. Von Lilienberg

The Crown Prince's 6th Infantry Regiment.

The Wurtemburg infantry formed a division within the 9th Army Corps according to the report on the Grande Armée made as at 1 April 1807.

1st Light Battalion. It was equipped with a rifled carbine.

Duke Ludwig's Chasseurs à Cheval.

From left to right and top to bottom. **Maréchal Mortier, General Dombrowski, Prince Jérôme Bonaparte and General Vandamme.** *(RR)*

bot, the bearer of an order to retreat in a tragically famous episode of the battle in which the 14th of the Line was almost wiped out, where 28 officers and 590 men were killed and 600 wounded.

— Lefranc's Brigade

Lefranc. He refused the rank of General in 1794 and was awarded a Sabre of Honour in 1801. He was made a General in 1803. Wounded at Eylau, he was replaced by Albert and returned to France. He went to serve in Spain where he was captured at Baylen and died in prison in Malaga in 1809.

Albert. He was awarded a Sabre of Honour for his conduct in the Western Pyrenees in 1794. He was Augereau's aide-de-camp from 1795 to 1805. He was promoted to General on 12 January 1807 and replaced Lefranc. He was wounded at Eylau. He commanded the 4th Brigade in Oudinot's Grenadier Division then took part in the siege of Danzig in April-May 1807. He was awarded the Couronne de Fer in 1809 and was made a Baron in 1810. He was wounded at the Berezina. He was made GdOLH in 1813 and Chevalier of SL in 1814. Aide-de-camp to the Duke of Orléans, he was put on the non-active list in 1818.

The 44th of the Line

Colonel Lafosse. He was Regimental Major before being appointed Colonel on 4 February 1807. Wounded at Danzig, he was made a Baron in 1808 and a General in 1811. He was made CSL then retired in 1815.

After Eylau, the regiment was assigned to the siege of Danzig.

The 105th of the Line

Colonel Habert. A veteran of the Egyptian campaign, wounded at Heilsberg, he was promoted to General in 1808, then Major-General and Baron in 1811. GdOLH in 1814, he fought at Ligny and was wounded at Wavre. He died in 1825.

● HEUDELET'S DIVISION

Heudelet de Bierre. Major-General, he replaced Maurice Mathieu in 1806. Wounded at Eylau. His division was disbanded on 12 February 1807 and he returned to France to convalesce. He was made a Count in 1808 and was at Danzig with Rapp in 1813, then on the Rhine — still with Rapp — in 1815. He retired when he received the news of Waterloo; he supported Ney and then was put on the non-active list in 1815. Peer in 1832, he was retired in 1825, then again in 1848. Made GdCxLH in 1836, he was put in the reserve in 1853.

— Amey's Brigade

Amey. Made a General in 1793, he took part in the St Domingo expedition and was made CtLH in 1804; Wounded at Eylau, he went over to the 2nd Brigade of the 2nd Division (Carra-Saint-Cyr) under Soult on 1 April 1807. Made a Baron in 1808, he was present in Russia, distinguished himself at Polotsk and was promoted to Major-General. Made GdOLH the following year, he retired in 1815.

The 7th Light

Colonel Lamaire. Wounded at Auerstadt, he was made OLH in 1807 and a Baron the following year. Wounded twice at Thann and Wagram, he was retired because of his wounds.

— Sarrut's Brigade *(see Bernadotte's First Corps)*

All the regiments of the corps were crushed at Eylau. When the corps was disbanded, they were spread out among the rest of the army.

— Durosnel's cavalry Brigade

Durosnel. Ecuyer Cavalcadour to the Emperor in 1804, he was promoted to General after Austerlitz. He took command of Augereau's cavalry on 27 July 1806 then joined Lasalle when the 7th Corps was disbanded. He was made a Count in 1808 and became aide-de-camp to the Emperor before being wounded and captured at Essling. He commanded the Gendarmerie of the Guard in Russia and was captured at Dresden the following year. During the Hundred Days he was once more again aide-de-camp to the Emperor and was made a peer. He retired in 1816, but was nonetheless aide-de-camp to Louis-Philippe and GdCxLH in 1832.

The 7th Chasseurs

Colonel Lagrange. Wounded at Valmy, he was made Regimental Colonel in February 1801. Wounded at Heilsberg, promoted to General on 25 June 1807, he was captured at Baylen. He lost an arm at Essling but was made Major-General on 29 June, then a Baron in 1811, he was retired in 1815.

The regiment was at Eylau, Königsberg and Heilsberg.

The 20th Chasseurs

Colonel Castex. Regimental Major since 1803, he was promoted to Colonel in October 1806. Promoted to General in 1809, he was in Russia and wounded at the Berezina. He was Major of the Grenadiers à Cheval and was promoted to Major-General in 1813. After serving in the Army of the North under Maison in 1814, he was on the non-active list. Made GdOLH in 1820, he was available in 1830.

The regiment was at Eylau, Guttstadt and Heilsberg.

When the corps was disbanded, the brigade was attached to Lasalle's division in the Cavalry Reserve and reinforced the 1st Corps at Friedland.

MORTIER'S 8th CORPS

The 8th Corps was assigned to protect the northern flank of the French army. In concert with Maréchal Brune, it was entrusted with defending the Baltic coast and covering Lefebvre during the siege of Danzig and the capture of Kolberg. The corps was reorganised in the spring of 1807.

The headquarters staff included **General Camus.** He had served with Mortier since 1805, when he was made CtLH. He was made a General in 1806 and a Baron in 1808. With Victor's headquarters in 1814, he was wounded at Craonne. He served in 1815, was put on the non-active list in August. Retired in 1825.

Colonel d'Halancourt. Was on Mortier's staff for a year, died in 1808.

Mortier's first aide-de-camp was **Colonel Gouré.** He served under Mortier from 1800. He was made OLH in 1804, General in 1811 and Baron in 1813. He was killed Lützen.

● MICHAUD'S DIVISION

Michaud. He was promoted to Brigadier then Major-General in 1793. After fighting in Italy, he commanded the Army of Holland in 1805. He was made a Baron in 1808 and GdOLH in 1814. He was retired in 1832.

The division was made up of the Desenfans, Gency and Grandjean brigades. In November 1806, Michaud was needed as Governor of the Hanseatic towns. On 21 March 1807, he took over command of the 2nd Division in Lefebvre's Corps besieging Danzig. His brigades were spread out as follows: Desenfans went over to Marchand's division in the 6th Corps and Gency and Grandjean made up the 2nd and 3rd Brigades of the Dupas Division respectively.

● DUPAS DIVISION

Dupas. He was in the Allobroges in 1792, at Toulon, in Italy at Mantua and in Egypt. He was made a General in 1803 then CtLH in 1804; he was promoted to Major-General in 1805. He was at Straslund and Friedland. He was a Count in 1809, and retired in 1813.

— Veaux's Brigade

Veaux. A veteran of the Egyptian Campaign, he was made a General in 1797 and CtLH in 1804. He served under Dupas from November 1806. He was made a Baron in 1809, then Major-General; he was elected in 1815. Imprisoned the same year then outlawed, he committed suicide in 1817.

The 4th Light

Colonel Bazancourt. A veteran of the Egyptian Campaign where he was wounded at St-John of Acre. He was one of the Duke of Enghien's judges. He served at Austerlitz and was made CtLH on

25 December 1805. He left for Spain after the Polish Campaign. He was made a General in 1808, a Baron the following year. He was retired in 1815.

— Gency's Brigade

Gency. A veteran of the Sambre and the Meuse, he was made a General in 1795. He was at Montebello and Marengo and was made CtLH in 1804. Made a baron in 1809, he served under MacDonald in 1814 and was wounded at Chalons-sur-Marne. He was made GdOLH and CSL the same year. He was put on the non-active list in 1815 and was retired in 1825.

The brigade comprised the **15th** and **58th of the Line**.

The 15th of the Line
Colonel Reynaud. CtLH in 1804, he was wounded at Friedland and promoted to General in 1808. He was made a Baron and Couronne de Fer in 1809.

The 58th of the Line
Colonel Arnaud. He was wounded at Friedland. He was promoted to General and made OLH in 1808, then a Baron in 1809. He was retired in 1815.

— Grandjean's Brigade

Grandjean. A veteran of the Sambre and the Meuse, he was made a General in 1803 and CtLH the following year. He went to Spain in 1808 but was put on the non-active list in 1809 and retired in 1811.

The brigade was made up of the **1st** and **2nd Regiments of the Paris Guard**.

On 29 April 1807, on Napoleon's instructions, the division was brought up to strength with the Würtzburg and the Grand-Duchy of Berg Regiments.

● LOISON'S DIVISION

Loison. A General since 1795, he was promoted to Major-General the following year. He was promoted to GdOLH in 1804. He was assigned to the siege of Kolberg on 1 February 1807, but only took command on 1 April. He took part in the Portuguese and Spanish Campaigns. Made a CSL in 1814, he was put on the non-active list then retired in 1815.

The division was composed of the **Teulié** and *Ronfanti Brigades* which were made up of the following units:

1st and **2nd Italian Light Infantry**, **1st** and **4th Italian Regiments of the Line**, **1st Polish Infantry Regiment**, **Seckendorff's Wurtemburg Regiment**, a **Saxon battalion**, a **squadron of Dragoons**.

● DOMBROVSKI'S POLISH DIVISION

The recently formed Polish division was assigned to the 8th Corps. It was made up of the following units:

2nd, **3rd** and **4th Polish Infantry regiments**, **2 regiments of Sokolnicki's cavalry**. Three Artillery batteries and a detachment of Polish Engineers

● DUMONCEAU'S DIVISION

Dumonceau. Born in Brussels, he took part in the revolution in Brabant. He went to serve France in 1792 with the rank of Lieutenant-Colonel. He was promoted to General in 1794 and commanded the Batavian Army from 1797 to 1799. He distinguished himself at the crossing of the Danube. He was made GdCx of the Dutch Order of Merit and Marshal of Holland in 1807, Major-General in France in 1810, Count in 1811 then GdCx of the Reunion in 1812. He was captured at Dresden and retired in 1815 before becoming a member of the Dutch Estates-General.

The division was made up as follows. **2nd** and **3rd Dutch Chasseur à Pied Regiments**, **2nd**, **3rd** and **7th Dutch Regiments of the Line**, **2nd Regiment of Dutch Hussars**. One Artillery battery

Under Mortier's command since 1805, Dunonceau was transferred, as was most of his division, to Brune's in March 1807. Only a few elements such as the Dutch Hussars remained with the 8th Corps.

— The cavalry Brigade

At first the 8th Corps cavalry was made up of two regiments of Dutch cavalry, the **2nd Hussars** and the **2nd Cuirassiers**.

On 4 June, the brigade was changed and then commanded by Frésia who had been recently promoted to Major-General.

Frésia. He was an Italian serving in the Sardinian Army before commanding the Piedmont cavalry in French service. He was made a General in 1802 then GdOLH in 1804. His appointment to the rank of Major-General took effect from 3 June 1807. He was made Baron of Oglianico in 1808. Two years later he was Governor of Veni-

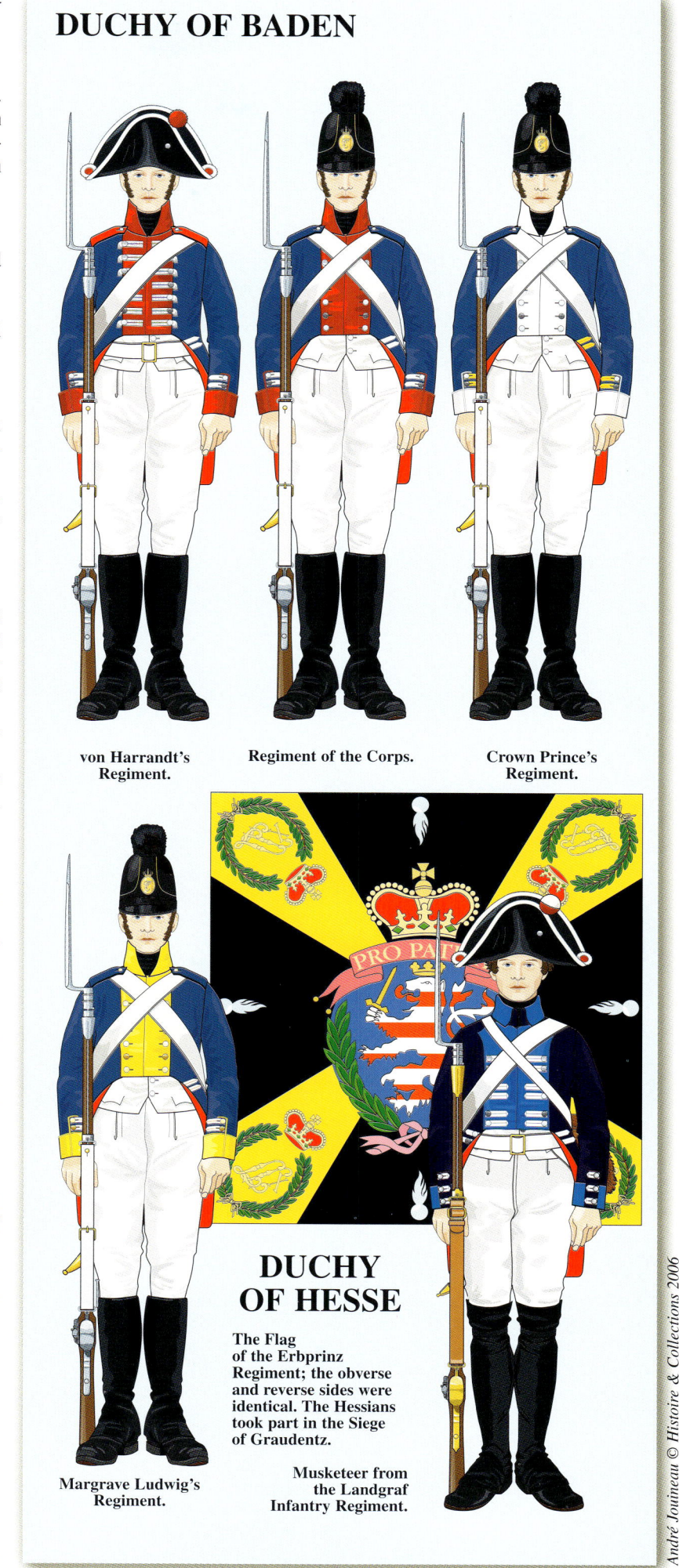

DUCHY OF BADEN

von Harrandt's Regiment.

Regiment of the Corps.

Crown Prince's Regiment.

DUCHY OF HESSE

The Flag of the Erbprinz Regiment; the obverse and reverse sides were identical. The Hessians took part in the Siege of Graudentz.

Margrave Ludwig's Regiment.

Musketeer from the Landgraf Infantry Regiment.

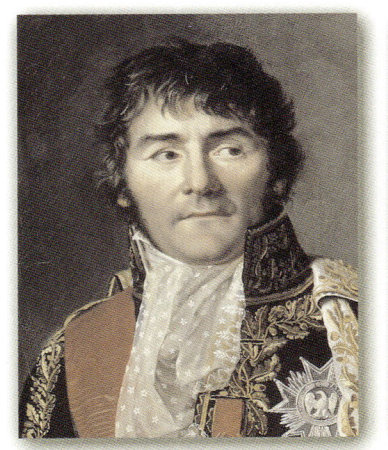

From left to right and top to bottom. Maréchal Lefebvre and maréchal Brune, General Molitor who was made a Maréchal in 1823, and Maréchal Lannes. (Dr and RMN)

ce. Retired in 1814, he was made a French Citizen in 1815.

The cavalry brigade was made up of the **5th** and **6th Polish Cavalry** and the **2nd Dutch Cuirassier Regiments**.

JÉRÔME'S 9th CORPS

Jérôme Bonaparte was Napoleon's youngest brother. He served at first in the Navy in which he rose to the rank of Rear-Admiral in 1806. He was made a Prince of France and Gd Aigle of the LH on 24 September of the same year. He then joined the Grande Armée where he took command of the 9th Corps which was made up of Bavarians and Wurtemburgers. He was made a Major-General and was declared King of Westphalia by the Senate on 16 August 1807. He died in 1860, during the reign of Napoleon III.

Jérôme's Chief-of-Staff was **General d'Hédouville**. He was made a General in 1793 and Major-General the following year. He distinguished himself as Hoche's chief-of-staff and was awarded three weapons of honour. He was GdOLH in An XII (1804), Senator in 1805 then Napoleon's Chamberlain. Retired 1807, Count in 1808. He voted for Napoleon to be deposed and for Ney to be executed in 1815.

● DEROY'S BAVARIAN DIVISION

5th and **6th Light Infantry Regiments** (one battalion each)
5th Regiment of the Line (two battalions)

● VANDAMME'S WURTEMBURG DIVISION

Prince Royal's Regiment (two battalions), **Lilienburg Regiment** (two battalions), **Duke William's Regiment** (two battalions), **Schroder's Regiment** (two battalions), **1st** and **2nd King's Chasseurs**, **1st** and **2nd Light Infantry battalions**, a battalion of Fusiliers

● LEFEBVRE-DESNOUETTE'S BAVARIAN DIVISION

Guards' Regiment (two battalions), **6th** and **10th Infantry regiments of the Line** (two battalions each), **Neimenschet's Saxon Regiment** (two battalions).

— Zand's Light Cavalry Brigade

Bavarian Chevau-Légers, **1st Bavarian Dragoon Regiment**, two squadrons of **Bavarian reserves**, **Wurtemburg Chevau-Légers**, **Duke Ludwig's Wurtemburg Chasseurs**.

This corps operated in Silesia with a total strength of 25 battalions and 14 squadrons, almost 17 000 men.

LEFEBVRE'S 10th CORPS

The chief-of-staff of the 10th Corps was **General Drouet**, already encountered in Lannes' Reserve Corps. The Artillery was commanded by **General Lamartinière**, and the Engineers by **Battalion Commander Larcher-Chaumont**.

Napoleon decided that Maréchal Lefebvre should have the assistance of the two best experts in the Imperial Army, the Artillery General Lariboisière and the Engineer General Chasseloup-Laubat for the siege of Danzig.

Boyvin de la Martinière served in America with Rochambeau from 1780 to 1783. Promoted to General in February 1805. He commanded the 10th Corps' artillery and was awarded the LH in March 1807. He was made a Baron in 1809 and retired the same year.

● MICHAUD'S DIVISION (See Mortier's 8th Corps)

12th Lights, **1st Regiment** from the **Northern Legion** (Prince Radziwill), **1st Battalion of Saxon Grenadiers**, **1st Battalion of Prince Anthony's Saxon Regiment**, two battalions from **Saenger's Saxon Regiment**, one battalion from the **Saxon Bevilaqua Regiment.**

● THE CROWN PRINCE OF BADEN'S DIVISION

19th of the Line (French), **the Corps Baden Regiment** (two battalions), **the Margrave Ludwig's Baden Regiment** (two battalions), **Harrant's Baden Regiment** (two battalions) and **Baden Chasseurs à pied**.

● GIELGUTT'S DIVISION

2nd Lights (one battalion), **44th of the Line**, **the Regiment of the Paris Guard**, **2nd** and **3rd Regiments of the Northern Legion**.

● GARDANNE'S DIVISION (see Ney's 6th Corps)

2nd Lights (2nd Battalion), one battalion of Saxon Grenadiers, one battalion of **Prince Maximilian's Saxon Fusiliers**, **Prince Anthony's Saxon Regiment** (2nd Battalion), **2nd** and **4th Polish Infantry Regiments**.

● POLENTZ'S CAVALRY DIVISION

— Duprez's Brigade

19th and **23rd Chasseur à cheval Regiments** (French)

— Besser's Brigade

King's Regiment of Saxon Cuirassiers (three squadrons), the **Saxon Chevau-Légers** from **Prince John's** and **von Polentz's Regiments** (one combined squadron), **Baden Hussars** (one squadron), **Baden Light Dragoons** (two squadrons).

— Sokolnicki's Brigade

1st and **2nd Regiments of Polish Cavalry**, a squadron of Polish nobles was attached to the brigade. The 10th Corps was under the command of Maréchal Lefebvre and was made up in order to keep an eye on the coast and especially for the capture of Danzig which was vital for the evolution of the campaign. Speaking German fluently, he had no communication problems with the large Saxon and Baden contingents. The corps was disbanded after Danzig was captured and some of its elements took part in the Battle of Friedland.

The flag of the Crown Prince of Baden's Regiment. The Baden contingent's baptism of fire took place at the siege of Danzig.

ITALY, BELGIUM, POLAND and BERG

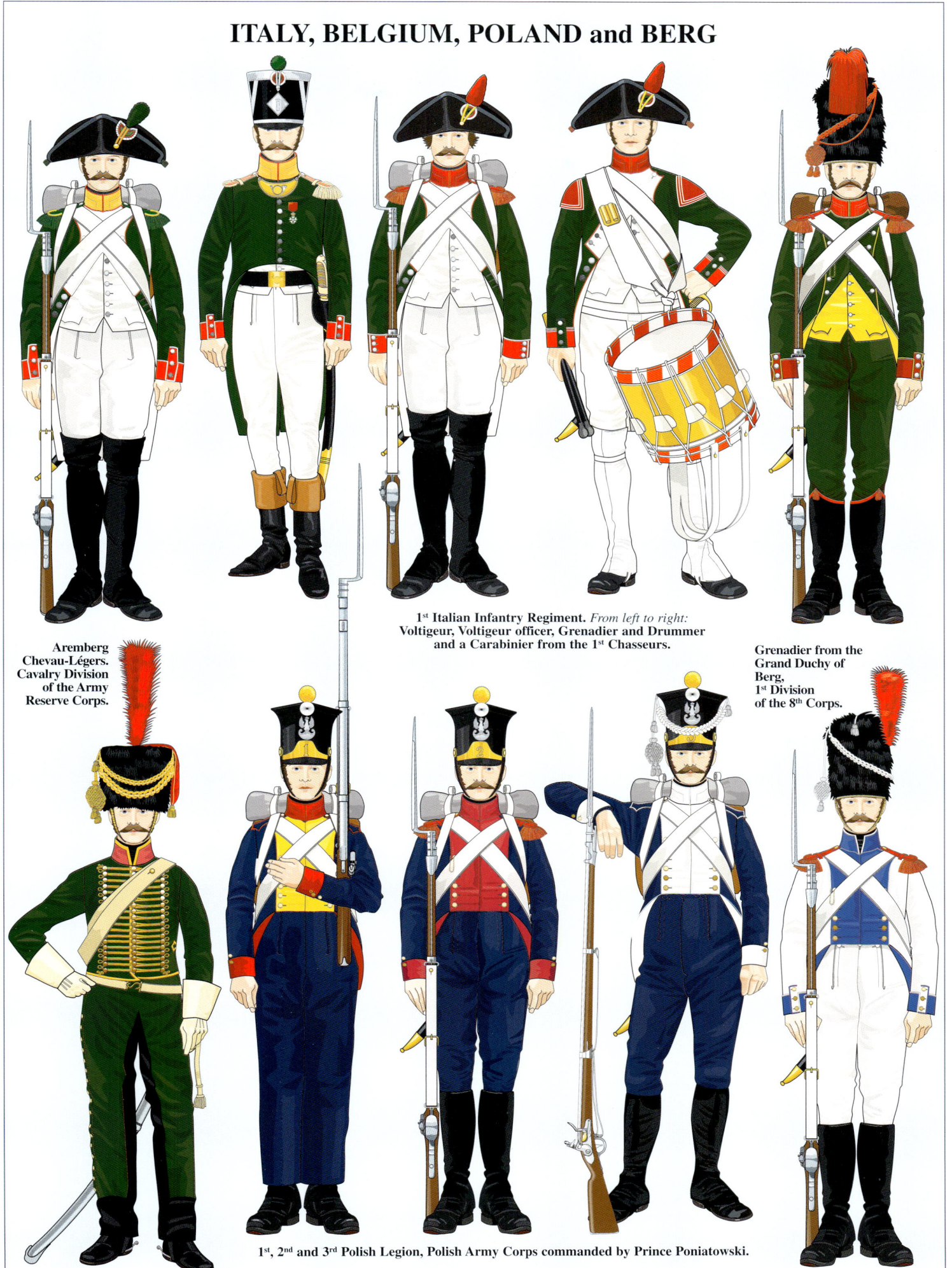

1st Italian Infantry Regiment. *From left to right:* Voltigeur, Voltigeur officer, Grenadier and Drummer and a Carabinier from the 1st Chasseurs.

Aremberg Chevau-Légers. Cavalry Division of the Army Reserve Corps.

Grenadier from the Grand Duchy of Berg, 1st Division of the 8th Corps.

1st, 2nd and 3rd Polish Legion, Polish Army Corps commanded by Prince Poniatowski.

137

BRUNE'S OBSERVATION CORPS

Brune. A Captain in the Paris National Guard in 1789, he was made a General in 1793. He distinguished himself in the Army of Italy in which he was promoted to Major-General in 1797. He became the Commander-in-Chief instead of Masséna in 1800. Ambassador to Turkey in 1802, he was made Maréchal and GdOLH in 1804. He commanded the Observation Corps but was replaced and disgraced for having spoken of the French army and not the Imperial army during a conference with Sweden. He remained available until 1814 when he rallied to the Bourbons. He joined the Emperor nevertheless when the latter returned from Elba. Captured by the Royalists in August of the same year, he was savagely murdered and his body thrown into the Rhone. His Chief-of-Staff was **General Rostollant.** A former artilleryman, he was made a General and Brune's chief-of-staff in 1799. He was made CtLH in 1804 and CSL in 1814. He was allowed to retire in 1815.

● BOUDET'S DIVISION

Boudet. A veteran of the Italian Campaign, he was made General in 1800 and was at Lodi and Marengo. He was present at Straslund and Kolberg in 1807. He was made a Count in 1808. The next year, following on his brilliant conduct during the defence of Essling, he was made GdOLH and Couronne de fer. He committed suicide after Napoleon told him off severely for losing his artillery on 6 July.

— Fririon's Brigade

Fririon. He was at Stralsund and Kolberg in 1807. He just avoided being slaughtered by the Spaniards at La Romana the following year. He was at Essling in 1809 and was promoted to Major-General the same year. He was made a Baron and Grand Cross of the Sword of Sweden in 1810.
3rd Lights

— Valory's Brigade

Valory. Promoted to General in 1803, he was made a Baron five years later. He was at Essling and Wagram. He was wounded and captured at Leipzig in 1813. Made CtLH in 1814, he did not serve in 1815, and then retired. 56th and 93rd of the Line

● MOLITOR'S DIVISION

Molitor. Made a General in 1799, he was made a Major-General in Italy in 1800. He was in Pomerania and at Stralsund. Made a Count in 1808, he distinguished himself at Essling and Wagram. He served with Rapp in 1815 and was made GdCxLH and Peer in the same year. He was again made a Peer and Maréchal de France in 1823. Grand Chancelier of the LH in 1848, he died the following year.

— Leguay's Brigade

Leguay. He was made CtLH in 1804, then Baron in 1810. He was with Dessaix in Russia and died of inanition on the Kowno road on 16 December 1812.
2nd and 16th of the Line

— Castella's Brigade

Castella. He commanded the stronghold at Königsberg in 1812, then that at Pillau the following year. He was made OLH on 19 November 1812.
37th and 67th of the Line

● THE ROMANA SPANISH DIVISION

The Prince and Asturias Regiment, Barcelona Light Battalion and The King's and the Infanta's Cavalry Regiments

● 2nd SPANISH DIVISION

Zamora and Guadalajara Regiments, 1st Battalion Catalonian Lights, Algarve Cavalry Regiment, Villaviciosa Dragoon Regiment.

● DUMONCEAU'S DUTCH DIVISION

— Van Heldring's Brigade. 3rd Chasseurs and 3rd and 4th of the Line

— Gras' Brigade. 6th and 9th of the Line

● GRATIEN'S DUTCH DIVISION

— Van Hasselt's Brigade. 2nd of the Line

— Duzy's Brigade. 7th and 8th of the Line

● CARTERET'S CAVALRY DIVISION

3rd Dutch Hussar Regiment and The Duke of Aremberg's Belgian Chevau-Légers
This observation corps really was a tower of Babel, with a strength of 44 000 men spread out among 46 battalions and 17 squadrons.

LANNES' RESERVE CORPS

Lannes. A veteran of Arcola and Lodi, he was promoted to General in 1797. He took part brilliantly in the Egyptian Campaign and was promoted to Major-General in 1800. He was made a Maréchal among those in the very first series, in 1804. He commanded the left of the French army at Austerlitz and was made Gd Aigle of the LH in 1805, then Commandeur of the Couronne de Fer the following year. He commanded the 5th Corps at Saafeld and Jena. Wounded at Pultusk, ill and depressed, he had to withdraw to convalesce. He designated Suchet as his successor in command of the corps, but Napoleon chose Savary however, who took over during this interim period until Masséna, coming from Calabria, could take command of this corps. Lannes recovered and returned to service by commanding the reserve corps which had just been formed; he distinguished himself at Heilsberg then at Friedland where he commanded the centre. He was made Duke of Montebello in 1808; he went to Spain and won at Tudela then at Saragossa. During the Austrian Campaign, he took over the 2nd Corps and was at Eckmühl and Regensburg. He was mortally wounded at Essling on 22 May 1809 and is buried in the Pantheon in Paris.

Drouet, Comte d'Erlon, was Lannes' Chief-of-Staff. He was present at Zurich and Hohenlinden and was promoted to Major-General in 1803. He was seriously wounded at Friedland. He was made Count of Erlon in 1809 and GdCxLH in 1814. He took part in the Lallemand plot upon Napoleon's return and commanded an army corps at Waterloo. He was outlawed and then pardoned in 1825. Governor-General of Algeria in 1834, he was promoted to Maréchal in 1843.

Le Tellier. A Captain attached to the Staff, he was Oudinot's aide-de-camp in 1809. General in 1813, he was captured at Dresden. He served in 1815 and committed suicide in 1818.
Lannes' Aide-de-camps

Guéhéneuc. His brother-in-law. Wounded at Friedland, he was a Baron and an aide-de-camp to Napoleon in 1809. Promoted to General in 1812, he served in Morea in 1831. Lieutenant-General in 1836, he served in Africa and was made a Count in 1838. He was retired in 1848.

Thomières. A Marengo veteran, he was made a General in 1807. He died at Los Arapiles in 1812.

Bussière. Aide-de-camp since 1805, he was wounded at Eylau. He was made a Chevalier in 1809. In 1814, he was Colonel of the 133rd of the Line and was blocked inside Landau. CrLH in 1827, he was retired in 1832.

● OUDINOT'S MIXED GRENADIER DIVISION

Oudinot. Major-General in 1799, he was made GdOLH in 1805. He was at Ostrolenka then at Danzig. He was ordered to organise a reserve division in Berlin and led it at Friedland. He was made a Count and Chevalier of the Croix de Fer in 1806. He took part in all the big campaigns during the Imperial period. He went over to Louis XVIII and was made a Peer in 1814. He was made GdCxSL in 1816 and Duke in 1827. He was in Spain in 1823; he was made Gd Chevalier of the LH and Governor of the Invalides and died in 1847.

The so-called Grenadier divisions such as the ones commanded by Oudinot at Friedland, were elite units and constituted a very high quality reserve which could be used at all moments on the battlefield. Each of the battalions it comprised was made up by grouping together six elite companies – grenadiers, voltigeurs or carabiniers – from the Light Infantry or from the Line regiments. These battalions were formed up into temporary regiments. Although these regiments did not have the status of 'Guards' because of their origins and their temporary organisation, they were nevertheless valuable units.

Ruffin's Brigade

Ruffin. Made a General in 1805, he was at Austerlitz and was made CtLH. He was at Ostrolenka and joined Oudinot on 5 May 1807. After Friedland, he was made a Major-General on 3 November 1807 and replaced Dupont under Victor after Baylen. Wounded and captured in Spain, he died two months later off Portsmouth in 1811.

The 1st Regiment
1st Battalion. Battalion Commander Launier. **Carabinier Companies** from the 6th, 7th, 9th, 16th, 25th and 27th Light: 440 men. ***2nd Battalion.*** Battalion Commander Broyer. **Voltigeur Companies** from the 6th, 7th, 9th, 16th, 25th and 27th Light: 450 men

The 2nd Regiment
3rd Battalion. Battalion Commander Fondousse. **Grenadier Companies** from the 8th, 30th, 33rd, 51st, 95th and 96th of the Line: 420 men. ***4th Battalion.*** Battalion Commander Chabert. **Voltigeur Companies** from the 8th, 30th, 33rd, 51st, 95th and 96th of the Line: 420 men

138

THE DUTCH

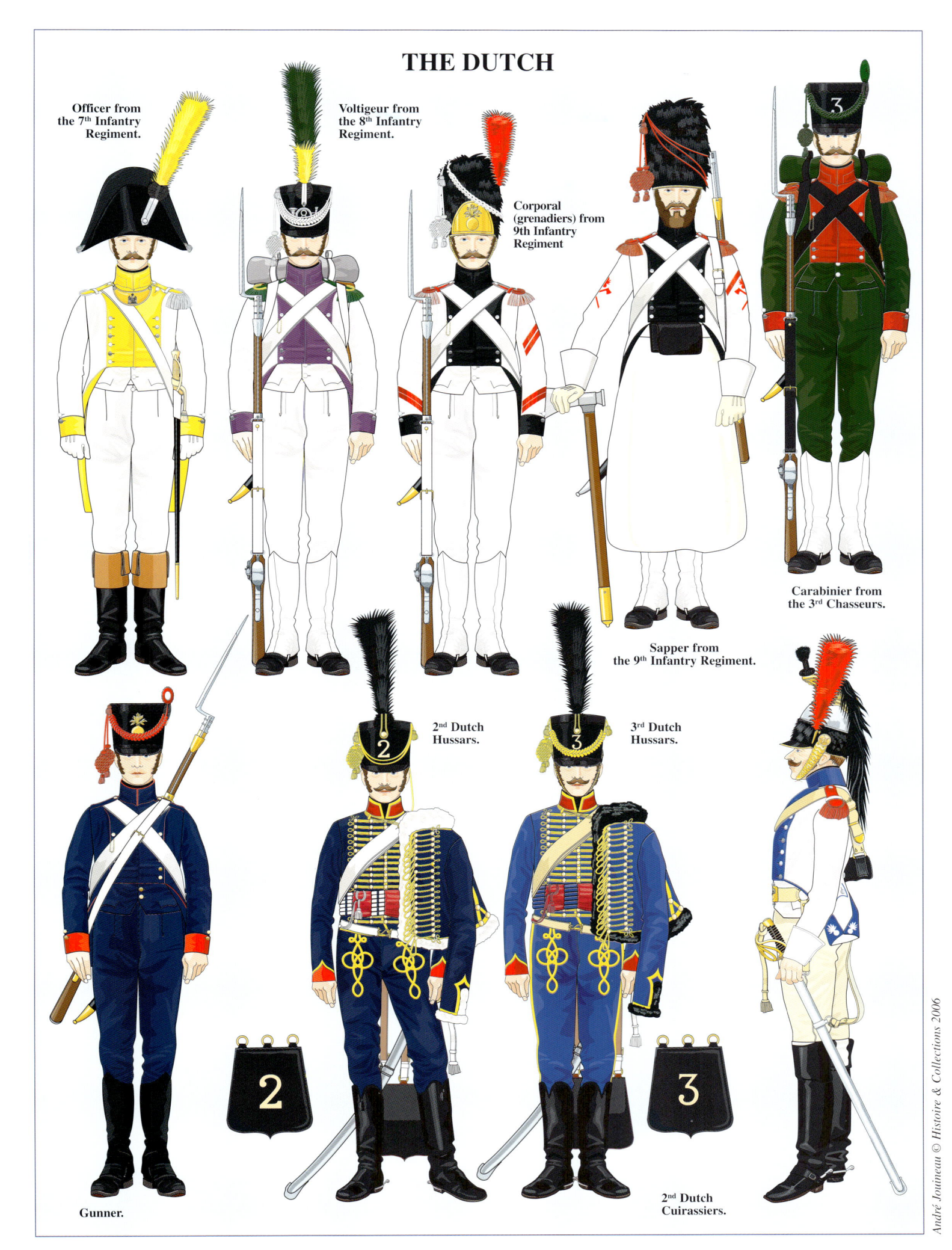

Officer from the 7th Infantry Regiment.

Voltigeur from the 8th Infantry Regiment.

Corporal (grenadiers) from 9th Infantry Regiment

Sapper from the 9th Infantry Regiment.

Carabinier from the 3rd Chasseurs.

Gunner.

2nd Dutch Hussars.

3rd Dutch Hussars.

2nd Dutch Cuirassiers.

Generals Coëhorn and Verdier. (RR)

— Conroux's Brigade

Conroux. A veteran of Italy, he was made a General on 24 December 1805. He joined Augereau and was wounded at Jena. In 1807, he was at Ostrolenka, Danzig, Heilsberg and Friedland. He was made a Baron in 1808 then Major-General in 1809. He went to Spain where he was mortally wounded at Ascain in November 1813.

The 3rd Regiment

5th Battalion. Battalion Commander Arnauld. **Carabinier Companies** from the 10th, 17th, 21st, 24th, 26th and 28th Light: 400 men. *6th Battalion.* Battalion Commander Franchot. **Voltigeur Companies** from the 10th, 17th, 21st, 24th, 26th and 28th Light: 390 men

The 4th Regiment

7th Battalion. Battalion Commander Coquereau. **Grenadier Companies** from the 4th, 18th, 34th, 40th, 64th and 88th of the Line: 410 men. *8th Battalion.* Battalion Commander Monnet. **Voltigeur Companies** from the 4th, 18th, 34th, 40th, 64th and 88th of the Line: 420 men

— Coëhorn's Brigade

Coëhorn. He was at Austerlitz and wounded at Auerstadt. Appointed General in March 1807, he replaced Jarry on 22 April. Wounded at Friedland, he was made a Baron in 1808 and CtLH in 1809 for his decisive action at Ebersberg; he was wounded at Wagram. Wounded and captured at Leipzig, he died as a result of the amputation of his left thigh.

The 5th Regiment

9th Battalion. Battalion Commander Dauger. **Grenadier Companies** from the 27th, 39th, 45th, 59th, 69th and 70th of the Line: 420 men. *10th Battalion.* Commander Comminet. **Voltigeur Companies** from the 27th, 39th, 45th, 59th, 69th and 70th of the Line: 450 men

The 6th Regiment

11th Battalion. Battalion Commander Vaugrignaude. **Grenadier Companies** from the 22nd, 44th, 45th, 63rd, 94th and 105th of the Line: 460 men. *12th Battalion.* Battalion Commander Boidot. **Voltigeur Companies** from the 27th, 39th, 45th, 59th, 69th and 70th of the Line: 420 men

— Albert's Brigade

Albert. Awarded a Sabre and Pistols of Honour for his conduct in the Western Pyrenees. He was an aide-de-camp to Augereau in 1799. He was at Jena and at Golymin; he was made a General under Augereau. He was wounded at Eylau. He was made a Baron in 1810, Chevalier of the Couronne de Fer and Major-General in 1812. Wounded at the Berezina, he was on the non-active list in 1818.

The 7th Regiment

13th Battalion. Battalion Commander Cornebise. **Carabinier Companies** from the XXX and the 25th Light and **Grenadier Companies** from the 22nd, 32nd, 57th and 65th of the Line: 360 men. *14th Battalion.* Battalion Commander Boulon. **Voltigeur Companies** from the 22nd, 32nd, 57th and 65th of the Line: 360 men

The 8th Regiment

15th Battalion. Battalion Commander Jouan. **Grenadier Companies** from the 3rd, 61st, 85th and 111th: 300 men. *16th Battalion.* **Voltigeur Companies** from the 3rd, 61st, 85th and 111th: 300 men

The division's artillery was made up of a battery of eight pounders and one of four.
The **9th Hussar Regiment** was detached to Oudinot's Division from May.

● VERDIER'S DIVISION

Verdier. A veteran of Italy, he fought at Arcola and was made a General in 1796. He went to Egypt, was awarded a Sabre of Honour and was made a Major-General in 1800. He took part in Heilsberg and Friedland. He was made Cr of the Couronne de Fer and a Count in 1808. He was at Polotsk in 1812 and in Italy in 1814. He served in the Var and was made GdCxLH in 1815. Retired in 1832.

The divisional staff included **Bourcet.** Assistant to the Staff, he was Verdier's aide-de-camp until 1818. He was retired in 1832.

Bosset. Captain attached to the staff, he transferred to Berthier on 24 May 1807. He commanded a battalion at Neuchâtel. He died at Smolensk in 1812.

Hutin. Squadron Commander, he was killed at Friedland.

Verdier's aide-de-camp was **Baillot**. He took part at Austerlitz and was made a Chevalier in 1809 and OLH in 1813. He served in the Pyrenees in 1814. He was retired in 1821.

— Vedel's Brigade

Vedel. Wounded at Rivoli he was at Austerlitz and promoted to General on 24 December 1805. Wounded at Pultusk, he was made CtLH. Wounded at Heilsberg then at Friedland, he was made a Major-General in 1807. He went to Spain and was ordered to lay down his arms by Dupont after the capitulation of Baylen. Disgraced, he was nevertheless taken back in December 1813 and served in Italy then under Augereau in 1814. He was made CSL. Put on the non-active list in 1815. He was in reserve in 1818.

The brigade was made up of the 2nd and 12th Light.

The 2nd Light

Colonel Brayer. Received a Sabre of Honour for Hohenlinden. He commanded the regiment since Austerlitz. Wounded at Friedland, he was made a General in 1809 and a Baron in 1810.

The 12th Light

Colonel Jeanin. Italian and Egyptian Campaigns. A Colonel since 1805, he was in Dupas' division in 1806 then with Michaud on 21 March 1807. Wounded at Heilsberg, he was made CtLH in 1808 and General in 1809. Promoted to Lieutenant-General in 1815, he was present at Waterloo.

— Harispe's Brigade

Harispe. He was made a General in 1807 and was at Guttstadt, Heilsberg and Friedland where he was wounded. He was made Major-General in 1810. He was awarded the Order of the Couronne de Fer, made a Count and GdCx of the Reunion in 1813. He fought at Toulouse in 1814 with Soult and was at Strasbourg in 1815. He was made a Maréchal in 1851 and was a Senator.

The brigade consisted of the 72nd of the Line only.

The 72nd of the Line

Colonel Ficatier. Seriously wounded at Friedland, he was made a General in 1808 and CtLH in 1809. He was retired in 1813.

Major Martineau. LH in 1804, he was battalion commander in the 72nd of the Line then Major in the 25th of the Line. Retired in 1811, he was made OLH in 1814. He was a Colonel in 1815 and finally retired in 1833.

— Schramm Brigade

Schramm (Senior). A veteran of Italy and Egypt, he was made a General in 1805 and CtLH in 1807. Couronne de Fer and Baron. He was made Maréchal de Camp in 1815 and retired in 1816.

His aide-de-camp was his son who was a General in 1813 with the Young Guard in Dresden. He served in 1815 then was put on the non-active list. He was taken back and made a Viscount in 1827 and Lieutenant-General in 1832. He was in Antwerp, then in Lyon for the Canut insurrection in 1834. He was elected Deputy in 1836 and made a Peer in 1839. He was in Algiers in 1840; He was made GdCxLH and a Count in 1841. He was awarded the Military Medal in 1852.

The 3rd of the Line was the only unit in the brigade.

Colonel Schobert. He succeeded Mouton at the head of the Regiment. Wounded and captured at Heilsberg. He was freed after Tilsitt. Baron in 1809, he was made a General in 1811 with Saint-Hilaire and was awarded the Order of the Couronne de Fer. Captured in Stettin in 1813, he served in 1815 and was put on the non-active list in 1821.

The division was supported by two artillery batteries.

● GENERAL VON POLENTZ'S SAXON DIVISION

— Infantry Brigade

Winkelman's and von Larisch's Grenadier Battalions
Prince Anton's and von Saenger's Infantry Regiments
Prince Maximilian's and Bevilaqua's Fusilier Battalions

— Von Besser's' cavalry Brigade

The King's Cuirassiers
Two squadrons of Chevau-Légers from the Prince Johan and von POLENTZ Regiments
Two batteries of artillery.

THE DUTCH

In the 1 April 1807 report on the Grande Armée, the Dutch had three divisions in the observation corps, i.e. two infantry and one cavalry, rein-

GETROUWHEID AAN DEN KONING
MOED **KRYGSTUCHT**
INFANTERIE VAN LINIE

DE KONING AAN HET 5de REGIMENT INFANTERIE VAN LINIE 2de BATAILLON

The new Kingdom of Holland infantry flag.

At the time, the former blue uniform of the Batavian Republic was still used alongside the white uniform of the Kingdom of Holland.

Grenadier from the 2nd Infantry Regiment.

Grenadier from the 3rd Infantry Regiment.

Fusilier from the 4th Infantry Regiment. The bayonet was always fixed to the barrel of the rifle, which is why there was no sheath with the uniform.

Grenadier form the 5th Infantry Regiment.

Grenadier from the 6th Infantry Regiment.

Sapper from the 7th infantry Regiment. As well as the traditional axe, he is also carrying a spade on his back.

André Jouineau © Histoire & Collections 2006

SAXONY

The Saxons were incorporated into the 3rd Division of the Reserve Army Corps.

Officer from Prince Anthony's Infantry Regiment.

Flag and soldier from von Bevilaqua's infantry regiment. The flag is identical on both reverse and obverse sides.

Von Saenger Infantry Regiment.

Prince Maximilian's Infantry Regiment.

The King's Cuirassiers.

Prince John's Chevau-Légers.

Von POLENTZ's Chevau-Légers.

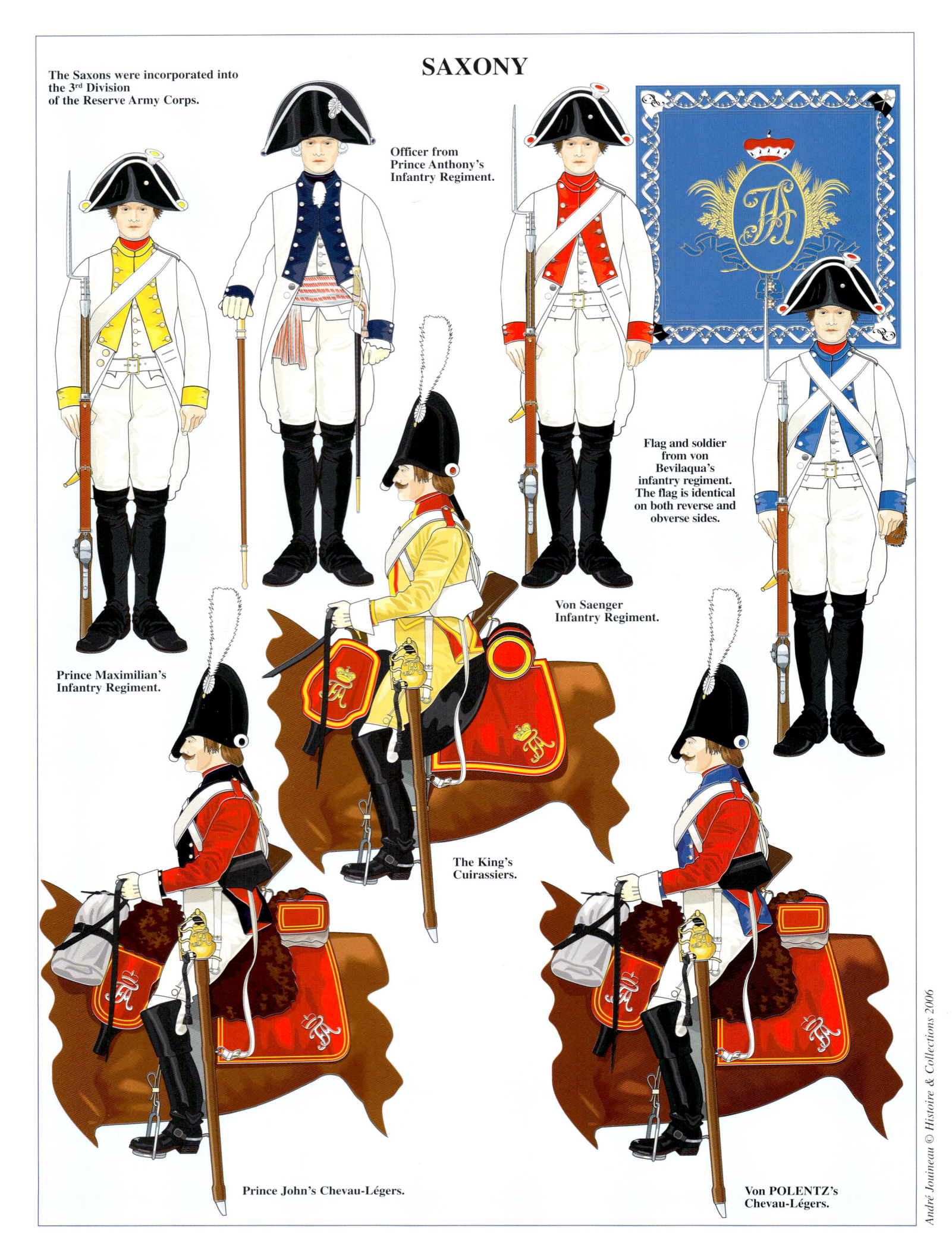

Murat and Soult pushed the Allies back to Könisgberg. Davout who was marching towards them was called back to Friedland with part of the cavalry just in case there was a second day's fighting, and also to cut off the Russian army's retreat along the banks of the Alle. The Emperor thought that Soult with a division of Dragoons would be enough to control Könisgberg.

On 14 June Soult enjoined the town to surrender, and was turned down. The men of the 4th Corps started investing it. Legrand took the left suburb; the 8th Hussars captured 400 horses and 6 cannon. At Labiau, the 1st Chasseurs captured 60 Hussars and 1 000 infantry. Marulaz with the 2nd and 12th Chasseurs from the 3rd Corps captured 260 horses and 2 500 men.

Lestocq decided he would abandon the town and rejoin the Russian army, leaving some 200 men in the town which was in no state to stand a siege anyway. English boats were there with a lot of equipment and 16 000 new rifles. In the hospitals there were 3 000 ill or wounded. Saint-Hilaire was in front of Pillau where a cease-fire was decided.

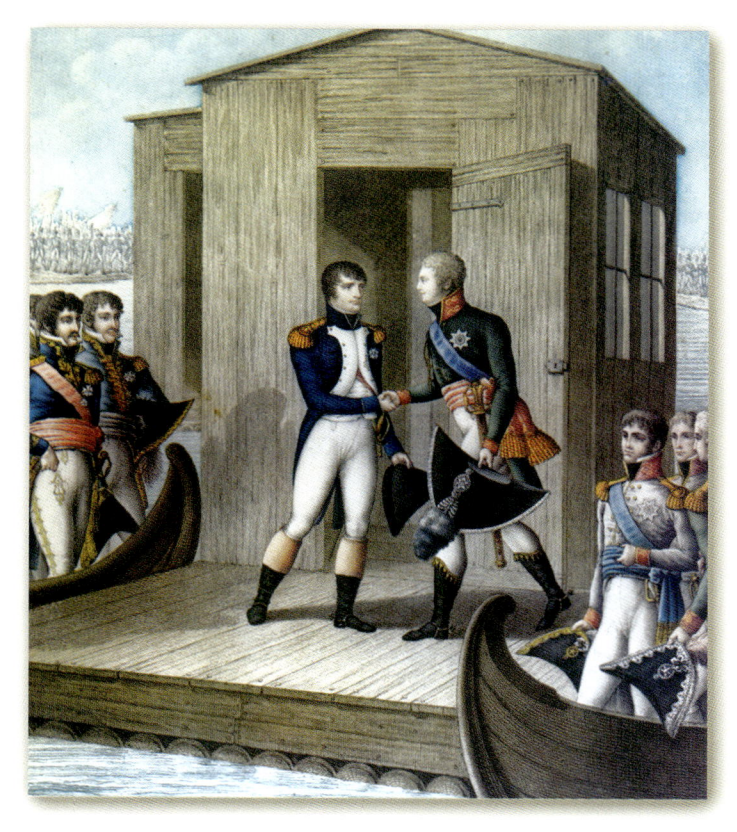

The two Emperors meet on a raft in the middle of the Niemen. They shared the whole of Europe, but their friendship neither stood the test of time nor did it especially resist political events. (RR)

divisions with the Bavarians under de Wrède and Deroy, together with the Wurtemburgers and Beker's cavalry (replaced by Lorge on 25 May 1807).

Montbrun was mentioned in despatches, as were the 28th Light and the 25th Dragoons at Glatz where Lefebvre-Desnouettes distinguished himself as did the Bavarians and the Wurtemburgers.

Claparède repulsed the Russians who fled back to Russia via Ostrolenka.

One has to insist on the role played by Davout at Eylau. It was the 3rd Corps which decided the outcome, and victory, by blocking the Friedland road.

The arrival of Ney towards 4 o'clock completed the encircling manoeuvre. He pushed Benningsen into a retreat, aided unwittingly by Lestocq who attempted to retake Kuschitten, which was occupied by Marulaz first, then by the 51st under Morand, who were obliged

THE EMPIRE AT ITS ZENITH

The Russians' retreat

The routed Russian army moved to Allenburg and Tilsitt.

Ney picked up deserters and laggards brought in every day by peasants. He said that enemy losses from laggards were higher than during the battle. Lasalle crossed the Alle and the Pregel and chased the Russian rearguard whilst Colbert captured a train and its escort.

The bridge at Welhau which had been destroyed by the Russians was rebuilt by the evening of the 16th. Frère and the vanguard crossed the Pregel with barges but they were charged by the Cossacks, Kalmucks and Baskirs armed with bows and arrows. These colourful irregulars were nicknamed *"amours"* and *"cupids"* by the soldiers.

Lasalle was sent towards Tepplaken which he captured and then pushed on to Tilsitt, where the armistice was signed.

In front of Trunkenstein, the 20th Chasseurs and the 7th Chasseurs under Bruyère were caught in an ambush. Parquin was wounded by five lance thrusts and captured, as was Sourd of the 7th—the future hero of Waterloo where he was a General and a Baron. Platov congratulated the 20th for its conduct at Eylau, saying, *"The Russians are today learning so much from their French teachers, but soon the Russians will be better than their masters."*

Left out by Benningsen in his memoirs, this fighting found Masséna up against Tolstoi and Essen on the Narev and the Omulev. Recalled from Italy, Masséna had arrived at Osterode where Napoleon had entrusted him with the 5th Corps instead of Savary replacing Lannes, who was depressed. As related, the latter later took on another command and marched to Friedland where he distinguished himself.

Masséna disposed his Suchet and Gazan

Banquets were organised for the Russian and French Imperial Guards to fraternise with each other. (RR)

to fall back towards the wood held by Friant, helped by Gudin's 12th. Davout's daughter, the Marquise de Blocqueville, quotes verses by Collot written to the glory of her father which end by saying that it was he *"who settled the victorious outcome."*

Benningsen in his memoirs present his battles as victories and he quite rightly exalted the valour of the Russian soldiers and the effectiveness of the Cossacks. He did however retreat everywhere, except at Pultusk and at Heilsberg where he put up a stern resistance before cautiously falling back. If he kept withdrawing like that it was, according to him, because of the formidable masses of French soldiers. At Eylau he claimed that it was his victory.

But he nevertheless just happened to forget that he would have been surrounded had Ney arrived earlier and that he had been obliged to withdraw even further again, before being routed at Friedland. He was given supreme command, all the more so since the Tsar remembered that he had been present at the assassination of Paul I, the Tsar's father, and that he was an embarrassing witness.

After the famous meeting on 25 June on the Niemen, the armistice between Napoleon and Alexander, and the parades made by the two Guards, peace was signed on 8th July. Nothing separated the two continental empires any more except the waters of the Niemen.

This brilliant campaign marked the apogee of the Empire and of the Grande Armée. The Tsar, Alexander I, for a while under Napoleon's spell joined the Continental Blockade aimed at suffocating England.

In less than two years the French had brought the whole Continent to its knees. All alone, far away at the other end of the continent, Portugal continued to trade with England. Napoleon decided to stop all that and launched himself into his Spanish adventure, which in the end was to be his downfall.

It was during the 1812 Russian campaign that his luck finally turned. ❐

A WORD ON FRENCH MILITARY TERMINOLOGY

In the many biographical notices to be found in this book (especially pp. 91 to 143 and), the following rules have been adopted.

Translation of ranks

In order to avoid confusion, the French officers rank of '*Chef de bataillon*' (foot troops) or '*Chef d'escadron*' (cavalry) has been translated as 'Battalion commander' or 'Squadron commander' respectively. For the Napoleonic period, this rank could not be translated as 'Major' (in English), as there existed also a rank of '*Major*' (in French) immediately above it. When the rank 'Major' is used in this book, it always refers to the original French rank above Battalion commander and below Colonel – cf. plate p. 23).

- '*Général de brigade*' has been translated merely as 'General', or in some cases as 'Brigadier General' (only in the biographical notices).
- '*Général de division*' has been always translated as 'Major General' in the biographical notices.
- '*Lieutenant général*' (in the Royal French Army) has been translated as 'Lieutenant General'. This rank did not exist in the Army of Napoleon.
- '*Maréchal*' has been retained in French or translated in English as 'Marshall'.
- '*Maréchal de camp*' (in the Royal French army) has been retained in French. This rank did not exist in the Army of Napoleon.

Abbreviations used for orders and decorations

LH : Légion d'honneur *(chevalier de la)*.
OLH : officier de la Légion d'honneur.
CtLH : commandant de la Légion d'honneur.
CrLH : commandeur de la Légion d'honneur *(it replaced the 'commandant' mentioned above, on the 17th February 1815)*.
GdCxLH : grand-croix de la Légion d'honneur *(it replaced the 'grand-cordon' on the 21th June 1814)*.
GdOLH : grand-officier de la Légion d'honneur.
CrSL : croix de Saint-Louis *(chevalier de la)*.
GdCxSL : grand-croix de Saint-Louis.

Design and lay-out by Jean-Marie Mongin and Denis Gandilhon
© Histoire & Collections 2007

All rights reserved.

No part of this publication can be transmitted or reproduced without the written of the Author and the Publisher.

ISBN: 978-2-35250-021-6

Publisher's number: 35250

© Histoire & Collections 2007

a book published by
HISTOIRE & COLLECTIONS
SA au capital de 182 938, 82 €
5, avenue de la République
F-75541 Paris Cedex 11 - FRANCE
Fax +33 1 47 00 51 11
www.histoireetcollections.fr

This book has been designed, typed, laid-out and processed by Histoire & Collections fully on integrated computer equipment.
Pictures integrated by Studio A&C
Printed by Zure,
Spain, European Union

August 2007